DEVELOPMENT AND COMMUNICATION IN INDIA

Elitist Growth and Mass Communication

DEVELOPMENT AND COMMUNICATION IN INDIA

Elitist Growth and Mass Deprivation

G. N. S. RAGHAVAN

GIAN PUBLISHING HOUSE
5, Ansari Road, Darya Ganj
NEW DELHI-110002

Development and Communication in India

Rs. 540

ISBN: 81-212-0406-2

First Published in 1992
Reprint in 2005
Gyan Publishing House
5, Ansari Road, Darya Ganj, New Delhi-110002
Phones : 23282060, 23261060, Fax : (011) 23285914
E-mail : gyanbook@vsnl.com
Website : http://www.gyanbooks.com

Laser Typesetting at : Shree Vaishnavi Creations, Delhi
Printed at : Chawla Offset Press, Delhi

CONTENTS

Part 3: As Communication, so Development

Part 4: An Agenda for Renewal

PREFACE

It was in the winter months of 1943-44 that I first saw the face of rural destitution while travelling through the Khulna, Jessore and 24-Parganas districts of the then undivided province of Bengal in British India as member of a students' delegation from different parts of the country. We carried some relief supplies, and the message of sympathy and solidarity from fellow-Indians to the people of Bengal afflicted by famine and epidemics. The experience stimulated my interest in movements for the political independence and economic reconstruction of the country.

Entering journalism after leaving college, I had the opportunity in the late 1940's of observing and reporting, for the English weekly *Swatantra* of Madras, situations of class conflict such as agrarian unrest and police repression in the North Malabar district of the then Madras Presidency, and a prolonged strike by textile workers in Coimbatore. During the 'fifties the Planning Commission was part of my beat in Delhi as a special correspondent of *Indian Express*. I also visited numerous Plan projects in various parts of the country and wrote about their progress and problems. The projects ranged from multi-purpose river dams and big industrial plants to the village-level programme of community development. They seemed to hold the promise of a transformation of the economy and of the condition of the masses.

Subsequently, from the late 'fifties I served in various media units of the Ministry of Information & Broadcasting. I had the opportunity, as director of the field publicity organisation (1970-73) of initiating an effort to make development communication area-specific, intelligible and relevant to the common people. This was attempted in the north-eastern region and in Kashmir Valley through the recruitment of local personnel who could use local speech, and the preparation of localised information material--films, posters, calendars and pamphlets. These experiments, like others such as by the socially concerned among scientists of the Space Applications Centre, Ahmedabad, who ran a local-interest and development oriented television station at Pij, were at variance with and made no difference to the dominant pattern of centralised and top-down communication through the official media and extension agencies.

Though the picture today of development and of communication related thereto is depressing, the compulsions of meeting the aspirations of the masses in a democracy hold the promise of a correction of the elitist bias. If the present work serves as a reminder of the pre-independence vision of a just and egalitarian society, and to draw attention to the possibilities of development communication as part of social engagement, it will have justified the support extended to me by the Indian Council of Social Science Research through the award of a two-year senior fellowship.

The project included field observation, on a modest scale, in some parts of rural India. The health programmes conducted in the Vidisha and Hoshangabad districts of Madhya Pradesh by official agencies, and by a voluntary organisation in Hoshangabad were studied by the late Taruna Tanwar. A former colleague of mine on the faculty of the Indian Institute of Mass Communication, she was at that time head of the department of communication in the Institute of Forest Management, Bhopal. Taruna Tanwar also organised, in twelve villages in the two districts, a questionnaire-based survey of local needs.

Meenakshi Ganguly, a young journalist friend, studied the working of the development broadcasting unit at the Kota station of All India Radio. She also interviewed a cross-section of students in a Navodaya school in order to test the claim that these schools cater for children from poor rural families.

Waheeduddin Ahmed Qazi, a former colleague in the field publicity organisation who is now Reader in the Indian Institute of Mass Communication, gathered data on the working of some of the media units of the Ministry of Information & Broadcasting. He made a content analysis of newspapers circulating in the two districts of Madhya Pradesh where field studies had been conducted, to ascertain the contribution made by the Press to drawing attention to the problems of the rural poor.

I am thankful to these three co-workers as well as to Dr. T.N. Banerji, Director of the Centre for Area Development and Action Research Studies (CADARS), New Delhi, the institution to which I affiliated myself for carrying out the ICSSR project.

My thanks are due also to the several experts and officials of the Planning Commission, Department of Rural Development, National Sample Survey Organisation, Central Statistical Organisation, and of the Media units of the Ministry of information & Broadcasting whom I interviewed. My discussions with them helped to clarify many issues.

I am grateful above all to ICSSR for enabling me to carry forward my study of a subject that has held my interest for many years, and to make this summative presentation of the challenges of development communication as perceived by me. The study confirms the hypothesis that development communication is effective when it is part of engagement in social action, rather than as communication *per se*.

New Delhi

G.N.S. RAGHAVAN

INTRODUCTION

Except in the state of dreamless sleep, every one of us is constantly engaged in communication. Much of it finds little overt expression, being internal and private: dreams; the wakeful activity of memory and anticipation; the ceaseless turning of the wheel of silent thought, trivial and profound. Such private communication is outside the purview of this work. Also outside its scope is creative communication, which at its intensest is almost private even if it is not oblivious of an audience, and serves an educative purpose as a by-effect.

The territory surveyed in this work is intentional communication. It includes induction into the practices, beliefs and prejudices of the religion of one's birth;formal secular education; the news (much of it pertaining to conflicts based on religion, caste or political affiliation), exhortation (including advertising with its heavy reliance on sex appeal and child appeal) and entertainment (much of it mindless) carried by the mass media of print, film, radio and television; and periodical bursts of electioneering. Considered in particular is the symbiotic relationship of socio-economic development and communication: the effect of a given type of development on the pattern of growth and on the content of communication, and the effect of consciousness-raising communication on development.

Development in a democracy is sought to be promoted, if not undertaken to a large extent, by elected governments. And where elections are held on the basis of universal adult franchise, as in India, the democratic process should be expected to result in a pattern of development that benefits all, not only a few. Yet so dormant is the political consciousness of the majority of our people that, at the end of seven Five Year Plans, they remain condemned to poverty and illiteracy. They give their votes to demagogues rather than to true spokesmen of their interests. The present study suggests that the political consciousness of the masses needs to be raised through action-related communication, that is, communication as part of mobilisation of the deprived masses for the improvement of their condition.

The nexus between development and communication is illustrated by the very notion of development that is entertained by the ruling elites in most of the developing countries including India. The international communication that the intelligentsia in developing countries (drawn mostly from the upper and middle classes) are exposed to is largely from the industrially advanced countries of the West. Their vision of development is a replication of the good life as lived in the affluent countries of the West, which they have come to know through books and films, magazines and television programmes, and during personal visits abroad as students or officials (in both cases, very often, on foreign scholarships or aid programmes) or as business men.

Politicians and administrators in the developing countries have been much influenced by the literature on the subject of development and communication that burgeoned in the wake of decolonisation following World War II. To the typical Western writer, development meant agricultural modernisation and industrialisation, on the Western model. Development thus conceived was to be promoted by the ruling elites in the newly free countries of the Third World (the First World being the industrially developed market-economy countries of the West, the Communist countries constituting the Second World.) Development literature till the 'seventies was predominantly American in authorship. So was it in its inspiration even when the writers were from countries of Asia or Africa. Development theorists avoided political questions such as 'Whose development?', and 'Who defines development ?'

We know now that it is the political clout wielded by, or not available to, different sections of the population that determines who benefits most from the development process, and who are passed by. The upper and middle classes have been the principal beneficiaries of planned development in India because it is they who occupy, or have access to, the corridors of power, at the Centre and in the States. They have reaped benefits in numerous forms: subsidised fertiliser and irrigation water for owners of agricultural land; tax concessions to industrialists for setting up in backward districts high-tech production units which make no difference to the condition of the local poor; the expansion of massively subsidised institutions of higher education for the fast-growing middle class; regular upward revision of the emoluments of employees of the government, the organised private sector and the public sector, college teachers and newspaper staff; perquisites like leave travel concession; and, for those in the higher rungs, expense account air travel and chauffeur-driven office cars.

As for communication, it was assumed by Western scholars in the 'fifties and 'sixties that development required support from the modern mass media which are pervasive in the industrialised countries. Theorists of development communication did not see that a country might be communication-rich even if media-poor. They under-rated the role of oral transmission of information and of values of life. They knew little about the powerful role of traditional communication modes such as song and dance, dramatic narration and folk art, in largely pre-literate societies. The prescription of mass media promotion by Western communication gurus suited the privileged classes in developing countries who were hungering for radio and television entertainment.

Shying away from a fundamental, and necessarily political, analysis, communication pedagogues have tended to discuss the role of the mass media in an academic vacuum. The function of the media, it is said, is to "inform, educate and entertain". There is little exploration of questions such as: (i) 'Inform and educate whom? Only those with the economic and educational capability of access to the Press, films, radio and TV?'; (ii) 'Entertain with what? The trash of Doordarshan's song-and-dance compilations from films?'

Another academic exercise is the division of Communication into Information, Publicity and Propaganda. The fact is that, depending on the political structure, information flow in a society may be either free and comprehensive, or censored and selective--serving the purpose of propaganda in the pejorative sense. Publicity can promote emulation of examples of individual and community self-help, and of selfless service, or it may be propagandist image-building of a person or party for the time being in power. Propaganda itself need not necessarily be narcissistic, let alone Hitlerian or Stalinist; it can be in the caring and loving spirit of a Buddha, the early Christian apostles or of a Gandhi or a Vinoba.

Fortunately there have been exceptions to the rule of holding out the industrially advanced nations of the West as models for the developing countries in respect of development and communication. Since the 'seventies, both in the West and in the Third World, the more perceptive among analysts have called attention to the real nature of decision making with regard to the pattern of development, as well as the pattern of growth and the content of communication.

Rajni Kothari has written in deprecation of "the gospel of modernisation--that package of urbanisation, achievement motivation, mass media exposure, specialised education, spatial mobility, and a rising consumption of finished goods" which has intoxicated the westernised middle class in developing societies.[1] He said in another work, 'Footsteps in the Future': "In this model of modernity the area of freedom and choice (of politics as Aristotle used the term) becomes increasingly limited...Emphasis on economic development through the historicist model of industrial growth and urbanization produces an elite (economic, bureaucratic and technocratic) that is intimately tied to the metropolitan areas of the world, and treats the vast rural hinterlands in its own country as colonies that provide cheap food, raw materials and surplus labour. It, no doubt produces impressive increases in GNPs (and hence also in the aggregate per capita incomes) without really benefiting anyone except a very small fragment of the large humanity huddled in the 'countryside'."[2]

This kind of political critique of an imitative and inegalitarian pattern of development has had counterparts in critical writing on communication. The MacBride Commission (or, to give its title in full, the International Commission for the Study of Communication Problems) established by UNESCO said in its report (1980) that the expansion of communication media is not an end in itself: "Everything depends on the use made...It can serve the end of either liberation or of oppression." The Commission's own value preference was unequivocal: it was informed by social conscience. Recognising that the full potential of communication depends on "the surrounding political, social and economic conditions, the most vital of these being democracy within countries and equal, democratic relations between them", it called for "elimination of gross inequalities which may threaten social harmony"; for the "democratisation of communication at national and international levels"; and for recognition of "the larger role of communication in democratising society".[3] This was remarkable, considering that the Commission included members form the Soviet bloc where at that time the term democracy used to be suspect unless it was qualified by such epithets as "people's " or "socialist".

Also apposite are the remarks--quoted more fully in Chapter V-- by Wilbur Schramm (1907-87) on communication as part of social action: "Activity at the village level is the only means, I would say, of effective village change. And whereas communication has to travel down, it has got to travel up and much more important, it has got to travel round at the village level. People have to work together and discuss together; they have got to make their changes together... The idea of big media, of talk-down communication, is something which is not going to work."

It was precisely such participatory and action-oriented communication at village level that was attempted in the mid-'seventies by the television centre at Pij in the Ahmedabad district of Gujarat. Run by socially conscious scientists of the Space Applications Centre, the Pij station pioneered the preparation of research-based programmes in local speech, dealing with local problems. But Pij was forced to fall in line with the rest of the government-operated network of Indian television. On 10th April,1983, the station began to telecast feature-films--the staple of popular entertainment designed to maximise the audience for televised advertising, commercial and political.

Paulo Freire, the Brazilian educator, has spoken of the political implications of literacy and illiteracy. Illiteracy, he says, is much more than just being unable to decode written language. It is "one of the concrete expressions of an unjust social reality...It is not strictly a linguistic or exclusively pedagogical problem. It is political."[4]

Violence erupts when communication breaks down. This is as true of wars between countries as of group conflicts within a country. A communicator earnestly desiring to promote broad-based human development must therefore be as mindful of the politics of war and peace as of domestic policies which aid or disrupt social harmony. Though expenditure on armament and armed forces is inimical to development, it is rarely that, even in countries where freedom of expression is allowed, foreign policies are subjected to critical scrutiny. It suits all rulers for the time being in power to invoke the mystique of the Nation State and to call for loyalty to it. The fact is that a 'nation' is a product of historical circumstances and is subject to alteration of frontiers (witness India's partition and the subsequent emergence Bangladesh which used to be part of Pakistan, and the erstwhile two Germanys). The Nation State is as liable to error as the fallible human beings in charge of its governance. The development publicist cannot therefore accept the demand of a country's rulers for unquestioning loyalty to the 'Nation State' whose interests, according to the rulers, transcend all differences and inequalities including class and sex.

Emmeline Pankhurst (1858-1928), the English suffragette, organised militant demonstrations in the early part of this century to enforce the demand that women should have equal political and other rights with men. The movement was at its peak when the first world war broke out in 1914. Emmeline and her daughter Christobel, an equally militant feminist, stopped the agitation and joined the war effort. It showed how the ruling classes can invoke national solidarity to override protest movements against domestic oppression. Only a tough mind like George Bernard Shaw's could see the war between rival imperialisms for what it was. And he had the courage to oppose it. Shaw wrote in *Common Sense* about the war, published as a supplement to the 'New Statesman' of 4 November 1914: "Militarism must not be treated as a disease peculiar to Prussia. It is rampant in England. I see both nations duped by their Junkers and Militarists...Will you now at last believe, O stupid British, German and French patriots, what the socialists have been telling you for so many years: that your Union Jacks and tricolours and imperial eagles are only toys to keep you amused, that there are two real flags in the world henceforth--the red flag of Democratic Socialism and the black flag of Capitalism, the flag of god and flag of Mammon." For expressing these views, Bernard Shaw had to face obloquy and social boycott by fellow-writers.

The primacy of politics in determining the course of development, and in generating communication--whether supportive or critical of the Establishment--will be evident from the above paragraphs. It is for this reason that the political framework of development and communication in India, and public policies which call for the development communicator's attention insofar as they promote or impede broad-based human development, are discussed at some length in this work.

NOTES

1. *State and Nation Building in the Third World*, ed. Rajni Kothari, Allied, 1976.
2. Quoted by Edward W. Ploman in 'Development Approaches and Implications for Communication Policy', *Rural Development and Communication Policies* (p.47), ed. G.N.S.Raghavan, Indian Institute of Mass Communication (1980).
3. *Many Voices' One World : Communication and Society Today and Tomorrow*', Kogan Page, London; Unipub, New York (1980).
4. Quoted by Paul Jurmo in *Development Communication Report* No. 68, Arlington, Va., U.S.A.

PART I

Vision and Reality

The course of India's post-independence development and of communication related thereto is best considered in the context of the vision entertained by the leaders of the national resurgence in the modern period.

Chapter I

CONTEXT OF HISTORY

India was not only the largest among the Asian and African colonies of the European powers, and the earliest to manifest patriotism; Indian nationalism was remarkable for being more than a gut reaction against foreign rule. The leading personalities, men and women, of the renascence which began in the first half of the 19th century strove for social reform at the same time as they pressed the colonial authorities for changes that would lead to self-government and eventual independence. They envisaged a free India that would achieve material progress without cultural uprooting.

(i) Rammohun Roy to Gandhi and Nehru

Thus Rammohun Roy (1772-1883) campaigned against social evils such as Sati (immolation of the widow on the husband's funeral pyre) that prevailed in certain parts of the country. He advocated modern education through the English language so that India could progress by acquiring knowledge of the sciences and of contemporary political thought in Europe and U.S.A. But Rammohun Roy was not swept off his feet by the new winds from the West. Defending the Vedantic core of Hindu religion against derisive attacks by Christian missionaries, whose brash tactics he had the courage to criticise, he advocated a synthesis of the best values of India's cultural heritage and of Western civilisation.

It is noteworthy that the initiator of India's reawakening was a great communicator. Rammohun Roy utilised the new medium of the printed journal, introduced by the British East India Company and the Christian missionaries who came in its wake.

Mahatma Gandhi (1869-1948) and Jawaharlal Nehru (1889-1964), who led the national resurgence to its culmination, were also great communicators. They spoke and wrote ceaselessly in advocacy of ending untouchability, promoting women's education and other reforms. Both envisioned an India that would not only be politically independent but be the home of a just society free of poverty and injustice.

Gandhiji dedicated himself, as he put it in 1931, to working "for an India in which the poorest shall feel it is their country, in whose making they have an effective voice, an India in which there shall be no high class and low class of people, an India in which all communities shall live in perfect harmony... There can be no room in such an India for the curse of untouchability or the curse of intoxicating drinks and drugs...Women will enjoy the same rights as men. Since we shall be at peace with all the rest of the world, neither exploiting nor being exploited, we should have the smallest army imaginable. This is the India of my dreams."[1]

In August 1947, the month of India's independence, Gandhiji wrote out the following 'talisman': "I will give you a talisman. Whenever you are in doubt, or when the self becomes too much with you, apply the following test. Recall the face of the poorest and the weakest man whom you may have seen, and ask yourself if the step you contemplate is going to be of any use to him. Will he gain anything by it ? Will it restore to him a control over his own life and destiny? In other words, will it lead to Swaraj for the hungry and spiritually starving millions? Then you will find your doubts and your self melting away".[2]

Mahatma Gandhi tirelessly propagated this vision of comprehensive human development through public speeches across the length and breadth of the country and through the journals in which he wrote extensively: *Navajivan* (1919-31); *Young India* (1919-32) and *Harijan* (1933 till his martyrdom in 1948).

Jawaharlal Nehru, like Gandhiji, was a tireless communicator through the public platform as well as through books and newspapers. He envisaged India's political emancipation not as an end in itself but as the necessary condition for achieving economic progress on a socialist basis, with equality of opportunity for persons of both sexes and of all castes and religious communities.

It was largely at Jawaharlal Nehru's instance that the articulation of economic policy by the Indian National Congress began, from 1929, to acquire a socialist accent. In response to urgings by the Congress Committee of the United Provinces (now Uttar Pradesh), Nehru's home province, the All India Congress Committee at its meeting in Bombay in May 1929 adopted a resolution calling for drastic changes in the economic and social structure: "In the opinion of this committee, the great poverty and misery of the Indian people are due not only to foreign exploitation in India but also to the economic structure of society, which the alien rulers support so that their exploitation may continue. In order, therefore, to remove this poverty and misery and to ameliorate the condition of the Indian masses, it is essential to make revolutionary changes in the present economic and social structure and to remove the gross inequalities."

(ii) Karachi Congress Resolution

Two years later, the Karachi session of the Congress (1931) adopted a resolution on the Fundamental Rights and Duties, and the socio-economic objectives, which should be included in any future Constitution. The seventeen points of the Karachi Resolution were as follows :

"*Fundamental rights and duties* : This Congress is of opinion that to enable the masses to appreciate what 'Swaraj', as conceived by the Congress, will mean to them, it is desirable to state the position of the Congress in a manner easily understood by them. In order to end the exploitation of the masses, political freedom must include real economic freedom of the starving millions. The Congress therefore declares that any constitution which may be agreed to on its behalf should provide, or enable the Swaraj government to provide, for the following :

1. (i) Every citizen of India has the right of free expression and opinion, the right of free association and combination, and the right to assemble peacefully and without arms, for purposes not opposed to law or morality.
   (ii) Every citizen shall enjoy freedom of conscience and the right freely to profess and practise his religion, subject to public order and morality.
   (iii) The culture, language and script of the minorities and the different linguistic areas shall be protected.
   (iv) All citizens are equal before the law irrespective of religion, caste, creed or sex.
   (v) No disability attaches to any citizen by reason of his or her religion, creed or sex in regard to public employment, office of power or honour, and in the exercise of any trade or calling.
   (vi) All citizens have equal rights and duties in regard to wells, tanks, roads, schools and places of public resort maintained out of State or local funds or dedicated by private persons for the use of the general public.
   (vii) Every citizen has the right to keep and bear arms, in accordance with the regulations and reservations made in that behalf.

(viii) No person shall be deprived of his liberty nor shall his dwelling or property be entered, sequestered or confiscated, save in accordance with law.

(ix) The State shall observe neutrality in regard to all religions.

(x) The franchise shall be on the basis of universal adult suffrage.

(xi) The State shall provide for free and compulsory primary education.

(xii) The State shall confer no titles.

(xiii) There shall be no capital punishment.

(xiv) Every citizen is free to move throughout India and to stay and settle in any part thereof, to acquire property and to follow any trade or calling, and be treated equally with regard to legal prosecution or protection in all parts of India.

(2) *Labour:*

(a) The organisation of economic life must conform to the principles of justice, to the end that it may secure a decent standard of living.

(b) The State shall safeguard the interests of industrial workers and shall secure for them, by suitable legislation and in other ways, a living wage, healthy conditions of work, limited hours of labour, suitable machinery for the settlement of disputes between the employers and workmen, and protection against the economic consequences of old age, sickness and unemployment.

(3) Labour to be freed from serfdom and conditions bordering on serfdom.

(4) Protection of women workers and, specially, adequate provision for leave during maternity period.

(5) Children of school-going age shall not be employed in mines and factories.

(6) Peasants and workers shall have the right to form unions to protect their interests.

(7) *Taxation and Expenditure* : The system of land tenure and revenue and rent shall be reformed and an equitable adjustment made of the burden on agricultural land, immediately giving relief to the smaller peasantry by a substantial reduction of agricultural rent and revenue now paid by them, and in cases of uneconomic holdings exempting them from rent so long as necessary, with such relief as may be just and necessary to holders of small estates affected by such exemption or reduction in rent, and, to the same end, imposing a graded tax on net incomes from land above a reasonable minimum.

(8) Death duties on a graduated scale shall be levied on property above a fixed minimum.

(9) There shall be drastic reduction of military expenditure so as to bring it down to at least one half of the present scale.

(10) Expenditure and salaries in civil departments shall be largely reduced. No servant of the State, other than specially employed experts and the like, shall be paid above a certain fixed figure, which should not ordinarily exceed Rs.500/- per month.

(11) No duty shall be levied on salt manufactured in India.

(12) *Economic and social programme* : The State shall protect indigenous cloth; and for this purpose pursue the policy of exclusion of foreign cloth and foreign yarn from the country and adopt such other measures as may be found necessary. The State shall also protect indigenous industries, when necessary, against foreign competition.

(13) Intoxicating drinks and drugs shall be totally prohibited except for medicinal purposes.

(14) Currency and exchange shall be regulated in the national interest.

(15) The State shall own or control key industries and services, mineral resources, railways, waterways, shipping and other means of public transport.

(16) Relief of agricultural indebtedness and control of usury, direct and indirect.

(17) The State shall provide for military training of citizens so as to organise a means of national defence apart from the regular military force.

In April 1936 the Lucknow Congress adopted a resolution which reiterated the Karachi formulations and referred, in addition, to the worsening of rural poverty and indebtedness as the result of a slump in prices of agricultural commodities.

The Faizpur Congress in December 1936 said that the "final solution involves the removal of British imperialistic exploitation and a radical change in the antiquated and repressive land tenure and revenue systems." The resolution also said that "effort should be made to introduce co-operative farming."

(iii) National Planning Committee

After these formulations of the policy approach, it became practicable to draw up the broad outlines of a national economic plan after the Congress assumed office in 1937 in several parts of the country. This was in the wake of elections held under the Government of India Act of 1935 which introduced provincial self- government.

For the first time the people's elected representatives gained access to official data relevant to economic development. This was in contrast to the situation earlier, when pioneering Indian industrialists had to face official obstruction. For example Jamshedji Tata who wanted to start steel manufacture in India had to struggle against great odds. The government refused to give Tata the information available with the Geological Survery of India about iron ore and coal deposits that had been discovered in Bengal and Bihar. He had to hire geologists to prospect all over again, for several years, to secure data already in the possession of the government.

At a meeting in August 1937, the Congress Working Committee asked the newly formed popular Ministries to form committees of experts to collect information for framing schemes of "national reconstruction and social planning". They were also asked to initiate consultations with neighbouring provinces and princely states on the feasibility of inter-state river valley projects. In October 1938 a Conference of Industries Ministers of the Congress-ruled provinces, presided over by the then Congress president, Subhas Chandra Bose, adopted a resolution on planning for promoting development: "The problems of poverty and unemployment, of national defence and of economic regeneration in general, cannot be solved without industrialisation including heavy key industries, medium-scale industries and cottage industries. Steps should be taken to start manufacture of machinery and plant and tools of all kinds; automobiles, motor boats etc.; electrical plant and accessories; heavy chemicals and fertilisers; and metal production." For giving effect to this, the resolution called for the formation of a National Planning Committee whose personnel would be announced later by the Congress president. Jawaharlal Nehru was the natural choice for chairmanship of the National Planning Committee.

The preoccupation with industrialisation in the resolution quoted above was understandable against the background of the discouragement of indigenous industries by the British rulers. They treated India as a source of raw materials at low prices and as a captive market for the profitable dumping of their own manufactures. In a memorandum of 4 June 1939, Jawaharlal Nehru pointed out to members of the National Planning Committee that though the resolution adopted by the industries ministers' conference did not mention agriculture specifically, "it is impossible to conceive of any scheme of national planning in any country, and least of all in India, which does not include agriculture. Agriculture is and will remain the largest single industry of this country, and it is associated with a host of subsidiary industries."

Even earlier, in the mid-'thirties when he wrote his autobiography, Jawaharlal Nehru envisaged improvement of the quality of life in India's villages, rather than urbanisation for its own sake. He said that he did not "appreciate in the least the idealisation of the 'simple peasant life'. I have almost a horror of it, and instead of submitting to it myself I want to drag out even the peasantry from it, not to urbanisation, but to the spread of urban cultural facilities to rural areas."[3]

In *The Discovery of India,* written in 1944 while in Ahmadnagar Fort jail and when the National Planning Committee was still at work, Jawaharlal Nehru said: "It should be possible to organise modern industry in such a way as to keep men and women, as far as possible, in touch with the land, and to raise the cultural level of the rural areas. The village and the city should approach each other in regard to life's amenities, so that in both there should be full opportunities for bodily and mental development and a full all-rounded life."[4]

(iv) Defining Development

Mahatma Gandhi and Jawaharlal Nehru were the most eloquent and insistent, among leaders of the freedom struggle, in affirming that political independence was not an end in itself but the condition for bringing about social and economic transformation. Gandhiji said: "To me political power is not an end but one of the means of enabling people to better their condition in every department of life."[5]. And Nehru : "We wanted no change of masters from white to brown, but a real people's rule, by the people and for the people, and an ending of our poverty and misery."[6]

However, the two differed, specially in the early phase of the development of Nehru's thought, on the nature of the transformation to be sought. The differences centred on the concepts of class war and violence, on the one hand, and non-violence and trusteeship on the other; the uses and the dangers of industrialisation; and the extent of the role to be played by the State.

Gandhiji was as radical as the most radical of socialists in his passion for the removal of hunger and want. He said: "For the poor the economic is the spiritual."[7] Again, "I may as well place before the dog over there the message of God, as before those hungry millions who have no lustre in their eyes and whose only God is their bread. I can take before them a message of God only by taking the message of sacred work before them."[8] Gandhiji believed, it will be seen, in work and not in doles. This is the reason why he was opposed to reckless industrialisation at the cost of employment. Gandhiji was not against the application of science and technology for raising living standards. "What I object to", he said, "is the craze for machinery as such. I want to save time and labour, not for a fraction of mankind but for all. Mechanisation is good when hands are too few for the work intended to be accomplished. It is an evil where there are more hands than required for the work, as is the case in India."[9]

He thus rejected the pursuit of high technology for its own sake, and wanted industrialisation to be subordinate to and regulated by the provision of work and bread for all.

Gandhiji did not like the class hatred and violence associated with socialism, and distrusted the accumulation of power in the hands of the State. On the subject of capitalism, trusteeship and the State, he said: "The State represents violence in a concentrated and organised form. The individual has a soul, but as the State is a soulless machine, it can never be weaned from violence to which it owes its very existence. Hence I prefer the doctrine of trusteeship. I would be very happy indeed if the people concerned behaved as trustees; but if they fail, I believe we shall have to deprive them of their possessions through the State with the minimum exercise of violence. That is why I said at the Round Table Conference that every vested interest must be subjected to scrutiny, and confiscation ordered where necessary—with or without compensation as the case demanded. What I would personally prefer would be not a centralisation of power in the hands of the State, but an extention of the sense of trusteeship as, in my opinion, the violence of private ownership is less injurious than the violence of the State. However, if it is unavoidable, I would support a minimum of State ownership."[10]

Fresh from a visit to the Soviet Union on the occasion of the tenth anniversary of the October 1917 Revolution, Jawaharlal Nehru wrote to Gandhiji on 11 January 1928 : "You know how intensely I have admired you and believed in you as a leader who can lead this country to victory and freedom. I have done so in spite of the fact that I hardly agreed with anything that some of your previous publications--'Indian Home Rule' etc.--contained. I felt and feel that you were and are infinitely greater than your little books. Above everything I admire action and daring and courage, and I found them all in you in a superlative degree. And I felt instinctively that however much I may disagree with you, your great personality and your posession of these qualities would carry us to our goal...

"Khadi will grow slowly, and if war comes it will grow very fast, but I do not see how freedom is coming in its train...You have criticised strongly the many obvious defects of industrialism and hardly paid any attention to its merits. It is the opinion of most thinkers in the West that these defects are not due to industrialism as such but to the capitalist system which is based on exploitation of others."[11] Gandhiji replied to say that they had perhaps reached the parting of their ways. In a letter of 17 January 1928, he suggested "a dignified way of unfurling your banner. Write to me a letter for publication showing your differences. I will print it in *Young India* and write a brief reply."[12] Jawaharlal Nehru shrank back from the very thought. He wrote to Gandhiji on 23 January 1928 : There can be no question of our personal relations suffering. But even in the wider sphere, am I not your child in politics, through perhaps a truant and errant child ?"[13]

Though the young rationalist thus yielded to the Mahatma, a certain ambivalence continued on the part of Nehru. This is evident from the pages of his autobiography, written during 1934-35. At places he expresses his dismay at what he perceived as Gandhiji's softness towards capitalists and landlords. At the same time he is amazed and moved by Gandhiji's ability to identify with and to mobilise the masses. Chiding arm-chair Marxists for their doctrinaire assessment of Gandhiji, he wrote: "Some people wanted to make high socialist doctrine a refuge for inaction. These parlour Socialists are especially hard on Gandhiji as the arch reactionary, and advance arguments which, in logic, leave little to be desired. But the little fact remains that this 'reactionary' knows India, understands India, almost *is* peasant India, and has shaken up India as no so-called revolutionary has done."[14]

In 1938, in an article contributed to a foreign journal, Nehru said that "the principles of socialism, of cooperation and service to the community for the common good" were "not so unlike the old brahmin ideal of service." He expressed the hope that the new India would develop in tune with the culture and genius of the country: "It may be that when India puts on her new garment—as she must, for the old is torn and tattered—she will have it cut in this fashion, so as to make it conform both to present conditions and to her old thought. The ideas she adopts must be racy to her soil."[15]

Later, in 1944, Nehru discusses the uses as well as the limitations of science, and the need for ethical values to govern human conduct : "Science does not tell us much, or for the matter of that anything, about the purpose of life... Some kind of ethical approach to life has a strong appeal for me, though it would be difficult for me to justify it logically. I have been attracted by Gandhiji's stress on right means and I think one of his greatest contributions to our public life has been this emphasis."[16]

After independence and the martyrdom, soon after, of Mahatma Gandhi, Nehru increasingly stressed that the humanistic ethics of the religions of man are an essential complement to material progress through the application of science for industrialisation, and to socialism with its emphasis on equality of opportunity. He said in 1958: "In our efforts to ensure the material prosperity of the country we have not paid any attention to the spiritual element in human nature. Therefore, in order to give the individual and the nation a sense of purpose, something to live for and if necessary to die for, we have to revive some philosophy of life and give, in the wider sense of the word, a spiritual background to our thinking...We must not forget the ethical and spiritual aspects of life which are ultimately the basis of culture and civilisation and have given some meaning to life....We have to give a new direction to education and evolve a new type of humanity."[17]

The growth of Nehru's thought on the subject of human development reached its culmination and found its finest expression in the first Maulana Azad Memorial Lecture which he gave in 1959. His theme was that science and socialism were necessary but not enough, and needed to be leavened by the humanist ethical values which are at the core of true religion. "Poverty is a degradation," he said, "and the obvious reaction is to get rid of it. But too much wealth and affluence, whether in an individual or a society, has also its attendant evils which are becoming evident today. The mere piling up of material riches may lead to an emptiness in the inner life of man...There is a danger that socialism, while leading to affluence and even equitable distribution, may still miss some of the significant features of life. It is largely for this reason that stress becomes necessary on the individual."[18]

"Can we", Jawaharlal Nehru asked, "combine the progress of science and technology with the progress of the mind and spirit also? Four great religions have influenced India--two emerging from her own thought, Hinduism and Buddhism, and two coming from abroad but establishing themselves firmly in India, Christianity and Islam. Science today challenges the old concept of religion. But if religion deals not with dogmas and ceremonials, but rather with the higher things of life, there should be no conflict with science or *inter se* between religions. It might be the high privilege of India to help in bringing about this synthesis."

While expressing this hope, Nehru also warned against the consequences of failing to achieve such a synthesis. Speaking of the manifest differences and rivalry between the Western Powers and the Communist Powers, and the similarity at the same time of the industrial culture of both, and the challenge to life-values which they faced from technological change, he said: "We see the effects of these rapid technological changes more especially in young men and women today. The patterns of behaviour which were held by the adults are no longer accepted, and there is a rejection of the old moral standards. In extreme cases there is a tendency to criminality, alcoholism, destructiveness, eroticism, in addition to a cynical and negative attitude towards life and work. In a world of constant change and without any assurance or certainty, the hedonistic principles of life have a strong appeal. The continuity of national culture is threatened and a tendency towards social disintegration becomes evident. These tendencies are present more in the developed and advanced societies than in India or other under-developed countires. But it is important to note them because similar forces are likley to affect our life too."

In this study, development is considered in the sense in which it was visualised by Gandhiji and Jawaharlal Nehru, namely economic progress governed on the one hand by the socialist aims of full employment and equality of opportunity and, on the other, by the humanist and ethical values of the country's religious and cultural heritage.

(v) Scope of Development Communication

Two streams of communication are to be found in society at any time and place. One stream promotes conformism and socialisation, while the other questions existing norms and aims at raising the level of consciousness. Gandhiji and Jawaharlal Nehru were notable examplars of the second type of communication, which promotes human development in a comprehensive sense.

Conformist communication, which is at work right from songs crooned to infants, seeks to impart the values and customs dominant in a community at a given time. In an unjust society, conformist communication buttresses the existing order by idealising the oppressors and inculcating a low self-image among those--women, and supposedly low castes or inferior races--whose human dignity is violated.

Conscientising communication, on the other hand, proclaims human equality. It affirms the right of all persons, irrespective of sex, race or other circumstance of birth, to satisfaction of the material needs, and the flowering of the intellectual and aesthetic potential, of each. Development communication in its wide sense is another term, in our time, for such conscientisation.

Presented here are some examples of both types of communication, drawn from the history of India over the centuries, and from ancient Greece and Europe of the Christian era.

Conformist communication subserving male dominance is exemplified by this extract from the Padma Purana, one of eighteen religious texts compiled by Brahmin scholars from about 200 A.D. till 1000 A.D: "There is no other god on earth for a woman than her husband. The most excellent of all the good works that she can do is to seek to please him by manifesting perfect obedience to him. Be her husband deformed, aged, infirm, offensive in his manners; let him also be choleric, debauched, immoral, a drunkard, a gambler...let his defects be what they may, a wife should always look upon him as her god."

In sharp contrast to this Puranic injunction is the ancient Rig Vedic verse (composed around 1500 B.C.) meant to be recited during the marriage ceremony at the Saptapadi, the taking of seven steps together by the bride and the bridegroom, symbolic of a joint journey through life :

"May we two, who have taken together seven steps
Become companions. May I not be separated from
Your friendship nor you from mine;
I am the Rik (the text), you are the Saman (the tune);
I am the Saman, you are the Rik,"

And on the position of the newly wed young woman in the connubial home :

"Be thou a queen over thy father-in-law,
Be thou a queen over thy mother-in-law;
Be thou a queen over thy sister-in-law;
Be thou a queen over thy brother-in-law."

It is a pity that verses like these are recited only in Sanskrit. They have not been translated into regional speech, possibly because the officiating priests did not want their incantations to be demystified. To the couples who get married, the verses are so much gibberish. It is a case of words being used without communication taking place.

The sturdy humanism of the early Vedic period declined with the rise of Brahminical ritual. From an occupational classification the caste system became a rigid, hereditary stratification of society. The change had begun to take place by the time of the Upanishads (c. 600 B.C.) which are regarded as the culmination of Vedic literature. To an Upanishadic sage are ascribed these words which are still relevant: "It is not our religion, still less the colour of our skin, that produces virtue: virtue must be practised." There was a decline in the status of women along with the hardening of the caste system. Vedic learning came to be denied to women. They were classed in this respect along with the Sudras, the proletarians who ranked fourth and lowest in the caste order after the priestly class of Brahmins; the ruling and warrior class of Kshatriyas; and the Vaisyas who were agriculturists and traders.

The Jain and Buddhist movements of protest and reform marked a reaffirmation of humanism. Humanist values were communicated widely by Mahavira and Buddha (spanning the 6th and 5th centuries B.C.) who employed the local dialects, instead of Sanskrit, for preaching their doctrine. Mahavira recognised only one, namely the human, caste. Intellectual tolerance was a notable feature of the Jain creed which comprised Ahimsa or non-violence, Aparigraha or non-possessiveness, and Anekanta which may be translated as non-absolutism or non-dogmatism. Mahatma Gandhi, born in Gujarat where Jainism is widespread, was deeply influenced by the approach of Anekanta, of which he said: "I very much like the doctrine of the many-sidedness of reality. It has taught me to judge a Muslim from his standpoint and a Christian from his." Among the prominent disciples of Mahavira were several women.

Buddha, like Mahavira, promoted through precept and example the concept of human equality irrespective of sex and caste. A saying attributed to Buddha is: "No Brahmin is such by birth. No outcaste is such by birth. An outcaste is such by his deeds. A Brahmin is such by his deeds." Women were admitted to the Buddhist Order. Buddha is said to have told his favourite disciple Ananda: "Women are competent, if they retire from household life to the homeless state under the doctrine and discipline, to attain to the fruit of conversion, to sainthood." But Buddha is also said to have remarked to Ananda that the Sangha or the Buddhist order would have endured for a thousand years, but now that women had been admitted, it was likley to decay after five hundred years. Here is an instance of interpolation by the small-minded from which almost all the venerated texts of the Hindu tradition have suffered. These interpolations were effected mainly by Brahmin communicators of conformism in order to clothe with the authority of scripture such notions as male superiority and caste inequality. Hence the need, urged by Gandhiji, for pruning of the scriptures so as to remove the chaff and preserve the grain.

In ancient Greece, at about the same time as Mahavira and Buddha in India, Socrates as reported by Plato advocated humane and egalitarian values. A notable practitioner of communication as dialogue rather than one-way harangue, Socrates held that women and men of the same aptitude should be given the same kind of education, and the same responsibilities, to act as guardians of an ideal republic. The Greek dramatist Aristophanes, a contemporary of Socrates, had the courage to write a play ridiculing the war party in his native city-state of Athens. In the comedy Lysistrata ('She who disbands armies'), he depicts an international sex strike by women of the Greek states which were wasting themselves in the Peleponnesian War. They refuse their men sexual intercourse till peace is negotiated.

Jesus Christ's teaching, 'love thy neighbour as thyself', was truly revolutionary. Soon, however, the humanist teaching of Jesus was buried under dogma and the church became the advocate of oppression based on sex and race. St. Paul said: "I would have you know that the head of every man is Christ; and the head of the woman is the man...Every man praying or prophesying, having his head covered, dishonoureth his head. But every woman that prayeth or prophesieth with her head uncovered dishonoureth her head: for that is even all one as if she were shaven."

Martin Luther of Germany said in the first half of the 16th century: "An earthly kingdom cannot exist without inequality of persons. Some must be free, others serfs; some rulers, others subjects...There is nothing more poisonous, noxious and utterly diabolical than a rebel. You must kill him as you would a mad dog."

As late as in 1727, the Bishop of London wrote to the slave-owners of the southern American colonies to assure them, with regard to the Negroes, that "as to their outward condition, whatever that was before, whether bond or free, their being baptised and becoming Christians makes no manner of change in them".

Both the types of communication, anti-humanist and humane, have flourished in India over the centuries. In the south, the poet Kaniyan Pungunranar of the Sangam age of Tamil literature (2nd and 3rd centuries A.D.) affirmed: "Every city is my city; all people are my people." A great Tamil poet after the Sangam age is Tiruvalluvar, of the 5th century, born in a so-called low caste. One of the verses in his Kural, a string of ethical verses, reads: "He alone lives who knows that he is one with all; the rest have their place among the dead." The sayings of an 11th century woman sage, Avvai, are regarded by Tamils as the quintessence of wisdom. There is an ethical injunction of Avvai by which to teach children each vowel of the alphabet: *aram seyya virumbu* ('Yearn to do right'), *aaruvadu sinam* ('Cool your anger'), and so on. But the esteem in which Avvai is held does not prevent the wide prevalence of sayings derogatory to women, such as: 'Even a fifty-year-old woman must bow before a five-year old boy'; and 'Should one get a licence from anyone to beat one's own wife?'

Among the greatest propagators of humane values in India's history are the egalitarian saints of the Bhakti movement which originated in the south in the tenth century and travelled to the north. There it was to find a counterpart in the soft face of Islam which revealed itself with the coming of the Sufis, in happy contrast to the marauding raids by Mahmud of Ghazni and Muhammad Gori who had brought Islam with sword in hand.

The saint poets of Karnataka have been described as "great voices of a sweeping movement of protest and reform in Hindu society."[19] They spoke and wrote in the colloquial form of the regional language. Their *vachanas* (literally 'sayings') in Kannada are lyrics which affirm the possibility of every individual, irrespective of sex or social origin, attaining spiritual realisation without priestly intervention. This devotional movement appealed to the artisans and cultivators who ranked low in the Brahminical hierarchy. The extensive spread of the sayings and songs of these saint poets--who included women--in Karnataka and in other parts of the country illustrate the power of the spoken word. This traditional mode of oral communication has transmitted information and wisdom across the generations in pre-industrial societies, without benefit of literacy or the mass media of our time. Socially concerned as they were, the saint poets expressed themselves in the everyday speech of the common people because they needed to get their message through to them. Their communication was effective for the reason that it was part of what we would describe today as social activism.

Devara Dasimayya of the 10th century, earliest of the *vacana* poets of Karnataka, made light of the difference of sex :

> If they see
> breasts and long hair coming
> they call it woman,
> if beard and whiskers
> they call it man:
> but, look, the self that hovers
> in between
> is neither man
> nor woman.

Basava said :

> To the servant of God, who could eat if served
> They say, 'Go away!'
> But to the image of God, which cannot eat,
> They offer dishes of food...
> Sweet words are equal to all prayers and penances.
> Good behaviour is what pleases God
> Kindness is the root of all righteousness.

Lalleshwari of Kashmir, popularly known as Lal Ded, a woman mystic of the 14th century, has been held in reverence by both Muslims and Hindus. She deprecated idol worship: "An idol is but stone and temple is but stone." Lal Ded also denounced animal sacrifice, calling it folly "to offer a living sheep to a lifeless stone."

Kabir, born in the weaver caste in Banaras, was claimed on his death in 1518 by Hindus and Muslims as one of their own. The devotional verses he composed in Hindi reflect strong Sufi influence on traditional Hindu belief :

> Hari is in the East; Allah is in the West.
> Look within your heart,
> For there you will find both Karim and Ram.
> All the men and women of the world
> Are His living forms.
> Kabir is the child of Allah and of Ram.

(Four centuries later, Mahatma Gandhi was to invoke the same Bhakti-Sufi strain in the Indian ethos when he popularised the verse, 'Iswar and Allah are both your names; Grant us all concord.')

The Bhakti-Sufi movement, in which the most sensitive minds among Hindus and Muslims reached out towards each other, culminated in the emergence of a new religion, Sikhism, based on the teachings of Guru Nanak (1469-1538). He affirmed the equality of humankind and rejected notions of high and low based on caste, sex or wealth, and stressed the importance of good conduct.

In the modern period beginning with the British advent, it is remarkable that almost all the leaders of the national re-awakening were great communicators. It is noteworthy also that they stressed social reform and self-improvement as much as the need to get rid of foreign rule. The development communication practised by them was comprehensive in its scope.

Raja Rammohun Roy, the initiator of India's renascence, was also the father of the Indian Press. The three journals brought out by him in the early 1820's--*Brahmunical Magazine* in English, *Sambad Kaumidi* in Bengali and *Mirat ul Akhbar* in Persian--were the first to be published by an Indian and addressed to Indians. There was nothing Indian about Hicky's *Gazette,* brought out in Calcutta much earlier, in 1780, except that it was published on Indian soil. It was a weekly newspaper brought out by an Englishman and addressed exclusively to Europeans temporarily resident in India.

Rammohun Roy was not a nationalist in the modern sense of advocating an immediate end of foreign rule. It was too soon for that, with an entrenched imperial power and a people steeped in illiteracy and ignorance and with little sense of any larger identity beyond caste. But his consciousness of India's unfortunate status as a subject country, and his readiness to assert national self-respect are evident from his courageous criticism of the tactics of foreign missionaries who, accompanied by policemen, poured ridicule at the market-place on the beliefs and practices of Indians, both Hindus and Muslims. "It is true", Rammohun Roy said, "that the apostles of Jesus Christ used to preach the superiority of the Christian religion to the natives of different countries. But we must recollect that they were not the rulers of those countries where they preached. Were the missionaries likewise to preach the Gospel and distribute books in countries not conquered by the English, such as Turkey, Persia, etc., which are much nearer England, they would be esteemed a body of men truly zealous in propagating religion and in following the example of the founders of Christianity. In Bengal, where the English are the sole rulers, and where the mere name of Englishman is sufficient to frighten people, an encroachment upon the rights of her poor, timid and humble inhabitants and upon their religion cannot be viewed in the eyes of God or the public as a justifiable act."

At the same time Rammohun Roy was deeply attracted by the humanist teaching of the gospels. He made a careful study of Vedanta, the Bible and the Quran and was struck by the fundamental unity in their teaching. He has been described by Monier Williams, the Indologist, as "perhaps the first earnest-minded investigator of the science of comparative religion that the world has produced."

Rammohun Roy utilised his journals on the one hand to appeal to his countrymen to free themselves from cruel customs such as Sati, to discard the rigidities of caste, and to equip themselves with modern knowledge; on the other he kept making demands on the authorities such as the opening of modern schools, improvement of sanitary facilities in Calcutta, and making the services of European physicians available to Indians. A century later, Mahatma Gandhi's journals were to perform the same dual role of social self-criticism and of pressing for self-government.

The impulse of national awakening generated by Rammohun Roy in Bengal soon spread to other parts of India. It resulted, by the mid-19th century, in the formation of political associations by educated Indians. Alongside these, newspapers sprang up in various parts of the country. Many of them advocated political and social reform. The Marathi journal *Kesari*, brought out by V.K. Chiplonkar from Pune, said in its first issue in January 1881 : "A continuous flow of writing in the newspaper from various places have the same value as the street lights and the regular police patrol in the night have. The honesty of government officers is maintained so long as their functioning is brought before the eyes of the people from time to time...One can well imagine how much benefit will accrue by discussing in newspapers matters like which old practices are worth giving up, and which new ones worth taking up."

Most of the Indian-owned newspapers were broadly nationalistic in their approach, though some of them took a moderate position in politics and others were radical. This difference notwithstanding, the editors of the nationalist newspapers had in common the quality of moral earnestness which they brought to the practice of journalism, and the perception of their responsible role as non-formal educators of the reading public. This is illustrated by the instances of Annie Besant, Gandhi and Nehru.

British by birth and Indian by choice, Annie Besant wrote in her autobiography: "Very solemn is to me the responsibility of the public teacher, standing forth in Press and on platform to partly mould the thought of his time, swaying thousands of readers and hearers year after year. No weightier responsibility can any take, no more sacred charge."

Gandhi likewise approached his task as a communicator with great earnestness. "I have taken up journalism," he said,"not for its sake but merely as an aid to what I have conceived to be my mission in life. My mission is to teach by example the matchless weapon of Satyagraha which is a direct corollary of non-violence. To be true to my faith, I may not write in anger or malice. I may not write merely to excite passion. The reader can have no idea of the restraint I have to exercise from week to week in the choice of topics and my vocabulary." Again, in his autobiography: "One of the objects of a newspaper is to understand the popular feeling and give expression to it; another is to arouse among the people certain desirable sentiments; and the third is fearlessly to expose popular defects."

Radically nationalist newspapers like the *National Herald* launched by Jawaharlal Nehru in 1938 not only lacked adequate advertising revenue but had to face demands for large amounts of security from the British authorities during the freedom struggle. Nehru interpreted the world to India, and India to the world through his books and the articles he contributed to foreign journals, as part of his practice of educative journalism.

The sense of mission which Annie Besant, Gandhi and Nehru brought to journalism was shared by scores of editors across the length and breadth of the country. The Indian Press in the first half the 20th century adhered by and large to the role which Rammohun Roy set for his journals--as instruments of popular education. There was a place for ephemeral news of local and 'human' interest, but the emphasis was on providing significant information on problems of public importance.

Non-verbal communication played its own part in rousing nationalist consciousness and mobilising mass participation in the freedom struggle. Gandhiji was a master of non-verbal as of verbal communication. The loin cloth of hand-spun Khadi that he wore and the Charkha which he plied were symbols of identification with the rural poor. He wanted men and women working in the national movement to give up ostentation and to live simply.

Gandhiji's choice of the tax on salt as the issue on which to focus the civil disobedience movement in the early 'thirties showed an uncanny instinct for symbolic communication. Salt is a basic need, and a free gift of nature. But even the poorest had to pay tax on it. As far back as in August 1844, in Gandhiji's native Gujarat, a new duty on salt had met with resistance in Surat where a mob attacked the courthouse. When he gave the call for the making of salt by the people in defiance of the law, some of his followers were puzzled. Kamaladevi Chattopadhyaya (1903-89) recalls that "we had always thought that a revolution was a big uprising of the people" and therefore wondered "how this could be brought about by breaking the salt laws." She expressed her doubt to Jawaharlal Nehru, and asked him if he could think of some alternative form of civil disobedience. Jawaharlal told her: "Gandhiji is a very intuitive person and his instincts are fruitful. We are not always able to see what he is leading up to, but usually he is able to achieve something. Therefore we shall have act accordingly."[20] The Salt Satyagraha turned out to be the biggest anti-imperialist mass movement till then.

The reach and impact of Gandhiji's message was increased manifold by the many poets and novelists in various languages of the country who were deeply influenced by him. Krishana Kripalani writes: "The eminent Hindi novelist Premchand has described in an autobiographical essay how, inspired by the Mahatma, he resigned from government service and settled down in a village to see life in the raw and to write about it. His later career as the foremost novelist in Hindi (as also in Urdu), his insight into the life ofthe village folk, his abounding sympathy with their unhappy, stunted lives...reflects the impact of Gandhi on modern literature in India. Among other writers of note who responded to this impact, each in his fashion, may be mentioned the gifted Gupta brothers, Maithilisharan and Siyaramsharan, as well as Jainendra Kumar, in Hindi; Kaka Kale lkar, 'Darshak' and Umashankar Joshi in Gujarati; Sane Guruji, Khadekar and Mama Warerkar in Marathi; Nilmani Phookan in Assamese; Kalindi Charan Panigrahi in Oriya; Annadashakar Ray in Bengali; Bharati in Tamil; Vallathol in Malayalam; and many more in these and other languages."[21]

The wide range of the development communication in which they engaged, covering social and economic besides political emancipation, is illustrated by the following lines from a poem by Subramania Bharati (1882 - 1921). The poem celebrated the coming liberation of India from foreign rule as well as the freeing of women, low-caste toilers and all the oppressed. This 'song of freedom', set for the 'Kummi' dance of south India, was rendered from Tamil into English by the poet himself:

> "Gone are they who said to woman: 'Thou shalt not open the Book of Knowledge.' And the strange ones who boasted saying: 'We will immure these women in our homes' -- Today they hang down their heads. Dance the Kummi, beat the measure. Let this land of the Tamils ring with our dance, For now we are rid of all evil shades; We have seen the Good."[22]

(vi) Early Years of Promise

Planned development could not be undertaken immediately after the country attained independence on 15 August 1947. This was because of the circumstances of the sub-continent's partition, which marked the culmination of the British rulers' encouragement of Muslim separatism.

Partition was reluctantly accepted by the leaders of India's freedom movement because of the murderous clashes between Hindus and Muslims which rocked northern Indian following the 'Direct Action Day' observed by the Muslim League on 16 August 1946 when thousands were killed in Calcutta. The rioting did not stop with the partition. Millions of Hindus moved from Pakistan to seek refuge in India and, likewise, millions of Muslims left India for Pakistan. The rehabilitation of refugees claimed the first priority. Nevertheless, the early years of independence held the promise of a people-oriented process of development.

(a) Approach to Development: Three major steps were initiated for restructuring the feudal-colonial agrarian economy: (i) abolition of Zamindari intermediaries and conferment of land ownership on the cultivating peasants who would now pay land revenue directly to the state; (ii) security of tenure for tenant cultivators and fixation of the maximum rent that a landlord could demand; and (iii) imposition of a ceiling on land holdings with a view to distributing of the surplus among the landless. The Constitution which came into force in January 1950 was amended in 1951 to protect Zamindari abolition from challenge in the courts as being violative of the fundamental right to property.

A community development programme was launched on 2 October 1952, birth anniversary of Mahatma Gandhi, for the reconstruction of village life on the triple bases of the panchayat (elected village council), the school and the co-operative. Agricultural productivity was to be stepped up through irrigation that would be provided by the river valley schemes which accounted for a large part of the outlay on the First Five Year Plan (1951-56). The storage dams would also help control floods, and generate hydel power to supplement coal-based electricity for the many industrial plants that formed part of the Plan.

The First Plan was necessarily based on the projects on which preliminary work had begun as part of the post-war reconstruction envisaged before independence. The Secon Plan reflected more fully Jawaharlal Nehru's philosophy of planning. The Plan Frame drawn up at his instance by Prof. P.C. Mahalanobis, the renowned statistician and thinker, envisaged the setting up of machine-making or mother industries which would fabricate the equipment needed for large-scale production of articles of mass consumption.

A study team appointed in January 1957 under the chairmanship of Balvantray Mehta made far-reaching recommendations for a decentralised administrative system for rural development. In place of nominated advisory committees at the level of the development blocks into which each district was divided, the study team recommended the establishment of elected bodies. "Development", its report said, cannot progress without responsibility and power. Community development can be real only when the community understands its problems, realises its responsibilities, exercises the necessary powers through its chosen representatives and maintains a constant and intelligent vigilance on local administration. With this objective we recommend an early establishment of statutory elective local bodies and devolution to them of the necessary resources, power and authority."[23]

A notable contribution to social transformation was the codification and reform of Hindu personal law which parliament effected in the mid-1950's through a series of enactments to improve the status of women. The Hindu Marriage Act which came into force in May 1955 ended the age-old institution of marriage as a one-sided sacrament. It enforced monogamy on both parties, not only the wife. Secondly, it granted the relief of divorce, for the first time, on specified grounds. Formerly the Hindu woman, specially of the so-called higher castes, had no right to divorce on any grounds--even if the husband took a second wife. If marriage proved unhappy, she could find release only in death. The Hindu Succession Act, which became effective from June 1956, gives the mother, window and daughter a share in succession to the property of Hindu males. Till this Act, property could pass only to sons or, in the absence of male issue, to brothers and other male agnates and cognates entitled to perform religious rites for the deceased. The line of succession bore no relation to the direction of natural love and affection.

Referring to the enactment of Hindu law reform, Jawaharlal Nehru said in the course of a letter to Chief Ministers of States on 10 May 1956: "The passage of this legislation marks an epoch in India. It indicates that we have not only striven for and achieved a political revolution, not only are we striving hard for an economic revolution, but that we are equally intent on social revolution. Only by advances on these three separate lines, and their integration into one great whole, will the people of India progress."

(b) Approach to Communication : Even as the approach to development had a mass orientation, so did the approach to communication in the pre-independence period and in the early years of independence.

Of the numerous sub-committees established by the National Planning Committee in the late 1930's one was, significantly, on communication. Television was at that time in an experimental phase even in the industrially advanced countries of the West. The report of the sub-committee on communication emphasised the role of radio as the only medium of mass communication, then available, which was free of the literacy barrier. The sub-committee regarded broadcasting as a necessity for modern development and, using the expression 'State propaganda' in the sense of what is now connoted by development communication, said: "The principal functions of broadcasting are: (a) dissemination of news and useful information; (b) adult education and fighting rural ignorance; (c) propaganda by the State; (d) entertainment." The sub-committee's report called for an innovative approach even to broadcasting hardware, stating that "many problems of communication engineering are peculiar to the country and their solution can only be obtained by carrying out investigations in the country itself." Broadcasting was envisaged as the most effective link between "the vast majority of the population who are still illiterate and a large section of the women who do not go out into the public, on the one hand, and the progressive part of India on the other." Radio, the report said, should provide "an easy channel for bringing to the masses useful information on agriculture, animal husbandry, current political thought, etc." The planning for broadcasting had to serve the objective of "providing populous regions of the country with first-grade service, and installing community receivers on a wide scale in the rural areas."[24]

The approach of the National Planning Committee's sub-committee on communication was thus oriented to rural development and showed a lively awareness of the need not only to put out broadcasts of relevance to the village population but to provide access to radio to the rural poor through the facility of community listening. It is a remarkable example of the pre-independence sensitivity to the need to make communication serve the interests of the majority of the common people of India who live in villages. The role of communication in development as envisaged in the document on the First Five Year Plan was in line with the approach of the National Planning Committee's sub-committee. The Plan document, published in December 1952, in Chapter VIII on 'Public cooperation in national development', had a section on 'Reaching the people' which said : "A widespread understanding of the Plan is an essential stage in its fulfilment .....An understanding of the priorities which govern the Plan will enable each person to relate his or her role to the larger purposes of the nation as a whole. The Plan has, therefore, to be carried into every home in the language and symbols of the people and expressed in terms of their common needs and problems...with the assistance of creative writers and artists, which has to be specially enlisted...All available methods of communication have to be developed and the people approached through the written and the spoken word no less than through radio, film, song and drama. Above all, steps have to be taken to provide literature and information for the people in simple language on a scale equal to the needs of the country." (Emphasis added.)

This early document is remarkable also for its recognition of the need for decentralisation of development planning and for candid feedback: "It is only in terms of local programmes that local leadership and enthusiasm can play their part...If obstacles are encountered and things go wrong anywhere, it would be helpful in every sense if information is imparted candidly and the people are acquainted with the steps being taken to set things right. It is an error to belittle the capacity of the common man to find out and accept what is good for him."

NOTES

1. Statement to Reuter at Aden, 3 September 1931. *Collected Works of Mahatma Gandhi*, Vol. 47, pp.388-9.
2. D.G. Tendulkar, *Mahatma* Vol. VIII, facing p.89.
3. Jawaharlal Nehru, *An Autobiography* (P.511), Jawaharlal Nehru Memorial Fund, New Delhi, 1984. (First published in 1936).
4. Jawaharlal Nehru, *The Discovery of India* (p.556), Jawaharlal Nehru Memorial Fund, New Delhi 1983. (First published in 1946).
5. *Young India*, 2 July 1931.
6. *The Discovery of India*, p.66.
7. *Young India*, 4 April 1929.
8. *Young India*, 15 October 1931.
9. *Harijan*, 15 November 1934
10. *Modern Review*, Calcutta, October 1935 (p.412).
11. *Selected Works of Jawaharlal Nehru* ed. by S. Gopal, Vol. 3, pp. 13-15.
12. *Collected Works of Mahatma Gandhi*, Vol. 35,pp. 469-70.

13. *Selected Works of Jawaharlal Nehru*, Vol.3, p.19.
14. Jawaharlal Nehru, *An Autobiography*, p.406.
15. *Asia* magazine, New York, June 1936.
16. *The Discovery of India*, pp.26, 28.
17. A note on 'The Basic Approach' by Jawaharlal Nehru in *AICC Economic Review* of 15 August 1958, New Delhi, reprinted in *Mainsteam*, New Delhi, of 27 May 1989.
18. Jawaharlal Nehru, *India Today and Tomorrow* (Azad Memorial Lecture, 1959), Indian Council for Cultural Relations, New Delhi.
19. A.K. Ramanujan, *Speaking of Siva* (p.12), Penguin, 1973.
20. Oral History transcript, Nehru Memorial Museum & Library, New Delhi.
21. Krishna Kripalani, *Modern Indian Literature*, Nirmala Sadanand Publishers, 1968.
22. *Subramania Bharati: Chosen Poems and Prose* ed. by Prof. K. Swaminathan, published by the Bharati Centenary Celebrations Committee, 1984.
23. Quoted in the Report of the Committee on Panchayati Raj Institutions headed by Asoka Mehta (pp.2-3), Department of Rural Development, New Delhi, August 1978.
24. Quotations in this páragraph are from *An Indian Parsonality for Television* (p.5), being the report of the working Group on Software for Doordarshan, Vol. I, Publications Division, New Delhi, 1985.

Chapter II

IMPEDIMENTS TO BROAD-BASED DEVELOPMENT

The promise of a people-oriented and broad-based, rather than an elitist and narrow, approach to development and to communication was soon belied.

(i) Lack of Committed Cadres

A major reason was the lack of committed volunteers. During the freedom movement such volunteers moved among the common people and spread through word of mouth the message of freedom, Swadeshi, the making of salt in defiance of the law, Khadi, Prohibition and other items of Civil Disobedience and of the Constructive Programme.

Even during the struggle for independence the Congress had not paid due attention to the building up of cadres. The party's programme required for its propagation and implementation large numbers of volunteers--men and women who would give their whole time to public work in return for a modest maintenance allowance, rather than seeking the maximisation of their income in the rat race of mercenary careers.

Jawaharlal Nehru recalls in his autobiography a suggestion made in 1924 that the Congress general secretaries should be paid: "I happened to be one of the secretaries then, and I welcomed the proposal. It seemed to me quite wrong to expect whole-time work from anyone without paying him a maintenance allowance at least. Otherwise some person with private means has to be chosen, and such gentlemen of leisure are not perhaps always politically desirable, nor can they be held responsible for the work...But there is in India an extraordinary and thoroughly unjustified prejudice against receiving salaries from public funds (though not from the State), and my father strongly objected to my doing so."

Widespread nationalist fervour made up, during the freedom struggle, for the absence of paid, trained and organised cadres. At one end of the social scale, leading lawyers and doctors gave up their lucrative practice and courted imprisonment during the non-cooperation movement of the 1920's. Among such were T.Prakasam and Dr. Muthulakshmi Reddi of Madras, C.R. Das of Calcutta, Motilal Nehru of Allahabad and Asaf Ali of Delhi. At the other end of the scale, even persons of limited means like school teachers, small peasants, workers and housewives joined the civil disobedience movement of the 1930's and subsequently the Quit India struggle, in their tens of thousands. They braved the rigours of prison life and disregarded the adverse economic consequences for themselves and their families. That kind of inspired self-sacrifice for a larger cause could not be expected to continue on any large scale after the objective of independence was achieved.

Gandhiji had always placed greater value on constructive work among the poor and the deprived than on the role of legislators and Ministers. After watching the performance of Congress legislators and Congress governments in the provinces for a year, he wrote on 3 Septemeber 1938: "It looks as if Congressmen are not able to digest the power that has come to the Congress. Everyone wants to have a share in the spoils of office. This is not the way to win Swaraj." Within a few months of independence, and just before he fell to the assassin's bullets, he advocated the transformation of the Congress into a Lok Sevak Sangh (Servants of the People Society).

In the draft of a new constitution for the Congress which Gandhiji prepared on 29 January 1948 and revised the following morning--on the day of his martyrdom--he suggested the disbandment of the Congress as a progaganda vehicle and parliamentary machine and the setting up of a Lok Sevak Sangh. It was not as if Gandhiji had no use for the political process. He wanted the Sangh's volunteers to check the voters' roll and encourage people to acquire the legal qualifications for the right of franchise. (This was before the coming into force of the 1950 Constitution which conferred universal adult suffrage.) The volunteers were to promote "equal respect and regard for all relgions and equality of opportunity and status for all, irrespective of race, creed or sex." On the question of funds for the Lok Sevak Sangh, Gandhiji's draft said: "The Sangh shall raise finance for the fulfilment of its mission from among the villagers and others, special stress being laid on collection of the poor man's pice."

It was not to be expected that the Mahatma's advice would be heeded by the Congress leaders who had in August 1946 entered the Viceroy's Executive Council and were, by January 1948, in full command of the government. But instead of relying entirely on the bureaucracy for the tasks of popular education and programme implementation, the Congress even while continuing as a political party could have raised a corps of Lok Sevak volunteers. They could have been trained to act both as an aid, and--through frank feed-back on the people's felt needs and their reactions to official programmes--as a corrective, to the administration.

Jawaharlal Nehru could have launched such an initiative. But an aptitude and capacity for organisation building was not among his strong points.

Moreover, unlike Gandhiji who approached every problem from the centre outwards--with the moral individual as the centre in relation to India, and India as the centre in relation to the world--Jawaharlal Nehru liked to study the larger context of a problem rather than the nuts and bolts required for solving it. Thus, according to Gandhiji, India would attain Swaraj when every Indian achieved freedom within and for himself. "Please do not carry unnecessarily on your head the burden of emancipating India", he wrote to his nephew Maganlal Gandhi. "Emancipate your own self. Even that burden is very great...In your emancipation is the emancipation of India. All else is make-believe."

Jawaharlal Nehru carried on his head the burden of saving the world from a turning of the Cold War into a nuclear holocaust. Had he concentrated on the eradication of poverty and illiteracy in India, he would have served both the country and the world better. By choosing to take charge of the portfolio of External Affairs in addition to his duties as Prime Minister and Chairman of the Planning Commission, Nehru applied a great deal of his time to the minutiae of the opening, staffing and running of embassies, and to visits abroad and the receiving of foreign dignitaries coming to India. He did not need to hold this portfolio personally either to carry through the decision that India as a sovereign republic would continue in the (no longer British) Commonwealth as an equal partner with the white Dominions, or to advocate non-alignment on the part of newly free countires, or to urge on all the cultivation of the temper of peace. He could have done all this as Prime Minister. Without the burden of handling external affairs personally from day to day, Nehru could have functioned more effectively as Chairman of the Planning Commission. He might have been able to ensure that the focus remained on human development rather than econometrics. This would have entailed the raising and training of a large cadre of volunteers throughout the country.

However, it is more profitable to remind ourselves of and derive inspiration from the best insights and endeavours of the great dead, than to deplore shortfalls in their achievement.

(ii) Disunity of Radical Forces

Not only did the Congress not raise a corps of volunteers, it lost such cadres as it had when, in February 1948, the Congress Socialists broke away from the parent body.

Leaders of the Congress Socialist Party, formed in 1934, were in the forefront of the Quit India struggle launched in 1942. Riding on the crest of popular esteem, and dissatisfied with the Congress leadership on account of its efforts since 1945 to make a compromise settlement with the Muslim League and the British rulers, the Socialists thought they could offer an alternative to the Congress. Their departure weakened the hands of Jawaharlal Nehru in relation to the conservative elements in the Congress.

As for the Communists, the other cadre-based party, they had alienated themselves from all sections of nationalist opinion by their People's War policy of collaboration with the British war effort. After the war they swung to the other extreme. Till the early 1950's they refused to acknowledge that India had become politically independent in August 1947.

Had there been a different electoral system based on proportional representation--this is discussed more fully in the next Chapter--the political groups who stood for radical economic change might have joined hands in coalition governments. Instead, they have remained frozen in confrontationist postures. As a result, Jawaharlal Nehru's hopes of land redistribution and co-operative joint farming by large numbers of small holders were frustrated. The Congress party passed under the control of large landlords, whose kin were entering trade and industry in a big way with the ending of British monopoly and the sale of many British enterprises to Indians. They nominally accepted radical resolutions drafted by Nehru, the party's indispensable vote getter, as at the Avadi session of the Congress in 1955 which adopted the objective of a socialistic pattern of society. The goal remained on paper since most of the Congress Ministers and legislators at the Centre and in the States had no use for socialism.

(a) Development Turns Elitist : The pattern of economic development took an increasingly elitist turn after the dealth of Jawaharlal Nehru in 1964. Land reforms ground to a halt, with many landlords retaining very large holdings under fictitious names. Industrial development has served largely to provide an increasing range of luxury goods and services to the middle and upper classes. Widespread destitution and illiteracy continue.

A major consequence of the fragmentation of progressive forces has been division and weakening of the trade union movement as well as the women's movement. Both remain largely confined to urban centres. Strike actions and threats have come far more from the relatively well-paid, such as the officers and staff of the nationalised banks, airlines and life insurance, college teachers, doctors in government employment, journalists and other newspaper employees, than those, in rural occupations and in the unorganised sector of industry, who are most in need of improvement in their emoluments and working conditions. The urban orientation and embourgeoisment of the women's movement matches that of the trade unions. Though the education of women is the key to self-development and to participation on equal terms in decision-making in the home and in public life, women's education is among the bleakest areas of post-Independence India's record. Meanwhile a futile expenditure of hundreds of crores of rupees is being incurred each year on trying to limit population growth through family planning. It is not realised that the norm of a small family cannot be achieved without a significant rise in the living standards of the toiling masses and without the education and empowerment of women

Little difference has been made by the emergence of non-Congress governments in certain States since the 1967 elections, and the further growth since then of various political parties as rivals to the Congress. With the partial exception of the CPI (M), they reflect competition between different sections of the privileged minority: the rural bourgeoisie as against the English-educated and Westernised urban bourgeoisie; the non-Hindi bourgoisie as against the privileged from the Hindi belt who are dominant at the Centre; and aspiring leaders of parties based on religious, caste, linguistic or ethnic identity. All these are vertical divisions which hide disparities within each. They enable the competing sections of the privileged upper strata to mobilise the poor and the dispossessed as cannon fodder for the furtherance of their own interests.

It has been the experience of political democracies the world over that adult suffrage, with free elections and secrecy of the ballot, is a necessary but not sufficient condition for the economic, social and intellectual liberation of the masses. Emancipation of the disadvantaged requires united action, by all those who stand for progressive change, to organise them and to raise their level of political consciousness. Without this the poor and the exploited tend to give their votes to demagogues rather than to genuine representatives of their interests. The privilege of casting a vote once in five years, or even oftener, brings them only some crumbs from those seeking their votes. Democracy becomes a facade that hides gross inequalities. This is what has happended in India after independence.

The middle and upper classes who rule the country through the different political parties have, by and large, abandoned the Gandhi-Nehru vision of human development in favour of indices of economic growth that are irrelevant to the well-being of the masses. The very expression 'alleviation of poverty', as but one of many Plan programmes, is significant. Eradication of poverty is not the aim, let alone the central and governing aim of planning.

The focus in successive Plan documents has been on economic growth measured in terms of national income, which is no indicator of human development. National income statistics club together the value of all commodities produced in a country, be they consumer goods or military equipment. The consumer goods themselves may be either essentials like foodgrains and clothing, or non-essentials in the context of a poverty-ridden country like banquets in multi-star hotels, motor cars, toiletry, soft drinks, cigarettes and Indian-made versions of a wide range of foreign liquor. While national income estimates take into account the value of production in agriculture and in industries, the intangible value generated in the tertiary or services sector is measured by the income earned by those engaged in it. Thus every upward revision of the emoluments of the increasing number of employees in the civil, police and military services of the government, and in the Central and State public sector undertakings, inflates the figure of national income.

National income data tell us nothing about how that income is distributed among different classes in a country's population. The figure of per capita national income at a given point of time is worth no more than information on the average depth of a river to a person who is considering whether he can wade across it.

(b) Narrow Concept of Communication : Even as the concept of development has suffered elitist distortion, the concept of development communication has been distorted and trivialised.

Three different sources have contributed to the narrowing of the concept of development communication. One is the capitalist or market-economy West, where the industrial culture of individualism, multiplication of wants and of urbanisation is promoted by the modern media of mass communication which purvey and are sustained by commerical advertising. This culture is a negation of the simple communitarian living based on mutual help which a long line of egalitarian thinkers--from the Vedic and Upanishadic sages of India to the so-called Utopian socialists of Europe, and Tolstoy and Gandhi in recent times--have advocated. The former colonial powers have commended to the newly free and developing countries, along with their own pattern of industrialisation, an extremely narrow concept of development communication focussed on agricultural modernisation, health and family planning. A strong motive behind their propagation of ethno-centric notions of development and of communication, through aid programmes and scholarships and textbooks, is export promotion of their machinery and manufactures including the hardware--and even the software--of mass communication.

Another source is the Soviet model. An example of Communist 'development communication', narrowly conceived to mean that workers in agriculture and industry should maximise their output, was the glorification of Stakhanov, the Russian coalminer. The cult of Stakhanovism showed that the State as owner of the means of production needs, no less than the private capitalist, to extract surplus value from labour. This surplus value is needed for maintaining the rulers in comfort and for investment in further growth of the country's economy and of its military machine.

A third source of trivialisation of development communication has been Third World totalitarianism, more often without than with the fig leaf of socialist ideology. In the Philippines under the authoritarian and corrupt Marcos regime--now discredited even in the U.S.A. which propped him up for long years--the concept of 'development reporting' was promoted as a substitute for political debate. It became popular with the authorities in India during the internal emergency imposed by the Indira Gandhi government in 1975-76 when the democratic liberties of citizens were abrogated, free expression throttled, and censorship imposed even on the proceedings of Parliament.

But the misuse and degradation of the concept of development communication does not invalidate the possibility of employing communication to promote human development in the widest and profoundest sense. Those who entertain a holistic approach to development should rescue the concept of development communication from the notion that it is an appendage of government departments of agriculture, health and family planning. In the context of grave problems like the killings in and related to Punjab and Kashmir in recent years, the outbreaks of communal riots and caste wars, development communication in the narrow, government-departmental sense of the term sounds rather like Nero's fiddling while Rome burnt.

In the present study, communication is considered in the widest sense of the term. It comprehends, besides the mass media and the extension services, the shaping of attitudes by religion in both its aspects, fanatical and humanist; by formal education; by exposure to or participation in the work of voluntary organisations; and by the messages put out by diverse political groups competing for power in a democratic polity. Some of these messages are divisive, and incite hatred and strife. Development, on the other hand, requires an atmosphere free of senseless hatred and violence--as distinct from the creative tensions that are unavoidable in the course of correcting ancient injustices.

Development communication understood in the broad sense must therefore counter the divisive propaganda mounted by power- seekers in the name of the vertical divisions of religion, caste, region, language or ethnic origin. The fact that these vertical divisions hide inequalities and exploitation within each group needs to be relentlessly exposed.

In addition, development communication must at the workaday level take to the poor information of relevance in meeting their felt problems, in language that will be intelligible. It must be multi-way communication, enabling ordinary people to talk among themselves and to give expression to their needs. It should not be one-way, top-down 'publicity' for the government's achievements and intentions, or image-building of the head of the government for the time being in power, at the Centre or in a State.

It should make the toiling masses aware of laws and programmes of relevance to them--such as land reforms, employment schemes and minimum wages--and help them to organise themselves to realise the benefits.

If development communication does all this, it will play a liberating role in a democratic and developing country like India. It will raise the level of awareness of the masses, mobilise them for freeing themselves from exploitative social and economic structures, and help them to live in amity and cooperation.

(iii) Framework of Public Policies

Development in the humanist and egalitarian sense can be promoted only in a framework of public policies--political, social and economic--conducive to such a pattern of development.

In areas of concrete action like land reform and minimum wages, or adult education and health, there is necessarily a coherence, even if imperfect, between stated aim, on the one hand, and policy and programmes on the other. Communication can therefore play a direct role in helping to implement, and through feedback on the people's felt needs and their reactions to the manner of implementation, to modify and improve the policy and programmes.

However, in such intangible areas as the promotion of national unity and social harmony, there can be a lack of congruence between the government's ostensible aim and its policies and programmes. For example, the political party in power at the Centre or in a State may, in order to woo votes, pursue policies and programmes which reinforce the sense of separateness on grounds of religion, caste or ethnic origin. It would be disingenuous on the part of such a government to expect communication to put out the fires of separatism which it is stoking.

There is little that the communicator in the official sector can do in such a situation. But non-official publicists concerned about development can and should help to correct the mismatch between development aims and public policies. The development communicator's role in influenncing public policies will necessarily be indirect and limited, but it is no less signifcant than that of the legislator, the administrator and the jurist as lawyer or judge. The development publicist can help by exposing the low-level motivation and dangerous consequences of pursuing divisive public policies, and by educating public opinion on the need for correcting the policies and programmes.

The major issues of public policy that call for critical scrutiny by development publicists, in the circumstances prevailing in India, are surveyed in the ensuing sections of this Chapter.

(a) Constitution : Unequal Treatment of Religions : Certain provisions of the Consitution of the Indian Republic which came into force on 26 January 1950 have unwittingly served to promote social divisiveness on the grounds of religion, caste and ethnic origin and thereby to distract the attention of the masses of the poor and the exploited from the central problem of inequality of opportunity.

On the one hand, the 1950 Constitution was a remarkable document in the political evolution of mankind. It conferred on one-seventh of the human race, at one stoke, universal adult franchise irrespective of sex or religion, racial origin, educational or economic status. The older democracies had inched their way towards universal suffrage over a period of two centuries beginning with the industrial revolution. Women did not enjoy equal voting rights with men in an old and economically developed democracy like Switzerland when Indian women gained the franchise. Another notable feature of the Constitution was that, in fulfilment of Gandhiji's mission, it expressly abolished untouchability and made its practice punishable in accordance with law.

Along with these epoch-making provisions, the Constitution had some negative features, to which more were added through amendment, that have had the unfortunate effect of solidifying vertical social divisions. Religious fundamentalists and political opportunists have utilised these provisions of the Constitution to promote their own interests at the expense of national unity and social harmony. These negative features of the Constitution are : (i) Unequal treatment of Indian citizens professing different religions, in contradiction of the secular State which the Constitution purports to establish and sustain, through the conferment of special rights on religious minorities which tends to make them States within the Indian State; and (ii) Sanction of special provisions--which have in practice taken the form of reservation of seats in educational institutions and of posts in public employment--in favour of caste and ethnic groups, without a time limit and without the requirement of legislation specifying norms such as family occupation and income.

Though religious, caste and ethnic riots have disrupted normal life, and the development process, from time to time in various parts of the country, the constitutional provisions that abet divisiveness have received little attention from political analysts and development publicists. A critical review of these provisions is attempted here in the hope that it may stimulate a debate on desirable lines of constitution amendment so as to minimise the exploitation of religious, caste and enthic difference by unscrupulous, vote-catching politicians.

On the subject of religion, the Karachi Congress Resolution set out two principles. One was that every citizen would enjoy the right freely to profess and practise his religion, subject to public order and morality; the other was that "The State shall observe neutrality in regard to all religions." The 1950 Constitution, on the other hand, does not accord equal treatment to the majority who profess the Hindu faith and the minorities professing other religions. The latter are given speical rights in the matter of establishing and administering educational institutions of their choice. Religious instruction may be imparted in such institutions, even if they receive aid from State funds, whereas religious instruction is prohibited in educational institutions wholly maintained out of State funds.

Articles 25 to 28, in Part III enumerating the fundamental rights, deal with the 'Right to Freedom of Religion'. They are as follows :

> "**25. Freedom of conscience and free profession, practice and propagation of religion.**-- (1) Subject to public order, morality and health and to the other provisions of this Part, all persons are equally entitled to freedom of conscience and the right freely to profess, practise and propagate religion.
>
> (2) Nothing in this article shall affect the operation of any exisitng law or prevent the State from making any law--
>
> (a) regulating or restricting any economic, financial, political or other secular activity which may be associated with relgious practice;
>
> (b) Providing for social welfare and reform or the throwing open of Hindu religious institutions of a public character to all classes and sections of Hindus.
>
> Explanation I.--The wearing and carrying of kirpans shall be deemed to be included in the profession of the Sikh religion.
>
> Explanation II.-- In sub-clause (b) of clause (2), the reference to Hindus shall be construed as including a reference to persons professing the Sikh, Jaina or Buddhist religion, and the reference to Hindu religious institutions shall be construed accordingly.
>
> **26. Freedom to manage religious affairs.--** Subject to public order, morality and health, every religious denomination or any section thereof shall have the right--

(a) to establish and maintain institutions for religious and charitable purposes;

(b) to manage its own affairs in matters of religion;

(c) to own and acquire movable and immovable property; and

(d) to administer such property in accordance with law.

27. Freedom as to payment of extra taxes for promotion of any particular religion.--No person shall be compelled to pay any taxes, the proceeds of which are specifically appropriated in payment of expenses for the promotion or maintenance of any particular religion or religious denomination.

28. Freedom as to attendance at religious instruction or religious worship in certain educational institutions.--

(1) No religious instruction shall be provided in any educational institution wholly maintained out of State funds.

(2) Nothing in clause (1) shall apply to an educational institution which is administered by the State but has been established under any endowment or trust which requires that religious instruction shall be imparted in such institution.

(3) No person attending any educational institution recognised by the State or receiving aid out of State funds shall be required to take part in any religious instruction that may be imparted in such institution or to attend any religious worship that may be conducted in such institution or in any premises attached thereto unless such person or, if such person is a minor, his guardian has given his consent thereto."

Also relevant is Article 30 relating to 'Cultural and Educational Rights' in the Fundamental Rights chapter:

"30. Right of minorities to establish and administer educational institutions.– All minorities, whether based on religion or langùage, shall have the right to establish and administer educational institutions of their choice.

(2) The State shall not, in granting aid to educational institutions, discriminate against any educational institution on the ground that it is under the management of a minority, whether based on religion or language."

Religious instruction is thus expressly and absolutely prohibited in educational institutions maintained wholly out of State funds. Since the ban is not restricted to instruction exclusively in any one faith, it applies obviously even to instruction in the ethical values common to all religions. Ethical training is denied to the great majority of boys and girls in the country who go--if at all they do--to schools and colleges run by a panchayat, municipality, corporation, State or Central Government where education is available free or at nominal cost.

Other schools and colleges are of two categories: the so-called 'public schools' which are in fact highly private, being accessible only to children of the well-to-do; and those run by linguistic or religious minorities. The Constitution thus allows institutions run by the religious minorities to impart religious instruction, which will in the nature of the case be confined ordinarily to one religion only. There have been disturbing reports of fanatical fundamentalist indoctrination in some 200 schools run in Kashmir Valley by the Jamaat-e-Islami[1], and at other religious minority schools elsewhere in the country. It was only in Jaunary 1990, after the outbreak of insurrection by secessionist elements in Kashmir Valley, that the Jamaat-run schools were ordered to be closed down.

This unequal and discriminatory treatment of citizens professing different religions runs counter to the principle of a secular State. And yet, an anachronistic amendment of the Preamble to the Constitution was enacted in 1976 at the instance of the ruling Congress (I)[2], by a gagged parliament during the internal emergency. It proclaimed that India was a 'socialist secular' republic, and not just a sovereign democratic republic as it had been till then. Even more extraordinary is the requirement, under a law passed by parliament in 1988,[3] that no political party can be registered by the Election Commission of India for the purpose of contesting elections unless it pledges itself "to the principles of socialism, secularism and democracy". The Statement of Objects and Reasons appended to this Bill said inter alia: "At present there is no statutory definition of political party in the Election Law. The recognition of a political party and the allotment of symbols for each party are presenly regulated under the Election Symbols (Reservation and Allotment) Order, 1968. It is felt that the Election Law should define political party and lay down the procedure for its registration. It is also felt that the political parties should be required to include a specific provision in the memorandum or rules or regulations governing their functioning that they would fully be committed to and abide by the principles enshrined in the preamble to the Constitution." This extraordinary legislation thus requires that every political party should adhere to the same objectives as are professed--howsoever hypocritically--by the Congress (I).

What could have led the constitution-makers to incorporate the non-secular provisions with regard to religious instruction, which bear a striking resemblance to the British rulers' policy of discrimination in favour of the religious minorities?

The historical background may be recalled briefly. The British colonialists systematically promoted separatist feelings among different sections of Indian society in order to divide and weaken the national movement and buttress their own rule. Separate electorates were created for Muslims under the first legislation which introduced the elective principle, though on an extremely limited franchise, namely the Indian Councils Act of 1909. The Government of India Act of 1919 extended separate electorates to the Sikhs in Punjab and to Indian Christians in Madras Presidency. The 1919 Act, moreover, created reserved seats for non-Brahmins in Madras Presidency and for Marathas (also non-Brahmins) in Bombay Presidency. The Government of India Act of 1935 extended the principle of reserved seats to the Depressed Classes (the so-called untouchables, now known as the Scheduled Castes) and to women, with some constituencies reserved for Muslim women.

The 1950 Constitution did away with separate electorates based on religion. But it conferred special rights on religious minorities. It might have been due to persistence of the pre- independence habit of treating religious minorities with kid-gloves, from fear of driving them into the waiting arms of the foreign rulers. Or it might be explained by the controversy then raging over the accession in 1947 of the Muslim-majority State of Jammu & Kashmir to India. It was an issue on which almost all the Muslim countries backed Pakistan in the United Nations; India had to rely on the Soviet Union's repeated exercise of the veto in the Security Council. Special treatment of the large Muslim minority of India's population, it was perhaps hoped, would please not only the community's predominantly non-secular leadership within the country but Muslim opinion outside India.

The constitution-makers might also have wished to reassure the religious minorities that though the sub-continent had been partitioned at the insistence of the representatives of a majority of the Muslim population, those Muslims who remained behind in India, as well as other religious minorities, would be free to preserve their indentity. But, over the years, many political parties have come to treat the minorities as vote banks. The ending, with independence, of British patronage for the communal separatists among Muslim and Christian leaders has been made good by a new factor: the wooing of Muslim and Christian votes even by political parties that profess faith in secular democracy.

This would explain the confining to Hindus of the reform and codification of civil law to improve women's status. Successive Indian governments have refrained from interfering with the personal laws of the minorities, even though the framing of a common civil code is among the Directive Principles which form Part IV of the Constitution. Article 37 says that, though the provisions in this Part are not enforceable by courts, "the principles therein laid down are nevertheless fundamental in the governance of the country and it shall be the duty of the State to apply these principles in making laws." Hindu law was codified in the 1950's to effect various reforms including enforcement of monogamy on the Hindu male. But the Indian Muslim male continues to be free to practise polygamy.

A Muslim-majority district of Malappuram was carved out in Kerala, amidst controversy, when the State was ruled by a Communist-led coalition government. The Central Government, run by the Congress (I), sponsored a regressive Muslim Women's Act following protests by Muslim male chauvinists against a Supreme Court judgment of 1985 which held that Muslim men, like other Indians, were liable under the Criminal Procedure Code to pay maintenance to a divorced and needy wife.

The Ramakrishna Mission seeking the status of a religious minority, and securing legal recognition as such in 1985, is the *reductio ad absurdum* of the constitutional provisions conferring special rights on religious minorities. The judgement was delivered by a two-member bench of the Calcutta HIgh Court on 7 October 1985, in Madhab Chandra Bandopadhyaya and others vs. State of West Bengal and others. The issue was whether the West Bengal College Teachers (Security of Service) Act 1975 and the West Bengal College Service Commission Act 1978 were applicable to the Sri Ramakrishna Vivekananda Centenary College run by the Mission at Rehara. The High Court held that Article 30 (1) gives religious minorities the right to establish and administer educational institutions imparting not only religious instruction but general secular education; and that since non-Hindus are not required to renounce their own religion and embrace Hinduism in order to follow the Religion Universal of Ramakrishna, Ramakrishnaism is a minority religion in India like the Lingayat faith or Buddhism, Sikhism and Christianity.

It is curious that at a time when the new wave of thinking sweeping across the Soviet Union and several other socialist countries accepts the need to loosen the grip of the State and to allow greater scope for cooperative and individual effort, an institution like the Ramakrishna Mission should have to claim the status of a minority religion in order to aviod the attentions of the State.

(b) Caste-Based Reservations : Separatism based on caste, as in the case of religion, has a history of deliberate encouragement by the British regime during the pre-independence years.

The British rulers carried their flattery of Indian Muslims so far as to treat the basic Indian identity as Muslim and to describe other Indians as 'non-Muhammadan'. Thus the officially published proceedings of the Central Legislative Assembly during 1927 describe not only Lala Lajpatrai of Muslim-majority Punjab as member from 'Jullundur Division: Non-Muhammadan' but members from the south too, where the Muslims are a small minority. A. Rangaswami Iyengar is member from 'Tanjore-cum-Trichinopoly: Non-Muhammadan Rural', and C. Duraiswamy Aiyangar is member from 'Madras Ceded Districts and Chittoor: Non-Muhammadan Rural'.

The British likewise cultivated members of the upper economic strata of the non-Brahmin Hindu castes many of whom were leaders of loyalist political parties. Until the Congress accepted office in the provinces under the Government of India Act of 1935, the loyalist parties formed provincial Ministries with limited powers and subject to the British Governor's veto. In Madras Presidency, the provincial Ministry formed by the Justice Party framed rules for recruitment to, and promotions within, the provincial civil services which treated non-Brahmins preferentially as against Brahmins. This was on the ground, which had much justification in social history, that discrimination-in-reverse was necessary in order to correct the wrongs suffered by the non-Brahmins over the centuries when learning had been monopolised by the Brahmins. However, since caste was the sole criterion for preference, the preferential treatment helped the already well-off among the non-Brahmin castes rather than those who could not afford the education necessary for seeking to enter the civil services and who were most in need of assistance.

When the Constitution of free India came into force, there was the possibility of the preferential treatment of certain castes in admission to educational institutions and in public employment being struck down as violative of the Fundamental Rights of equality and non-discrimination. The Government did not wish the non-Brahmin castes to lose the special provision made in their favour, particularly with the first general elections due to be held soon on the basis of universal adult suffrage. The Constitution was amended in 1951 to protect discrimination-in-reverse, but without a time limit and without the requirement of legislation to prescribe norms such as family occupation and income. As in the case of the Constitution's special treatment of religious minorities, the provisions relating to backward castes and tribal groups have been found handy by vote-seeking politicians.

Articles 15 (4), 16 (4) and 335 which sanction protective discrimination have in practice served to perpetuate disunity and conflict among different castes, and between the tribal and non-tribal sections of the population. The articles are reproduced below in full :

> **"15. Prohibition of discrimination on grounds of religion, race, caste, sex or place of birth.--**
>
> (1) The State shall not discriminate against any citizen on grounds only of religion, race, caste, sex, place of birth or any of them.
>
> (2) No citizen shall, on grounds only of religion, race, sex, place of birth or any of them, be subject to any disability, liability, restriction or condition with regard to--(a) access to shops, public restaurants, hotels and places of public entertainment; or (b) the use of wells, tanks, bathing ghats, roads and places of public resort maintained wholly or partly out of State funds or dedicated to the use of the general public.
>
> (3) Nothing in this article shall prevent the State from making any special provision for women and children.
>
> *(4) Nothing in this article or in clause (2) of article 29 shall prevent the State from making any special provision for the advancement of any socially and educationally backward classes of citizens or for the Scheduled Castes and the Scheduled Tribes."
>
> **"16. Equality of opportunity in matters of public employment.--**
>
> (1) There shall be equality of opportunity for all citizens in matters relating to employment or appointment to any office under the State.
>
> (2) No citizen shall, on grounds only of religion, race, caste, sex, descent, place of birth, residence or any of them be ineligible for, or discriminated against in respect of, any employment or office under the State.
>
> (3) Nothing in this article shall prevent Parliament from making any law prescribing in regard to a class or classes of employment or appointment to an office under the Govern-

---

* This clause was added by the Constitution (First Amendment) Act, 1951. Article 29 (2) reads : "No citizen shall be denied admission into any educational institution maintained by the State or receiving aid out of State funds on grounds only of religion, race, caste, language or any of them."

> ment of, or any local or other authority within, a State or Union territory, any requirement as to residence within that State or Union territory prior to such employment or appointment.
>
> (4) Nothing in this article shall prevent the State from making any provision for the reservation of appointments or posts in favour of any backward class of citizens which, in the opinion of the State, is not adequately represented in the services under the State.
>
> (5) Nothing in this article shall affect the operation of any law which provides that the incumbent of an office in connection with the affairs of any religious or denominational institution or any member of the governing body thereof shall be a person professing a particular religion or belonging to a particular denomination."
>
> **"335. Claims of Scheduled Castes and Scheduled Tribes to services and posts.--** The claims of the members of the Scheduled Castes and the Scheduled Tribes shall be taken into consideration, consistently with the maintenance of efficiency of administration, in the making of appointments to services and posts in connection with the affairs of the Union or of a State."

The Fundamental Right to non-discrimination, which article 15 purports to guarantee, and the Fundamental Right to equality of opportunity in matters of public employment which article 16 purports to guarantee, are both thus seriously eroded by qualifying clauses which permit the State to disregard those Fundamental Rights.

There was an initial time-limit of ten years (subsequently extended to 50 years through successive amendments of the Constitution) in the provision made under articles 330, 332 and 334 for the reservation of seats in the House of the People and in the State legislatures for the Scheduled Castes and the Scheduled Tribes. Moreover, the reservation of seats was limited to the proportion borne by the population of SC and ST to the total population. In contrast, the special provisions permitted by the Constitution for the SC, ST and OBC can continue till the end of time. Nor is there any stipulation as to the quantum of the reservation of seats in educational institutions and of posts in public employment which may be made in favour of the SC, ST and OBC. Though articles 15 (4), 16 (4) and 335 permit abridgement of the fundamental rights to equality and non-discrimination, the State governments do not have to get legislation passed for the prupose. Executive orders are issued--usually on the eve of elections--setting off violent agitations by or against the castes whose votes are wooed. Unlike Hindu-Muslim riots which generally break out in congested urban localities, violent conflicts between castes affect rural India too, and to a greater extent. Often the conflict is between land-owing members of Other Backward Classes and the Scheduled Castes who are no longer prepared to be treated as beasts of burden. Sometimes it is between OBC castes, as when one OBC caste–like the Vanniyars in Tamil Nadu who repeatedly launched a blockade of roads as part of their agitation in 1988–feels that the more 'forward' castes among the Other Backward Classes have cornered the benefits of reservation. Hence the demand of the Vanniyars for compartmentalised reservation (i.e., caste-wise as between OBCs)--a trend that seems likley to spread elsewhere. The executive orders regarding reservations have been challenged in High Courts and the Supreme Court--each court giving different decisions at different points of time. This amounts to judicial legislation, which is fair neither to the judges nor to the citizens. In Balaji v. State of Mysore the Supreme Court held in 1963 that though "caste in relation to Hindus may be a relevant factor in determining the social backwardness of a group or classes of citizens, it cannot be made the sole dominant test in that behalf."[4]. After considering the criteria of educational and social backwardness, the Court said with regard to the quantum of reservation in favour of the SC, ST and OBC that the interests of the weaker sections of society had to be adjusted with the interests of the community as a whole: "Speaking generally and in a broad way, a special provision should be less than 50 per cent. How much less than 50 per cent would depend upon the relevant prevailing circumstances in each case."

The relevance of a means test for the purpose of reservation of college seats and public employment has also been considered by the courts. The Kerala Government accepted the recommendnation made by the State Backward Classes Commission that there should be a means-cum-caste test. But in Shamim v. Medical College, Trivandrum, a Single Judge of the Kerala High Court quashed the government order, holding that irrespective of their economic status all families from the backward classes were entitled to protective discrimination as "the test of poverty cannot be the determining factor for social backwardness." However, on appeal, the Division Bench of the same High Court reversed this decision and upheld the government's order. The High Court held that economic backwardness plays a part in social and educational backwardness and, therefore, poverty or economic standard was a relevant factor. In appeal, in Jayasree v. State of Kerala, the Supreme Court upheld the decision of the Kerala High Court.

In addition to commending these broad approaches, the courts have also made some specific pronouncements which some citizens may, with respect, regard as odd. Thus, the Supreme Court held in 1971, in

Chanchala v. State of Mysore that "it is not unreasonable to extend that principle (namely, preferential treatment) to children of political sufferers and of Defence personnel and ex-Defence personnel." In 1964 the Kerala High Court, in Jacob Mathew v. State of Kerala, upheld reservation in favour of Ezhavas, Muslims and Latin Catholics on the ground that they belonged to socially and educationally backward classes; it also upheld the reservation in favour of outstanding sportsmen as being a valid classification, but struck down the reservation in favour of children of medical practitioners on the ground that it was based on a classification which has no rational relation to the object to be secured. In State of Uttar Pradesh v. Pradeep Tandon, Chief Justice Ray, speaking for the Supreme Court, held in 1975 that reservation for persons from the hill and Uttar Khand areas was valid, but not reservation for persons from the rural areas as a whole.[5]

West Bengal is the only State to have provided no reservations other than for the Scheduled Castes and Scheduled Tribes. The State Government led by the CPI (M) has resisted the temptation to seek votes by holding out caste-based inducements. The report of the second Backward Classes Commission headed by B.P. Mandal notes in Chapter II surveying the status of OBCs in the States :

> "Government of West Bengal set up a Committee on August 1st, 1980, to study whether it was necessary to invoke the powers vested in the State Government under Articles 15 (4), 16 (4) and 29 (2)...In its report submitted on August 30th, 1980, the Committee recommended that 'Poverty and low levels of living standards rather than caste should, in our opinion, be the most important criteria for identifying backwardness.' It also recommended the identification of occupational groups as backward, and formulation of comprehensive programmes 'for the economic development and educational advancement of those groups who are below the poverty line.' The committee was against reservation of quotas in government services for backward classes. The report of the Committee has been accepted by the Government of West Bengal in toto."

Of interest in this connection is a recent news report by the Press Trust of India about the estate, valued at over Rs. 50 lakhs, left by Babu Jagjivan Ram, the Scheduled Caste leader who served a long innings as Minister in the Union Government. The news agency reported an order made by the Delhi High Court on 19 May 1989 extending, till further orders, a temporary injunction restraining the wife and daughter of Babu Jagjivan Ram from disposing of his estate. This was in a suit filed by other relatives of the late Scheduled Castes leader.

The Mandal Commission has not recommended a means test, such as some State governments including Kerala and Karnataka have prescribed, in order to limit the benefit of caste-based reservations to the really backward and needy. On the contrary, the Commission has argued against a means test. The commission says in its report of December 1980: "It is no doubt true that the major benefits of reservation and other welfare measures for Other Backward Classes will be cornered by the more advanced sections of the backward communities. But is not this a universal phenomenon ? The chief merit of reservation is not that it will introduce egalitarianism amongst OBCs when the rest of the Indian society is seized by all sorts of inequalities. But reservation will certainly erode the hold of higher castes on the services and enable OBCs in general to have a sense of participation in running the affairs of their country."

In such a caste-based approach which altogether ignores the economic criterion right? Should reservation of posts in the public services be confined to the stage of initial recruitment or should it apply also--as it is being applied now--to posts filled by promotion? Within a Scheduled Tribe, should those living outside the tribal habitat and pursuing non-traditional occupations be treated on par with other members of the tribe? To what extent have the benefits from preferential treatment of SC and ST in the issue of permits, licences, allotment of shops and houses, and other concessions been cornered by others acting *benami*? It is unfortunate that questions such as these are rarely investigated and discussed.

(c) Nursing Vote Banks : Whether in relation to religious communities or castes, a certain ambivalence has marked the Central Government's policy. The ruling party's electoral calculations incline it towards treating religious minorities and castes as if they are homogeneous entities without internal class difference. On the other hand, the constraint of resources sometimes inducese the Government to adopt the rational apprach of limiting assitance to the truly needy. A few instances illustrate the ambivalence.

Though segregation is hardly the right approach for securing the integration of the Scheduled Castes and Scheduled Tribes with the rest of Indian society, the Central Government has sponsored a scheme of assistance to the States for the construction of hostel buildings for SC/ST girl students. Sumati Oraon, as Deputy Minister for Welfare, told the Rajya Sabha on 19 August 1988 in a written reply to a question that Central assistance is provided to the State Governments on 50:50 basis for the construction/expansion of hostel buildings for SC/ST girl students. She added that a similar scheme for SC/ST boys had been agreed to in principle.

The electoral pull is evident also in other Central schemes like the opening of polytechnics in areas with a concentration of the minority population (meaning Muslims). *Muslim India,* the monthly journal edited by Syed Shahabuddin, recalled in the December 1987 issue, under the heading 'Educational progress of minorities under PM's Directive', that the opening of community polytechnics in minority concentration areas, coaching classes for educationally backward minorities for competitive examinations, and training of teachers from minority-managed educational institutions were among the Prime Minister Indira Gandhi's 15-point programme (May 1983) for the minorities.

The Press Information Bureau on 27 October 1987 issued a news release on 'Education Foundation for the Benefit of Muslims'. It reported Rajendra Kumari Bajpai, Minister of State for Welfare, as announcing at a meeting of the Central Wakf Council that the establishment of a foundation to ensure educational and vocational training of Muslims was being thought of. She also said that the Central Government had so far given grants-in-aid totalling Rs. 488.64 lakhs to the Central Wakf Council. Speaking of the role of the State Wakf Boards, she said that the scholarship scheme of the Council had been decentralised "and now the grant of scholarships for technical diploma courses, higher secondary and Islamic Madarsa education were being operated through the State Wakf Boards." Subsequently, on 27 December 1988, the same Minister promised the early creation of an educational foundation exclusively for Muslim women.[6].

The annual report of the Department of Food for 1988-89 includes the following: "Programme for Minorities: The Mobile Food & Nutrition Extension Units (MEUs) and Food and Nutrition Extension Centres (FNECs) of the Department also organised educational programmes in nutrition and fruits and vegetable preservation for minority groups. The MEUs organised 848 Nutrition Education programmes in minority concentration districts covering 31,410 beneficiaries, while FNECs conducted 77 training courses on fruits and vegetable preservation benefitting 2405 persons during the period April to December 1988."

As against these instances of policies designed to catch votes, the Central Government applies a means test in the scheme for the pre-examination coaching of SC/ST candiates for posts and services under the Central Government and Public Sector Undertakings. More than 100 coaching centres are being run throughout the country. The annual intake is more than 8000. On 12 June 1989 the Central Government announced[7] that the income limit for free coaching had been increased from Rs. 18,000 as the income of the parents or guardians from all sources, to Rs. 24,000. This was a rational and necessary step in order to index the means test for inflation. Similarly sound is the priority given in the poverty alleviation programmes, to assisting SC families living below the poverty line.

The application of the economic criterion as a supplement and corrective to the criterion of caste or ethnic origin is, however, yet to become settled policy.

(d) The Tribal Scene : The policy of reservations in higher education and in public employment can help only those who have already attained a certain level of development. This is illustrated by members of those tribal communities in the North East, with a high rate of literacy initially promoted by Christian missionary activity, who are conspicuously present on Central university campuses, in Central Government offices and in public sector enterprises like Indian Airlines. On the other hand, the generality of India's tribal population have been victims more than beneficiaries of a process of development ungoverned by ethical values. They have suffered both moral and material damage.

In the predominantly tribal States of Nagaland and Mizoram in the North East, the moral damage has been considerable. Insurrection brought in large numbers of security forces from outside, whose prolonged presence has nowhere been good for either side. At the same time, both the States have received Central financial assitance of a high order per capita. With a large literacy base, the burgeoning urban middle class and the political leaders thrown up by it have been quick to absorb outside influences, not necessarily the best. Attaining Statehood and joining what is called the national mainstream, the two States now rival the rest of India in corruption at political and administrative levels, defections from one party to another, and the free flow of money and liquor during elections. In terms of the dominance of amoralism in public life, Nagaland and Mizoram stand fully integrated.

Elsewhere, the tribals have suffered both in material and moral terms. The State sacrifices them at the altar of development when forested hill-sides inhabited by tribal people atre submerged by large storage dams. Private entrepreneurs, often in collusion with corrupt officials and politicans, get forests cut down for mining or timber or for the manufacture of paper, plywood and packing material. Liquor vendors introduce bottled brews of venomous potency, and consequently drunkeness, among people who traditionally use home-made rice beer or other fermented beverages with a low alcohol content, harmless or even nutritious.

Over and above the economic exploitation of the tribal people who have been reduced to wage slavery by intruders into their habitats, a moral blot on the colonisers is the sexual exploitation by many of them of tribal women engaged in road building, quarrying or domestic labour.

Jawaharlal Nehru had a premonition of what was to happen. Referring to the disastrous effect of "the so-called European civilisation" on tribal peoples in other parts of the world. "putting to an end their arts and crafts and their simple ways of living", he said that "now, to some extent, there is danger of the so-called Indian civilisation having this disastrous effect, if we do not check and apply it in the proper way... There is no point in trying to make of them a second-rate copy of ourselves."[8]

(iv) Decline in Values

The ethic of hard work was preached tirelessly by Jawaharlal Nehru in the years following independence. He said to young men and women in the colleges and engineering institutes that they were fortunate "to be alive at this time, and more especially, to be young at this time. For before them lies the great adventure of building up this new and young, old and young, India of ours...It is a fascinating adventure. It is not an easy adventure, and no good adventures are easy. It is the hard adventure, the risky adventure, that takes something out of us, that demands of us our highest ability. It is only those adventures that are worthwhile. It is that adventure that waits for you, this task of joining with others in building this great nation."

Again, in an address to students at Lucknow University in January 1949: "Here is a time when work is required, labour is required, peace is required, cooperative effort is required, when all the concentrated energy that a nation possesses is required to be put to the great tasks of the nation...There is a time for work, and there is a time for play. Today it is the time for work in this nation. For this generation of ours, if I may say so, is condemned to hard labour."

(a) From Hard Work to Hedonism : From this high vision, we have sunk to the self-indulgent hedonism of consumerist culture propagated by commercial advertising through the media of mass communication, both those that are privately owned and those that are publicly owned and governmentally run.

Nehru had expressed the misgiving, in the course of the Azad Memorial Lecture of 1959: "I have no doubt that India will progress industrially and otherwise...But what I am concerned with is not merely our material progress, but the quality and depth of our people. Gaining power through industrial processes, will they lose themselves in the quest of individual wealth and soft living?"

A resounding 'yes' has been the answer of history to Nehru's question. But with a difference. Whereas the hedonistic culture of consumerism is being spread in the industrialised countries of the West by commercial advertising of luxury goods and services among people whose basic needs including education have been met, here in India consumerism is being promoted among a privileged minority who are in command of the State apparatus and who have appropriated to themselves the gains of post-independence development. Though it is among the upper classes that the craze for material acquisitions is growing, the consumerism spread by State-run radio and State-run television, besides newspapers and outdoor advertising, is seeping down the social scale. Pervasive corruption, dowry deaths and murders with robbery as motive are grim evidence of the collapse of values. So is the increasing incidence of sadistic ragging in educational institutions and of drug addiction among the young.

The dismal state of ethics in India's public life after four decades of independence was summed up by the then Prime Minister Rajiv Gandhi, in his other capacity as president of the Congress (I), in a remarkably candid address at the Congress centenary session in Bombay on 28 December 1985 : "Our economy owes much to the enterprise of our industrialists. But there are some reputed business and industrial establishments which shelter battalions of law breakers and tax evaders...The trade unions have a glorious heritage of nationalism and of socially relevant radicalism. Today, they are a mere shadow of their past. They now protect the few who have, oblivious of millions who have not...Teachers seldom teach and students seldom learn. Strikes, mass copying, agitations are more attractive alternatives...And what of the iron frame of the system, the administrative and the technical services, the police and the myriad functionaries of the State? They have done so much and can do so much more, but as the proverb says there can be no protection if the fence starts eating the crop. We have Government servants who do not serve but oppress the poor and the helpless, police who do not uphold the law but shield the guilty, tax collectors who do not collect taxes but connive with those who cheat the State, and whole legions whose only concern is their private welfare at the cost of society...

"We have looked at others. Now let us look at ourselves. What has become of our great organisation? Instead of a party that fired the imagination of the masses throughout the length and breadth of India, we have shrunk, losing touch with the toiling millions. On their backs ride the brokers of power and influence, who dispense patronage to convert a mass movement into a feudal oligarchy. They are self-perpetuating cliques who thrive by invoking the slogans of caste and religion and by enmeshing the living body of the Congress in their net of avarice."[9]

(b) Moral Vacuum : Article 28 (1) : Among the factors contributing to the collapse of values in public and private life, is the prohibition of religious instruction under Article 28 (1) of the Constitution, discussed earlier. This has created a moral vacuum which any rubbish may fill.

Writing in *Harijan* (16 July 1938), a decade before independence, Gandhiji said in response to a correspondent's query about the place or religious instruction in the Wardha Scheme of Basic Education: "I regard it as fatal to the growth of a friendly spirit amoong children belonging to the different faiths if they are taught that their religion is superior to every other, or that it is the only true religion." Describing as "too dreadful to contemplate" the consequences of banishing religion from schools, he said: "Fundamental principles of ethics are common to all religions. These should be taguht to the children."

Maulana Azad, who was Education Minister during the first decade of independence, consistently advocated the inclusion of instruction in the universalist values of religion as part of the curriculum of education. At a press conference on 18 February 1947, a month after assuming the Education portfolio in the Interim Government, he recalled that contrary recommendations on the question of religious instruction in schools had been made by two committees appointed by the Central Advisory Board of Education. Expressing his own view, Azad said: "The religious instruction often imparted in India in private institutions is of a kind which, instead of broadening the outlook and inculcating a spirit of toleration and goodwill towards all men, produces exactly the opposite results. The aim of all religious teaching should be to make men more tolerant and broadminded, and it is my opinion that this can be more effectively done if the State takes charge of the question than if it is left to private initiative."

Returning to the subject a year later, Maulana Azad said on 13 January, 1948: "At first it was considered that religious instruction would stand in the way of the free intellectual development of a child, but now it has been admitted that religious education cannot altogether be dispensed with. If national education was devoid of this element, there would be no appreciation of moral values or moulding of character on human lines...No doubt a foreign government had to keep itself away from religious education. But a national government cannot divest itself of this responsibility."[10]

The Commission on University Education headed by Dr. S. Radhakrishnan expressed itself in similar terms in the report it drew up towards the close of 1949. Religious instruction in the universities was one of the terms of reference of the Commission, which included distinguished humanist scholars as well as scientists, both Indian and foreign: Dr Tara Chand, historian; Sir James F. Duff, Vice-Chancellor of the University of Durham in the U.K.; Dr Zakir Hussain, of the Jamia Millia Islamia; Dr. Arthur E. Morgan, first chairman of the Tennessee Valley Authority in the U.S.A.; Dr. A Lakshmanaswami Mudaliar, vice-chancellor of Madras University; Dr Meghnad Saha, F.R.S.; Dr. Karan Narayan Bahl, zoologist; Dr. John J. Tigert, formerly Commissioner of Education in the U.S.A.; and Prof. Nirmal Kumar Siddhanta of Lucknow University, member-secretary.

The Commission referred to the Constitution of free India that was then being drawn up, and said: "The fundamental principles of our Constitution call for spiritual training. There is no State religion. The State must not be partial to any one religion. Each one is at liberty to approach the Unseen as it suits his capacity and inclination. If this is the basis of our Secular State, to be secular is not to be religiously illiterate. It is to be deeply spititual, and not narrowly religious."

The degree course, the Commission recommended, should include the teaching of the lives of the great religious leaders like the Buddha, Confucius, Zoroaster, Socrates, Jesus, Sankara, Mohammad, Kabir, Nanak and Gandhi. The study of selections of a universalist character from the scriptures of the world was also recommended. "A study of the great books, books that shame our smallness, that quell our fears, that fill us with hope, is essential in the university courses. A reverent study of all religions would be uniquely rewarding as a step towards harmony between religions long divided. This is in consonance with the spirit of our country."

The Constitution that came into force in January 1950 contained provisions relating to religious instruction that ran wholly counter to the advice of Mahatma Gandhi, Maulana Azad and Dr. Radhakrishnan. As if with a forevision of these constitutional provisions, Maulana Azad had said in his speech of 13 January 1948: "What will be the consequence if the Government undertakes to impart purely secular education? Naturally, people will try to provide religious education to their children through private sources. How these private sources are workig today or are likley to work in future is already known to you. I know something about it and can say that not only in villages but even in cities, the imparting of religious education is entrusted to teachers who, though literate, are not educated. To them religion is nothing but bigotry."

Maulana Azad's warning has proved true. The fact is that religion cannot be wished away. If it is not taught in the right way, it will get taught in the wrong way. As Dr. Radhakrishnan said in 1955: "The need for religion, for a system of thought, for devotion to a cause which will give our fragile and fugitive existence significance and value, does not require much elaborate argument. It is an intrinsic element of human nature. The question is, what kind of religion? Is it a religion of love and brotherhood, or of power and hate? The question is therefore not religion or no religion, but what kind of religion."[11]

A broadening of the curriculum to include the teaching of humanist ethical values has been urged recently by G. Parthasarathi, the distinguished diplomat and educationist. He said in the course his convocation address at the University of Hyderabad in 1987: "Now that the concept of a core national curriculum has been accepted, it seems to me that consideration might be given to the inclusion in it of a course covering the development of human values the world over and with special reference to India. Such a course would cover the contributions made to the development of a humanistic outlook by the various religions, by outstanding thinkers, by Marxism and the different schools of socialist thought, as well as by modern science many of whose findings are supportive of the concepts of humankind's oneness and of the ecological relatedness of all life on earth."

(v) Coping with Fundamentalism

The judiciary has not been altogether immune from the tendency evident in the Constitution, and in the policy pursued by the Government in the years after, as before, independence to treat religious minorities as sacred cows.

(a) Excommunication : In Saifuddin Saheb v. State of Bombay four Judges out of a five-member bench of the Supreme Court upheld, on 9 January 1962, the right of Sardar Syedna Taher Saifuddin Saheb, as the Dail-ul-Mutlaq, to excommunicate any member of the Dawoodi Bohra community on religious grounds. The sole dissenting judgment was by Chief Justic B.P.Sinha, who held that excommunication results in the treatment of a human being as a pariah and therefore offends Article 17 of the Constitution which abolishes untouchability and makes its practice in any form an offence punishable in accordance with law.

The case had a history going back to 1949 when the Bombay legislature adopted the Prevention of Excommunication Act (No. 42 of 1949). In a suit filed the same year, Justice J.C. Shah as a single judge of the Bombay High Court held on 21 February 1952 that the Act was not inconsistent with Article 26 of the Constitution, which had meanwhile come into force, guaranteeing the right of every religious denomination to manage its own affairs in matters of religion. On the Syedna appealing against this judgment, a bench of the Bombay High Court comprising Chief Justice Chagla and Justic Bhagwati upheld the judgment of the Single Judge though on different grounds. It was this 1953 judgment of the Bombay High Court that the Supreme Court overruled in 1962.

The majority judgment was based on the reasoning that excommunication is for the purpose of maintaining the strength of the religion and therefore forms part of the management by the community, through its religious head, "of its own affairs in matters of religion" (Article 26 b); that the Act was not saved by Article 25 (2) (b), namely "providing for social welfare and reform"; that a religion cannot be 'reformed' out of existence or identity; and that the Act rendered the Dawoodi Bohra community impotent to protect itself against dissidents and schismatics.

Chief Justice Sinha, on the other hand, said: "Though the freedom of conscience is guaranteed to every individual so that he may hold any beliefs he likes, his actions in pursuance of those beliefs may be liable to restrictions in the interest of the community at large, as may be determined by common consent, that is to say, by a competent legislature. It was on such humanitarian grounds, and for the purpose of social reform, that so-called religious practices like immolating a widow at the pyre of her deceased husband, or of dedicating a virgin of tender years to a god to function as a devadasi, or of ostracising a person from all social contacts and religious communion on account of his having eaten forbidden food or taboo, were stopped by legislation." Pointing out that excommunication not only excludes a person from places of worship and the beneficial use of the property of the denomination of which the Dai is the trustee but prevents burial of the dead in the burial ground of the community, Chief Justice Sinha held that Article 26 (b) must be read subject to Article 25 (2) (b).

Like the prohibition of polygamy for one section of Indian citizens and its sanction for another section, the abolition of untouchability among some and the sanction of excommunication among others is a contradiction which points to the need for review of the relevant constitutional provisions. It is indeed ironical that a progressive piece of legislation passed before the Constitution came into force should have been held void on the ground of the Fundamental Rights.

(b) Tensions over Proselytism : The Karachi Congress resolution said that every citizen would enjoy "the right freely to profess and practise" his religion. The 1950 Constitution added the right also to 'propagate' religion. Christian churches have for two centuries received substantial funds from abroad and are able to hold out inducements for conversion. Following the oil boom in the Muslim countries of West Asia since the early 1970's Islam too became a well-endowed multinational religious corporation. Tensions have been generated over the years by reports of money-induced conversions to Islam and Christianity in certain parts of the country, and by attempts at reconversion to Hinduism. The attempts at large-scale conversion and reconversion generally take place in rural areas, as in recent years at Meenakshipuram in Tamil Nadu and in the tribal areas of central and north-east India.

Three States with large tribal populations, among whom Christian missionaries have been particularly active, have found it necessary to enact legislation prohibiting conversion through force, fraud or inducement. They are Orissa, Madhya Pradesh and Arunachal Pradesh. The legislation in all the three States defines 'force' to include the threat of social excommunication.

The Orissa Freedom of Religion Act, 1967 (Act. No. 2 of 1968) defines 'inducement' to include "the offer of any gift or gratification, either in cash or in kind, and shall also include the grant of any benefit, either pecuniary or otherwise." An offence is punishable with imprisonment up to one year or fine up to Rs. 5000 or with both, "provided that, in case the offence is committed in respect of a minor, a woman or a person belonging to the Scheduled Castes or Scheduled Tribes the punishment shall be imprisonment to the extent of two years and fine up to Rs. 10,000."

The Madhya Pradesh Dharma Swatantrya Adhiniyam, 1968 (Act No. 27 of 1968) prescribes punishment on the same scale as in Orissa, with higher penalties for offences committed in respect of a minor, a woman or a person belonging to S.C. or S.T. The Madhya Pradesh Act requires, in addition, that whoever converts any person from one religious faith to another shall send an intimation to the District Magistrate of the fact of such conversion.

The Arunachal Pradesh Freedom of Religion Act, 1978 (Act No.4 of 1978) also requires intimation to the Deputy Commissioner of the District to which the person converted belongs.

There is no information on the working of these Acts: the number of prosecutions under the Acts, and of the number of conversions reported each year in Madhya Pradesh and Arunachal Pradesh. This is an area for useful further research.

Worthy of the attention of legislators, jurists and publicists are the observations made on the subject of proselytism by Justice Baharul Islam, a former Judge of the Supreme Court, in the course of the fourth Motilal Nehru Memorial Lecture delivered by him under the auspices of the Institute of Constitutional and Parliamentary Studies in New Delhi on 9 December 1987. He said: "In my opinion, guarantee (of the right) to propagate religion was excessive and unnecessary, if propagation of religion includes coversion of a person from one religion to another.

"There should be no objection if a person voluntarily renounces his or her religion and accepts another; but propagation of religion and conversion by persuasion or lure creates, and has created, a lot of misunderstanding between different communities and often creates considerable tension. I believe it will more conducive if Article 25 (1) is amended to the extent indicated above."

An all-India enactment with a bearing on proselytising activity is the Foreign Contribution (Regulation) Act,1976 (No. 49 of 1976). Its provisions, as modified up to 1 July 1985, are not stringent with regard to religious associations compared to political parties, the Press and those in public employment.

Section 4 (1) lays down categorically : "No foreign contribution shall be accepted by any--

(a) candidate for election,

(b) correspondent, columnist, cartoonist, editor, owner, printer or publisher of a registered newspaper,

(c) Judge, Government servant or employee of any corporation,

(d) member of any Legislature,

(e) political party or office-bearer thereof.

Explanation.--In clause (c) 'corporation' means a corporaton owned or controlled by Government and includes a Government company as defined in section 617 of the Companies Act, 1956."

Section 5 (1) provides : "No organisation of a political nature, not being a political party, shall accept any foreign contribution except witb the prior permission of the Central Government.

Explanation.--For the purpose of this section, 'organisation of a political nature, not being a political party' means such organisation as the Central Government may, having regard to the activities of the organisation or the ideology propagated by the organisation or the programme of the organisation or the association of the organisation with the activities of any political party, by an order published in the Official Gazette, specify in this behalf."

In contrast to these provisions pertaining to foreign money in public life, Section 6 (1) relating to religious associations read

"No association (other than an organisation referred to in sub-section (1) of section 5) having a definite cultural, economic, educational, religious or social programme shall accept foreign contribution unless such association--

(a) registers itself with the Central Government in accordance with the rules made under this Act; and

(b) agrees to receive such foreign contributions only through one of the branches of a bank as it may specify in its application for such registration, and every association so registered shall give, within such time and in such manner as may be prescribed, an intimation to the Central Government as to the amount of each foreign contribution received by it, the source from which and the manner in which such contribution was received and the purposes for which and the manner in which such foreign contribution was utilised by it: Provided that where such association obtains any foreign contribution through any branch other than the branch of the bank through which it has agreed to receive foreign contribution, or fails to give such intimation within the prescribed time or in the prescribed manner, or gives any intimation which is false, the Central Government may, by notification in the official Gazette, direct that such association shall not, after the date of issue of such notification, accept any foreign contribution without the prior permission of the Central Government."

It will be seen that there is no outright prohibition of the acceptance of foreign contributions by religious associations (unlike political parties, the Press and public servants). Secondly the good faith of religious associations will be assumed until the contrary comes to the knowledge of the Government.

An area calling for further research is the number of religious associations which have registered themselves for receiving foreign contributions; the number out of them belonging to different religious denominations and the amounts of foreign contributions received by them year after year; and the names of religious associations in respect of whom, and the dates with effect from which, the Central Government has been constrained to require that they should not receive foreign contributions without prior permission.

Another aspect of the contribution of proselytism to social tensions that calls for study is the variation in the proportion of the major religious communities in India's total population over the post-independence Censuses. The reasons could be: i) different rates of natural increase in population; ii) excess of in-migration over out-migration or vice versa; and iii) conversions.

It will be seen from the following table that there has been a steady decline in the proportion of Hindus in India's total population over the

1951-1981 Censuses. Of the two largest religious minorities, there has been a steady increase from Census to Census in the proportion of Muslims, and an increase in the case of Christians from 1951 to 1961 and again in 1971 but a fall in 1981 though the 1981 proportion of Christians still stands higher than in 1951.

Percentage of religious communities in India's total population

	1951	1961	1971	1981
Hindus	84.98	83.57	82.72	82.64
Muslims	9.91	10.69	11.21	11.35
Christians	2.35	2.44	2.60	2.43
Sikhs	1.74	1.79	1.89	1.96
Buddhists	0.05	0.74	0.70	0.71
Jains	0.45	0.46	0.47	0.48
Others	0.52	0.37	0.41	0.43

In absolute terms, the number of Hindus increased from 30,35,75,474 in 1951 to 54,97,79,481 in 1981; of Muslims from 3,54,14,284 in 1951 to 7,55,12,439 in 1981; and of Christians from 83,94,038 in 1951 to 1,61,65,446 in 1981.

The factors affecting the natural increase in population of the different religious groups include the following.[12]

Standard average no. of living children among

Hindus	2.65
Muslims	2.95
Christians	2.80

Marital fertility rates estimated on the basis of 1971 Census data

Hindus	5.19
Muslims	5.77
Christians	5.97
Sikhs	5.39
Buddhists	6.16
Jains	4.84

(c) Regulating the use of religious funds : There is no uniformity in the regulation by the State of the use of their funds by religious institutions of the different faiths, whether the funds are derived from abroad or within the country.

Statutory control over the utilisation of the funds of Hindu temples has a long history. It is the most stringent, compared to the laws for regulating the use of the funds of Muslim wakfs and Sikh gurdwaras, which too date from pre-independence days. There was no separate legislation in the British period for regulating the use of the funds of Christian churches nor is there any now.

Typical of the sweeping powers assumed by the Government in relation to Hindu religious endowments are the provisions of the Andhra Pradesh Charitable and Hindu Religious Institutions and Endowments Act,1966.[13]. Section 8, dealing with powers and functions of the Commissioner to be appointed by the Government in terms of the Act, says: "The administration of all chairtable and Hindu religious institutions and endowments shall be under the general superintendence and control of the Commissioner and such superintendence and control shall include power to pass any order which may be deemed necessary to ensure that such institutions and endowments are properly administered for the purpose for which they were founded or exist."

Other provisions of the Act provide inter alia that :

(i) The Commissioner (the expression covering also those acting on his behalf) shall appoint boards of trustees as well as executive officers for the Hindu religious institutions and endowments;

(ii) He shall prepare a code of conduct for the Archakas and other office holders, and for visitors and worshippers. Anyone who violates the code may be evicted from the premises.

(iii) The Commissioner may, with due regard to the religious practices and usages of the institution, enter and inspect its properties, correspondence and accounts. The only requirement is that he be a Hindu, in the case of a religious institution or endowment.

(iv) The budget of each institution and endowment is required to be submitted to the Commissioner. The auditor will be appointed by the Government and give his report to the Commissioner.

(v) Appeal against an order made by the Commissioner may be made to the Government.

The Andhra Pradesh Act has a special chapter on the Tirumala Tirupathi Devasthanams. It provides that the board of trustees will consist of not more than 11 persons of whom three shall be members of the State legislature, one shall be a person belonging to the Scheduled Castes and one shall be a woman.

In contrast to the direct, detailed and rigorous control of Hindu religious endowments by officials appointed by the Government is the superintendence of Muslim wakfs by State-level Boards and a Central Wakf Board consisting predominantly of non-officials.

The all-India Wakf Act 1954 (Act No. 29 of 1954), as amended from time to time, provides for the appointment by the State Government of a Board consisting of one or more of the following categories of persons:

(a) members of the State legislature and members of parliament representing the State;

(b) persons having knowledge of Muslim law and representing associations such as State Jamiat ul Ulama or State Shia Conference;

(c) persons having knowledge of administration, finance or law; and

(d) Mutawallis of wakfs situated within the State (not more than one from this category).

The Chairman of the Board is to be elected by the members from among themselves. There are to be separate Boards for Sunni and Shia wakfs if Shia wakfs constitute in number more than 15 per cent of all the wakfs in the State or if the income from properties of the Shia wakfs in a State constitutes more than 15 per cent of the total.

The functions of the State Board include scrutiny and approval of the budgets submitted by Mutawallis and arranging for the audit of accounts of the wakfs by auditors to be appointed by the Board; to appoint and remove Mutawallis; to inspect or cause inspection of wakf properties and accounts; and to give directions for the administration of wakfs.

The Central Wakf Council is to consist of a Chairman, who shall be the Union Minister in charge of wakfs, and other members to be appointed by the Central Government. The Council will administer the Central Wakf Fund consisting of the prescribed contributions from the State Boards and other donations and grants. It will advise the Central Government on matters concerning the working of the State Boards and the due administration of wakfs.

The role of the Commissioner of Wafks and his deputies, to be appointed by the State Governments, is limited to data collection regarding the number, objects, income and other particulars of each wakf in a State.

In the case of Sikh gurdwaras, the legislation has from the beginning been based on the principle of democratic self-management. The reform was the outcome of a non-violent struggle launched in the early 1920's by the Akalis, in the words of Jawaharlal Nehru in his autobiography, "to purge their gurdwaras by driving out corrupt Mahants and taking possession of the places of worship and the property belonging to them."

The Sikh Gurdwaras Act of 1925 provided for compensation to hereditary office-holders for pecuniary loss owing to a gurdwara being 'notified' under the Act and undergoing a change in management. The Act provided for a Central Board with a majority of elected members, and for annual election of the Board's executive committee. There was to be a Chief Commissioner, Gurdwara Elections, who would supervise the elctions. Every constituency would return one member, with the Central Government selecting 20 costituencies as plural-member, each returning two members of whom one shall be a Sikh belonging to a Scheduled Caste notified as such under Article 341 of the Constitution. Only Sikhs qualifying by virtue of their observing the prescribed disciplines could vote. The Punjab Act was amended from time to time, among other things to provide for the 'extended territories' after the merger of Patiala and of the East Punjab States Union in 1956, and again after the separation of Haryana in 1966.

The Central Board was itself to act as the committee of management in respect of the major Takhats in the country, with committees of management being formed for every other gurdwara on the recommendation of the Board. Gurdwaras were to contribute a prescribed part of their income to the Board and spend the balance on religious and charitable purposes including social welfare but excluding political purposes. The Act provides in Section 129: "The Board in any meeting may consider and discuss any matter with which it has power under this Act to deal, and any matter directly connected with the Sikh religion, but shall not consider or decide, discuss or pass any resolution or order upon any other matter."

A separate Delhi Sikh Gurdwaras Act was passed by parliament in 1971 "to provide for the proper management of the Sikh Gurdwaras and Gurdwara property in Delhi and for matters connected therewith." The Delhi Sikh Gurdwara Management Committee was to consist of 46 members to be elected from various wards of Delhi, with a few additional nominated members. Section 26 provided that the Management Committee may not contribute any amount or amounts: a) to any political party; b) for the benefit of any political party; of c) for any political purpose to any individual or body.

But there have been allegations of the Central Government itself playing politics with the Act. Section 16 (3) prescribed for office-bearers a minimum qualification in terms of formal education. It was alleged that this requirement was designed by the Congress (I), which was in power at the Centre, to keep out certain persons, in particular Jathedar Santokh Singh. A decade later, when Jathedar Santokh Singh had moved close to the Congress (I), the Central Government issued an ordinance on 21 January 1981 to remove the educational qualification.

Another way of playing politics with laws is to refrain from acting in accordance with their provisions. Elections have not been held by the Government for years together, under the Punjab Act as well as the Delhi Act.

(d) Misuse of Religious Places : A major reason for the tragedy of Punjab since the 1980's is the failure of the State governments of different political hues, including the Congress (I) and Akalis, and of the Central Government during the periods of President's rule, to enforce laws providing punishment for the incitement of enmity on religious grounds.

Chapter VIII of the Indian Penal Code of 1860, as modified from time to time, deals in Sections 141 to 161 with 'offences against the public tranquillity'. As far back as in 1969, Section 153-A of the I.P.C. was strengthened, through the Criminal and Election Laws (Amendment) Act, 1969 (Act No. 35 of 1969). The definition of the offence was widened, and the penalty made more stringent if it was committed in any place of worship. The amended Section read :

> "153-A.(1) Whoever--
>
> (a) by words, either spoken or written, or by signs or by visible representations or otherwise, promotes or attempts to promote, on grounds of religion, race, place of birth, residence, language, caste or community or any other ground whatsoever, disharmony or feelings of enmity, hatred or ill-will between different religious, racial, language or regional groups or castes or communities, or
>
> (b) commits any act which is prejudicial to the maintenance of harmony between different religious, racial, language or regional groups or castes or communities, and which disturbs or is likley to disturb the public tranquillity, shall be punished with imprisoment which may extend to three years, or with fine, or with both.
>
> (2) Whoever commits an offence specified in sub-section (1) in any place of worship or in any assembly engaged in the performance of religious worship or religious ceremonies, shall be punished with imprisonment which may extend to five years and shall also be liable to fine."

Three years later, there was a further amendment through Act 31 of 1972. In the first place, a new offence was included in sub-section (1) of Section 153-A by adding the following:

"(c) organises any exercise, movement, drill or other similar activity intending that the participants in such activity shall use or be trained to use criminal force or violence or knowing it to be likley that the participants in such activity will use or be trained to use criminal force or violence, or participates in such activity intending to use or be trained to use criminal force or violence or knowing it to be likely that the participants in such activity will use or be trained to use criminal force or violence, against any religious, racial, language or regional group or caste or community and such activity for any reason whatsoever causes or is likely to cause fear or alarm or a feeling of insecurity amongst members of such religious, racial, language or regional group or caste or community"...

Secondly, the 1972 amendment added a new Section 153-B, which read :

"153-B. (1) Whoever, by words, either spoken or written or by signs or by visible representations or otherwise,

(a) makes or publishes any imputation that any class of persons cannot, by reason of their being members of any religious, racial, language or regional group or caste or community, bear true faith and allegiance to the Constitution of India as by law established or uphold the sovereignty and integrity of India, or

(b) asserts, counsels, advises, propagates or publishes that any class of persons shall, by reason of their being members of any religious, racial, language or regional group or caste or community, be denied or deprived of their rights as citizens of India, or

(c) makes or publishes any assertion, counsel, plea or appeal concerning the obligation of any class of persons, by reason of their being members of any religious, racial, language or regional group or caste or community, and such assertion counsel, plea or appeal causes or is likely to cause disharmony or feelings of enmity or hatred or ill-will between such members and others persons,

shall be punished with imprisonment which may extend to three years, or with fine, or with both.

(2) Whoever commits an offence specified in sub-section (1) in any place of worship, or in any assembly engaged in the performance of religious worship or religious

> ceremonies, shall be punished with imprisonment which may extend to five years and shall also be liable to fine."

Had these provisions of the law been enforced, the Golden Temple at Amritsar could not have been turned by armed Khalistani extremists into a fortress from which they blared out virulently communal propaganda and incitement. The country might have been spared the sequence of grisly events which began with 'Operation Blue Star' in June 1984. It led on to mutiny by a section of Sikh soldiers of the Indian Army, the assassination of Prime Minister Indira Gandhi on 31 October, the retaliatory killing of upwards of 2500 innocent Sikhs in Delhi alone in the early days of November, and the continuing murder of innocent persons day after day by terrorists in Punjab, Delhi and elsewhere.

The tragic events of 1984 did not lead to any significant improvement in law enforcement. The Government armed itself with further powers under the Terrorist and Disruptive Activities (Prevention) Act of 1987. But the Golden Temple once again came under the control of armed Khalistani militants. 'Operation Black Thunder' was undertaken in May 1988 to flush them out.

Inability or unwillingness to enforce laws already on the statute book has not diminished the Government's pathetic faith in arming itself with more powers. On 26 May 1988 there was a further addition to the legal armoury with the promulgation by the President of the Religious Institutions (Prevention of Misuse) Ordinance. The sweeping powers that the Government gave itself came in for criticism from some quarters.

When a law for replacing the ordinance came up before parliament, a senior officer of the Union Home Ministry was asked, as part of the present study, for information on the action taken in Punjab under the ordinance. The query was intended to ascertain whether the exercise of the new powers had yielded results good enough to justify the replacement of the ordinance by a regular law. The surprising reply was that the Union Home Ministry had no information; only the Punjab Government would know. In answer to a further question, the officer confirmed that there was no system for the monitoring by the Centre of action taken by State governments under laws made by parliament.

This matter acquires added importance in view of an enactment connected with the then impending ninth general elections to the Lok Sabha. The Representation of the People (Amendment)Act passed by Parliament in 1988 (it become Act No.1 of 1989 on receiving the President's assent) disqualifies from candidature for election, persons convicted of offences under specified enactments, including the Religious Institutions (Prevention of Misuse) Act, 1988.

An area of useful research will be to ascertain whether the Government and the Election Commission have, or how they propose to secure, information regarding persons who, in the various States and Union territories, have been convicted under the laws enumerated in Section 4 of Act 1 of 1989, thereby standing disqualified for election. The Section provides for inclusion in Section 8 of the principal Act, namely the Representation of the People Act, 1951, of the following :

> "(1) A person convicted of an offence punishable under--
>
> (a) section 153-A (offence of promoting enmity between different groups on ground of religion, race, place of birth, residence, language, etc., and doing acts prejudicial to maintenance of harmony) or section 171-F (offence of bribery) or section 171-E (offence of undue influence or personation at an election) or sub-section (1) or sub-section (2) of section 376 or section 376-A or section 376-B or section 376-C of section 376-D (offences relating to rape) or section 498A (offence of cruelty towards a woman by husband or relative of a husband) or sub-section (2) or sub-section (3) or section 505 (offence of making statement creating or promoting enmity, hatred or ill-will between classes or offence relating to such statement in any place of worship or in any assembly engaged in the performance of religious worship or religious ceremonies) of the Indian Penal Code; or
>
> (b) the Protection of Civil Rights Act, 1955, which provides for punishment for the preaching and practice of 'untouchability', and for the enforcement of any disability arising therefrom; or
>
> (c) section 11 (offence of importing or exporting prohibited goods) of the Customs Act, 1962; or
>
> (d) sections 10 to 12 (offence of being a member of an association declared unlawful, offence relating to dealing with funds of an unlawful association or offence relating to contravention of an order made in respect of a notified place) of the Unlawful Activities (Prevention) Act, 1967; or
>
> (e) the Foreign Exchange (Regulation) Act, 1973; or
>
> (f) The Narcotic Drugs and Psychotropic Substances Act, 1985; or
>
> (g) section 3 (offence of committing terrorist acts) or section 4 (offence of committing disruptive activities) of the Terrorist and Disruptive Activities (Prevention) Act, 1987; or
>
> (h) section 7 (offence of contravention of the provisions of sections 3 to 6) of the Religious Institutions (Prevention of Misuse) Act, 1988; or

(i) section 125 (offence of promoting enmity between classes in connection with an election) or section 135 (offence of removal of ballot papers from polling stations) or section 135-A (offence of booth capturing) or clause (a) of sub-section (2) of section 136 (offence of fraudulently defacing or fraudulently destroying any nomination paper) of this Act,

shall be disqualified for a period of six years from the date of such conviction.

(2) A person convicted for the contravention of--

(a) any law providing for the prevention of hoarding or profiteering; or

(b) any law relating to the adulteration of food or drugs; or

(c) any provisions of the Dowry Prohibition Act, 1961: or

(d) any provisions of the Commission of Sati (Prevention) Act, 1987, and sentenced to imprisonment for not less than six months, shall be disqualified from the date of such conviction and shall continue to be disqualified for a further period of six years since his release.

(3) A person convicted of any offence and sentenced to imprisonment for not less than two years–other than any offence referred to in sub-section (1) or sub-section (2)–shall be disqualified from the date of such conviction and shall continue to be disqualified for a further period of six years since his release."

The development process will undoubtedly gain if criminals are prevented from trying to enter the legislatures--and becoming Ministers. The 1989 amendment to the Representation of the People Act, 1951, may prove in the long run to be a crucial step in retrieving the standards of public life from the depths to which they have sunk. Much will depend on the administration compiling regularly, and sharing promptly with the Election Commission's officials, data on persons who are convicted of the specified offences and who thereby stand disqualified for election.

(vi) Consequences of Electoral System

The divisiveness on grounds of religion, caste and ethnic origin inherent in India's heterogeneous society has been aggravated by the elctoral system. This system enables a political party to secure a majority of seats in the legislature with a minority of the popular vote. It therefore tempts political parties to hold out favours to the leaders of a religious minority here, a caste group there and a tribe elsewhere, as a vote bank that can tilt the balance in the party's favour.

It is understandable that, amidst the turmoil of Partition, the system of single-member constituencies introduced by the British was continued after independence without critical examination. However, the outcome of the very first elections held in 1951-52 on the basis of adult franchise, under the new Constitution, should have opened the eyes of political parties to the inequity of a system under which a person first past the post is declared the winner and takes all.

A candidate who secures, say, 40 per cent of the votes cast in a multi-cornered contest becomes the sole representative of the constituency, with no voice in the legislature for the other 60 per cent of voters who did not favour this candidate. Political parties, likewise, secure huge majorities in the legislatures on the strength of less than half of the popular vote, Perhaps because different political parties have benefited at different times and in different States from the present system, or hope to do so, few have questioned it. The Bharatiya Janata Party and the Communists, sometimes, are the only ones to have advocated proportional representation through a suitable variant of the List System in place of First-Past-the-Post.

(a) The Election Lottery : The Lok Sabha, the directly elected House of the Indian parliament, reflects public opinion like a distorting mirror, even as the 'mother of parliaments' does in Britain. In the 1987 elections to the House of Commons the Conservatives won 57.6% of the seats with only 42.2% of the votes. On the other hand, the Liberal-Social Democratic Alliance got only 3.3% of the seats through it won 22.5% of the votes. The distortion in the vote-seat ratio happened to be the least in the case of the Labour Party. The performance of the winning party in the successive elections to the Indian Lok Sabha has been as follows :

Elections to Lok Sabha

Year of election	Winning party	% of votes	% of seats
1952	Congress	45	74.4
1957	Congress	47.4	75.1
1962	Congress	44.7	73
1967	Congress	40.9	54.4
1971	Congress (I)	43.5	67.9
1977	Janata	43.2	52
1980	Congress (I)	42.7	66.8
1984	Congress (I)	49.1	77

The elections held in November 1989 resulted in a 'hung' Lok Sabha, with no party securing a majority of seats. Congress (I) emerged as the largest party, securing 194 of the 524 seats (37.02%) for which elections were held, with 39.33% of the popular vote. But the Janta Dal secured 27.1% of the seats with only 17.73% of the votes.

The results of elections at State level have also been anomalous. For example, in the 1984 elections to the Tamil Nadu State Assembly the Dravida Munnetra Kazhagam (DMK) secured only 24 seats with 29.5% of the votes, while the All-India Anna DMK won 133 seats with 37.1% of the votes. In the elections held in the State in January 1989, the vote-seat distortion worked the other way. The DMK won 151 seats with 33.44% of the votes, while the Anna AIDMK faction led by Jayalalitha secured only 27 seats with 21.68% of the votes.

In Haryana and West Bengal, the Congress (I) has much had fewer seats in the State Assemblies than it should have by virtue of its share of the popular vote. But the party desires no change in an electoral system which has given it, over the decades, a bonanza of seats in the Lok Sabha and absolute power at the Centre.

In Punjab, carved out in 1966 as a Punjabi-speaking State with a Sikh majority, a major reason for acrimony in public life has been that the Akali Dal, though it commands a substantial following, has been able to have a share in governmental power only intermittently and for short periods.

Instead of encourgaging political parties to work together in coalition governments, as they would have had to do much of the time both at the Centre and in several States if there had been proportional representation, the present system has promoted the politics of confrontation. Political parties under-represented in the legislatures tend to take issues to the streets. Bandhs (general strikes) and other forms of agitation disruptive of normal life have retarded development.

(b) CMs and PM as Demigods : The leader of a party that is over-represented in the legislature is given, and is glad to take, personal credit for the huge legislative majority. Deified by office-seeking sycophants, he or she develops a domineering style of Chief Ministerial or Prime Ministerial government.

At the Centre, the Prime Minister has for many years also been president of the ruling Congress (I) party. Since the time of Indira Gandhi, Chief Ministers of Congress-ruled States came to be nominated by the Congress Prime Minister, who could also remove them at will, acting in the name of the party's high command. Except for the Janata interlude of 1977-79, the Union Cabinet became little more than a rubber stamp.

Relations between the Centre and the States ruled by non-Congress parties worsened steadily. There were complaints of deliberate delay by the Centre in the clearance of the non-Congress States' development projects, and of hostile discrimination in the discretionary part of Central assitance, as in funds for disaster relief.

There were ugly confrontations between the non-Congress Ministries of some States and the persons, including retired civil servants, police and Defence Services officers besides Congress party activists, appointed by the Centre as Governors.

(c) Devaluation of High Offices : Though ordinarily confined to a ceremonial role, Governors of States are part of the delicate mechanism of checks and balances in a multi-party federal democracy. On crucial occasions they are expected to act as impartial umpires of the political power game. This has not happened in practice because the political party which is in power at the Centre on the strength of a minority of the popular vote is able to appoint as Governors persons who will be its pliant instruments.

Even the highest office of the land, that of the President of the Republic, was shorn of its dignity when the Union Cabinet adopted a resolution in 1987 declaring that the President's right to information relating to the administration of the affairs of the Union (expressly provided in Article 78 of the Constitution) was subordinate to Article 74 as amended during the internal emergency. The original article in the 1950 Constitution read: "There shall be a Council of Ministers with the Prime Minister at the head to aid and advise the President in the exercise of his functions." The amendment made during the internal emergency changed it to say: "There shall be a Council of Ministers with the Prime Minister at the head to aid and advise the President who shall, in the exercise of his functions, act in accordance with such advice." When, on relaxation of the emergency, elections were held early in 1977 and the Indira Gandhi government fell, the new government formed by the Janata party sponsored another Constitution amendment which, inter alia, sought to repair the damage done to the dignity of the President's office. It added the proviso: "Provided that the President may require the Council of Ministers to reconsider such advice, either generally or otherwise, and the President shall act in accordance with the advice tendered after such reconsideration."

If the system of legislative representation is changed so as to ensure that no political party secures much more--or much less--representation in legislatures than in warranted by its share of the popular vote, it will be difficult for a single political party to decide who the President shall be. With multi-party involvement in the country's governance and in the choice of a suitable person as President, the appointment of non-partisan Governors of States will be facilitated.

Reform of the electoral system is an area in which India can learn from neighbouring Sri Lanka. In the parliamentary elections held in the island on 15 February 1989 on the basis of a combination of the territorial constituency and party list systems, there was a fairly close correspondence between the percentage of seats secured and the percentage of votes won by the two leading political parties. Out of the total of 225 seats, the United National party won 125 seats (55.5%) with 50.7% of the votes, while the Sri Lanka Freedom Party secured 67 seats (nearly 30%) with 31.8% of the votes.

(vii) Security: A Grey Information Area

India has been no exception to the rule of the modern nation State withholding information, if not spreading disinformation, with regard to problems of security.

(a) Internal Disorder : An example pertaining to internal security relates to the operations against insurgency by a section of some ethnic groups in north-eastern India. There have been allegations from time to time of misbehaviour by some members of the security forces posted in that region. Some of these incidents would not have come to light but for the enquiries conducted by voluntary civil rights groups. Insurgency is only likely to get prolonged if things happen which estrange the people from the government instead of isolating the rebels from their sympathy. Investigation and reporting of the true state of affairs, by leading to corrective measures, can contribute to the return of normalcy that is necessary for development.

Another example concerns class conflict. In Bihar, Andhra Pradesh and elsewhere, there have been periodic outbreaks of agrarian unrest entailing clashes between landlords and agricultural labourers, sometimes resulting in deaths. Newspaper reports based on briefing by district officials and the police tend to attribute such clashes to incitement by Naxalites--so called because the killing of cruelly exploitive landlords as class enemies was originally advocated by a section of communists in the village of Naxalbari in West Bengal. There are also newspaper reports from time to time of the killing of Naxalites by the police in what are described as 'encounters'. It has been alleged by unions of agricultural workers and by civil rights activists that in many cases the encounters are fake, and a cover for the execution without trial of suspected Naxalites caught by the police.

"Journalists have to be on guard," the Second Press Commission said, "against attempts by the authorities or by landlords to pass off agrarian revolts against exploitation as Naxalite or other politically organised violence. An example of biased briefing resulting in questionable reporting or headlines was the police action against alleged 'Naxalite' elements in certain blocks of Patna district in October 1981. The police operation was not sudden; it was known to be in the offing. One of the English newspapers of the capital carried on 30 October 1981 a report headlined CRACKDOWN ON 'NAXALITES' IN PATNA IMMINENT which said inter alia that some of the villages were 'seething with discontent owing to the conflict between the landless and the landlords'; that 'additional police parties were being sent to augment the police already deployed in the area after violence erupted in the Lohsuna village on 2 September in the wake of the alleged rape of a maidservant by a landlord'; that the demands of the landless labourers comprising Harijans, Awadhiya Kurmis, Nonias and other backward castes included 'implementation of statutorily fixed minimum wages for farm workers and distribution of ceiling-surplus land acquired by the Government; and that they were also insisting that landlords be prevented from employing outside labourers for harvesting the standing paddy crop.' A local political worker, not belonging to the ruling party, was quoted in the same report as having warned that the police exercise would degenerate into a planned genocide against Harijans and other poor farm workers in the rural areas of Patna district.

"Yet the reports of the police firing of 30 October, which were prominently displayed by the English-language newspapers in the capital on the front page were, in four out of the six, under headlines which implicitly accepted the claim by the authorities that all the persons killed were extremists. It is an example which illustrates the need for caution, on the part of both reporters and sub-editors, in the handling of reports pertaining to 'encounters'. We have noted with appreciation that, in recent years, some newspapers have attempted to get at the truth behind incidents of law and order in rural areas."[14]

A third example of insufficient information on disturbed conditions within the country pertains to Punjab. In the grim tragedy witnessed in that State during years, many of the mass killings and the assassination of individuals prominent in public life were undoubtedly the work of Khalistani terrorists. But there is no knowing how many of the other killings were, as claimed by the police, the outcome of rivalry between different extremist groups, or murder committed out of vendetta or for robbery. Allegations of fake encounters have been made in Punjab too. There have been disturbing reports of the police in some cases extorting money as ransom for freeing persons held on suspicion of having links with terrorists. Any attempt on the part of the authorities to gloss over the truth with regard to these matters will be counter-productive in the long run.

If information on problems of internal security is a grey area, it is even more so in the case of external security.

The press itself is 1oth to share with its readers such information as it has on security matters, let alone commenting candidly. This is only partly from fear of the consequences of violating the Official Secrets Act, and is mainly due to notions of patriotic duty.

An early example which instilled fear into the Press was that of the price paid by S. Sadanand, intrepid publisher of the *Free Press Journal* of Bombay, for making public the movement of Indian naval ships and army units towards Junagadh in Septemeber 1947. This military move was in response to the feared induction of outside forces by the Muslim ruler of Junagadh, an overwhelmingly Hindu-populated State surrounded by Indian territory in the Kathiawad peninsula on the west coast, who had chosen to accede to Pakistan on the sub-continent's partition. Sardar Patel, who was Home Minister and held charge also of the Information portfolio, showed his anger at the publication of security information by denying to Sadanand the lease of teleprinter lines for the distribution in India of international news, for gathering which Sadanand had made expensive arrangements.[15]

Journalists, even those sharply criticial of the Government's internal policies, tend to identify with the Government on issues concerning the country's external relations. At a press conference of John Foster Dulles, then Secretary of State of the U.S.A., on 10 March 1956 in New Delhi, Indian journalists went on so persistently about Goa, Kashmir and Pakistan that the visitor said: "We have been here for a little time, and I think so far we talked about nothing really except Goa and Kashmir. A lot of interesting things are going on in the world and I do not think we have exhausted them. If you have no other question or topic, perhaps we better adjourn the conference." (Page 14 of 23-page transcript of the Press conference issued by the Press Information Bureau, Government of India.)

That the Indian Press, by and large, tends to be uncritical of the Government's handling of foreign relations out of a sense of patriotic duty has been attested by Girilal Jain, who was for many years editor of a leading Indian daily, *The Times of India*. He said: "Whenever national interests have been involved we have been less than frank. I would not like to illustrate the point because in doing so I may myself hurt the national interest. But anyone who knows anything about India, knows that on matters of national interest we have been more than willing to go along with the government. But on other issues we will not go along."[16]

An instance of the Press 'going along' with the Government was the black-out of information on what was an open secret--the training and equipping of cadres of the Liberation Tigers of Tamil Eelam (LTTE) on Indian soil for operations against the government forces in neighbouring Sri Lanka. It is a different matter that LTTE later turned out to be a Frankenstein's monster--like Jarnail Singh Bhindranwale of Punjab who was certified by Rajiv Gandhi, in his capacity as Congress general secretary when his mother was Prime Minister, as a non-political 'religious preacher'.

It is rarely that in an international dispute one party is a hundred per cent right and the other a hundred per cent wrong. Yet, the government of every country tends to indoctrinate its citizens into the belief that the adversary has no case. On the other hand, the peaceful settlement of international problems on the basis of give-and-take requires that the public should be aware of the facts and arguments adduced by the other country. If the government shuts out data presented by the rival, it will only disable itself from negotiating a peaceful settlement when and if the other side is ready for a compromise.

(b) The India-China Border

A case in point is the India-China border, in regard to which both sides have impressive evidence to support their respective claims. Yet the citizens of either country know next to nothing about the arugments in support of the claims of the other.

As pointed out by the Verrier Elwin, the British anthropologist who studied Indian tribal life with intelligent sympathy and took Indian citizenship after independence, "The former British Government tended on the whole to leave the tribesmen alone, partly because the task of administration, especially in the wild border areas, was difficult and unrewarding; partly from a desire to quarantine the tribes from possible political infection; and partly, I think, because certain officers sincerely held the Rousseau-Diderot doctrine that the people were better and happier as they were."

After independence, the Indian authorities continued to administer lightly the areas along the 2640 miles of the country's border with the Tibet region of China (the length including the frontiers of Sikkim and Bhutan which were attached to India by special treaties). So little was known about the undemarcated border that, in the early 1950's the report of a team of Indian power and irrigation engineers which visited China was published by the Government of India with a map which showed the North East Frontier Agency (as the present Arunachal Pradesh was then known) and the Aksai Chin region of Ladak--both of which were to be claimed by China--outside India's international border. Several other publications carried similar maps. It was only after the India-China hostilities of 1962 that the Union Home Ministry instructed all departments of the Government to remove the offending publications from libraries under their control and to destroy them.

In Ladakh, the Aksai Chin area claimed by India was administered so lightly--or not at all--that the Government came to know of the Chinese having constructed a Tibet-Sinkiang link road across Aksai China in the mid–1950's only after the event.

We knew as little about the culture of the Indo-Mongoloid people who live along the north-eastern frontier as about the terrain. For years after the India-China hostilities of 1962, All India Radio used to broadcast programmes in a series entitled 'India and the Dragon'. With our background of English education and of English literature grounded in the Bible, we assumed that the dragon, equated in Revelation 20:2 with "that old serpent, which is the Devil, and Satan", was an image that was bound to evoke aversion and disgust. We did not know that the dragon is a protective and beneficent symbol among the people of Sikkim, Arunachal and elsewhere in the north-east.

To refer to these facts is not to suggest that all of China's claims are valid, but only to point out that it is the path of good sense to seek a settlement based on the down-to-earth maxim according to which possession is nine-tenths of the law. In 1959, India was in possession of Arunachal Pradesh and China of Aksai Chin. Jawaharlal Nehru was unable to accomplish such a settlement because of the 'sacred territory' fervour worked up by the Indian Government's own handling of publicty. The Indian public was told about encroachments made by Chinese forces at certain points along the border, not about the fact that China likewise regarded the establishment of forward posts by Indian forces as 'encroachments'.

In a letter of 26 September 1959 to Chou En-lai, Nehru told the Chinese Premier that the Indian government had not given publicity till very recently to the information which it had about many encroachments by the Chinese on Indian soil, "in the hope that peaceful solutions of the disputes could be found by agreement by the two countries without public excitement on both sides. In fact our failure to do so has now resulted in sharp but legitimate criticism of the Government both in Parliament and the Press in our country."[17]

In this atmosphere, Nehru could not risk accepting the proposal made by Chou En-lai in his reply of 7 November 1959 that, pending talks between the two Prime Ministers, "the armed forces of China and India each withdraw 20 Km. at once from the so-called McMahon Line in the east and from the line up to which each side exercises actual control in the West." Precisely these were to be the terms of the cease-fire that was imposed by China following the military debacle suffered by India in 1962 after Prime Minister Nehru told newsmen in New Delhi on 12 October 1962 that the Indian Army had been instructed to 'throw the Chinese out of NEFA'.

Whether it is in relation to the border with China or with Pakistan, it is best to recognise and formalise the long-standing realities on the ground. Only so can the countries concerned wind down military expenditure, as the Soviet Union wisely began to do under the leadership of Mikhail Gorbachev, and apply the resources so saved to development.

(c) Facts about Kashmir : The religious demography of Jammu & Kashmir at the time of the sub-continent's partition is not widely known. At that time a princely State under a Hindu ruler, J & K consisted of three provinces: Jammu, Kashmir valley and Ladakh (including Gilgit and the Frontier Ilaqas). The population was overwhelmingly Muslim in each of the three provinces. (It was only after the hostilities of 1947-48, during which the heavily Muslim-populated areas of Jammu and Ladakh were occupied by Pakistan, that Jammu on the Indian side of the ceasefire line came to have a Hindu majority and there was a demographic shift in favour of the Buddhists in Ladakh.)

The strength of the two principal communities in the three provinces of J & K at the last two pre-1947 Censuses was as follows:

	JAMMU		KASHMIR VALLEY		LADAKH	
	Muslims	Hindus	Muslims	Hindus	Muslims	Buddhists
1931	10,91,021	6,65,246	14,78,287	69,296	2,48,328	38,212
1941	12,15,676	8,22,835	16,15,478	85,580	2,70,093	40,164

While J & K was contiguous both to India and to Pakistan, the economic lifeline of Kashmir Valley was the road that connected the capital city of Srinagar with Rawalpindi, in present Pakistan. There was no reliable road from Pathankot, in India, via Jammu to Srinagar. It was only after the State's accession to India that an all-weather road was constructed, including numerous bridges across rivers and a tunnel through the Banihal mountain range that separates Jammu from the Kashmir Valley. It is pertinent to recall that when Jawaharlal Nehru went to Srinagar along with barrister Asaf Ali in 1946 for the legal defence of Sheikh Abdullah, leader of the State's principal political party who had been imprisoned by the Maharaja's administration for demanding democratic rule, it was the road from Rawalpindi that Nehru took.

Thus, in terms of the communal logic of the sub-continent's partition as well as economic linkages, Pakistan saw itself as having a formidable cliam on J & K. Sheikh Abdullah's preference for India seemed to matter as little as that of Khan Abdul Ghaffar Khan, tallest among the leaders of the people of the North West Frontier Province, who too wanted his province to be part of a democratic, secular and progressive India rather than a theocratic and reactionary Pakistan. A referendum held in the NWFP had brought that province into Pakistan despite Ghaffar Khan.

The circumstances may be recalled briefly. The partition plan worked out by Lord Mountbatten as the last British Viceroy entailed, so far as British India was concerned, a process of consultation with the concerned provincial legislatures and plebiscites to be held in the NWFP and in the Sylhet district of Assam. In the case of the several hundred States of varying size that constituted princely India, it was for the rulers to accede to either of the two new Dominions of India and Pakistan. Though Mountbatten made it clear that accession should be based on geographical considerations and that there was no question of independence for the princely States, some of the rulers entertained the hope of establishing a direct Dominion link with the British Crown.

Till Jinnah's dram of Pakistan approached realisation with the drawing up of the partition plan, the fierce tribesmen of the NWFP had followed the leadership of Ghaffar Khan, known as the 'Frontier Gandhi' because of his loyalty to the Mahatma. Maulana Azad, the Congress president, and Ghaffar Khan were the only regular members of the party's Working Committee who, at its meeting on 2 June 1947 when the Mountbatten Plan was accepted, spoke against partition.[18]

Ghaffar Khan would have liked the NWFP to be part of India if partition became inevitable. If the proposed East Pakistan (as the area that now constitutes Bangladesh was then known) could be separated from the western wing by a thousand miles of Indian territory, there could be no objection to the NWFP, similarly separated by Pakistan territory, being part of India. But he knew that if his people were asked to opt between a Hindu-majority even if democratic India and an Islamic state of Pakistan, the religious pull would prove decisive. Ghaffar Khan therefore asked his colleagues to find out, as a small mercy, if the plebiscite in the NWFP could include the third alternative of independence as well.

The Congress president wrote to the Viceroy accordingly, and Gandhiji took Ghaffar Khan along to meet Mountbatten. But the Viceroy refused to consider the suggestion of independence as a third alternative, pointing out that it was Jawaharlal Nehru himself who had strongly objected to such an option for any province. Nehru had opposed the option because it could lead to a balkanisation of India much worse than partition into a diminished India and Pakistan. Not securing the option of independence, Ghaffar Khan's 'Red Shirts' boycotted the referendum in the

NWFP. In the result, more than 50 per cent of the electorate voted for merger with Pakistan.

Whatever the strength of Pakistan's claim on J & K, the cause was morally lost when it launched on military action. Early in October 1947, when the Maharaja was still sitting on the fence, raiders organised and equipped by the Pakistan army attacked the border town of Muzaffarabad and advanced into the Kashmir Valley. It was only towards the close of the month, when the raiders had reached Uri, barely 62 miles from Srinagar, that the Maharaja acceded to India and handed over the administration to an interim government headed by Sheikh Abdullah. India accepted the accession, but subject to the condition that the people's wishes would be ascertained. The Indian Army drove the raiders back but did not clear them entirely out of the State's territory since the Government accepted a ceasefire under United Nations auspices.

No plebiscite was held as in the NWFP, India holding that Pakistan's forces should first vacate the State. The outcome of the elections held in 1951 in the Indian portion of J & K, in which Sheikh Abdullah's party won all the 75 seats--73 of them without contest--was claimed as sufficient vindication and ratification of the State's accession to India. The moral complexity of the Kashmir issue deepened when Sheikh Abdullah was deposed and arrested in August 1953 on the suspicion of his wanting to make J & K an independent State--on the same lines and for the same reasons as Khan Abdul Ghaffar Khan had visualised independence in the case of the NWFP.

It is not widely known how unhappy Jawaharlal Nehru was at this turn of events. He knew that elections in J & K were never as free and fair as in the rest of India. Following the 1962 elections in which the party led by Bakshi Ghulam Mohammed (who succeeded Sheikh Abdullah) won almost all the seats, Nehru wrote to Bakshi: "In fact, it would strengthen your position much more if you lost a few seats to bona fide opponents."[19] Subsequently, on 7 August 1962, Nehru conceded in a letter to P.N. Bazaz that all that could be said for the Bakshi Ministry was that it was better than the autocratic rule of the Maharaja in the years before 1947. "It is true," Nehru wrote, "that political liberty does not exist there in the same measure as in the rest of India. At the same time, there is much more of it than there used to be."[20]

Shortly before his death, Jawaharlal Nehru in what his biographer S.Gopal describes as "a valedictory act of policy" ordered the withdrawal of the conspiracy case which had been dragging on for years. Nehru remarked, as recalled by Y.D. Gundevia, former Foreign Secretary: "If a damned thing can't be proved in four years, in six years, there is oviously nothing to be proved."[21] Sheikh Abdullah was released on 8 April 1964 and Jawaharlal Nehru invited him for talks. These talks resulted in Sheikh

Abdullah undertaking an exploratory mission of conciliation to Pakistan. The visit had to be cut short because of Nehru's death on 27 May 1964. Wider knowledge of these facts about Kashmir will help to secure acceptance by the public of any peaceful settlement of the issue that the Indian government may be able negotiate with Pakistan.

(viii) Armament v. Development

Even more galling to Jawaharlal Nehru than the humiliating military reverse suffered by India in the hostilities of 1962 with China must have been the tragic fact that he, an internationalist and a man of peace, should be leaving a legacy of conflict with the two largest of India's neighbours.

As early as in 1939, as chairman of the National Planning Committee, he had said in a note circulated to his colleagues: "A world union of free and equal nations may lead to a voluntary limitation of sovereignty; it will help planning within nations." In a letter of 1 August 1940 to J.R.Jayewardene, who was later to become President of Sri Lanka, Nehru said: "Personally I should like India to be closely associated in a future order with China, Burma and Ceylon as well as other countries which fit in. Our relations with China have become very close during the last year or two, and I am sure that the leaders of China look upon this possibility with favour."

It was characteristic of Jawaharlal Nehru that he convened an international conference in New Delhi on Asian Relations early in 1947, as head of the interim government, when independence was within sight and the sub-continent's partition, though feared, seemed possibly avoidable. He said to the participants in his inaugural address on 23 March 1947: "We stand at the end of an era and on the threshold of a new period of history...We have arrived at a stage in human affairs when the ideal of 'one world' and some kind of a world federation seems to be essential, though there are many dangers and obstacles in the way...But in order to have 'one world' we must also, in Asia, think of the countries of Asia cooperating together for that larger ideal."[22]

Within a few months, instead of movement forward to a new era, there was to be a throw-back to religious fanaticism when the Direct Action Day observed by the Muslim League on 16 August 1946 led to the killing of thousands in Calcutta and triggered a chain reaction of Hindu-Muslim massacres across northern India which made partition inevitable.

Jawaharlal Nehru's musings on the shadow that fell between his vision of One World and the reality of the conflict with Pakistan are significant. Speaking of the difference between a statesman and a saint, he said in the course of a speech on the birthday celebration of Ramakrishna Paramahamsa in New Delhi on 20 March 1949 that, in dealing with the problems of the world, even a good politician or statesman "has to be an opportunist in that he has to deal with the material he has. He cannot put across something which the people do not understand or cannot live up to. More especially in a democracy, the politician and the statesman has to make, very often, compromises with the truth because people's receptivity of truth is not enough. If he sought to do something else, he would be pushed away and others with a clear conception of the limitations of the majority will take his place."

India's militarisation has proceeded at an accelerated pace since the death of Nehru. This is a major reason for the frightening proportions which India's external and internal debt have assumed. Educators of public opiion concerned about developmet--as journalists, academics or political and social activists--should therefore try and create a non-hysterical climate of public opinion that will permit the settlement of disputes with neighbouring countries on the basis of give-and-take. Four decades have passed since Gandhiji who, though an apostle of non-violence, repeatedly affirmed his preference for violent resistance to evil over cowardly surrender, approved the despatch of an Indian armed force to Kashmir to defend it against aggression. But he quickly added: "A war will bring both the Dominions under the sway of a third power and nothing can be worse. I plead for amity and goodwill."[23] He said also: "If India and Pakistan are to be perpetual enemies and go to war against each other, it will ruin both the Dominions and their hard-won freedom will be soon lost. I do not wish to live to see that day."[24]

A major challenge for the development publicist is to fight the 'sacred territory' fetishism of the nation-state. What we mean by the term 'nation' is really the people living in a political state whose boundaries are the product of the accidents of history. Bangladesh and Pakistan formed one 'nation' from 1947 till 1971. West Bengal and Bangladesh, the Indian and Pakistan Punjabs, like the erstwhile two Germanys and the two Koreas, are examples of nations or sub-nations divided by the borders of political states which call themselves 'nation-states'

The humanism which is of the essence of Indian democracy and secularism cannot surely come to an abrupt halt at the political borders with Pakistan, China or other neighbours. Like other vertical divides--religion, race, caste, language and sex--the political state calling ifself a nation-state hides internal contradictions, and is a convenient rallying cry. The nationalism of a subjugated people is an assertion of self-respect and a heroic impulse entailing sacrifices and suffering. In contrast, nationalist feeling among the people of an independent country can be turned into chauvinism and exploited by demagogues and power-mongers for their profit at the expense of the common people. The point was made incisively by O.V.Vijayan, cartoonist of the *Statesman,* when he showed the late President Zia of Pakistan suggesting to the Indian Prime Minister, on the hot line telephone, 'How about a little cooperative war?' This was at a time when both the leaders were troubled by acute domestic problems. The miliatry-industrial-political complex is a reality in modern states of all ideological orientations. The decades after World War II have seen not only the U.S.A. and the U.S.S.R. but the U.S.S.R. and Communist China on the brink of war. Numerous Third World countries have been actually at war with each other, often with the same country acting as arms supplier to both sides in a conflict--like the U.S.A. in the case of India and Pakistan over the years, and the U.S.S.R. too for a brief while. Some Third World countries are themselves emerging as arms exporters on a modest scale, India and Pakistan among them.

In India, as in other countries, expansion of the armed forces offers opportunities to industrialists, construction contractors and traders, as well as to educated youth in terms of careers. There are also, for the unscrupulous among politicians, officials and business middle-men, kick-backs in the multi-crore deals of domestic contracts as well as foreign armament purchase. And sophisticated apologists for higher defence spending are not lacking who argue that investment in Defence research and development yields spin-off benefits for civilian industry. This, as a participant in a PTI-TV programme on Disarmament and Development put it, amounts to saying, "Spend a billion to get a million".

Leaders of Third World countries including India are eloquent while commending to the Big Powers a reduction in their expenditure on armament, so that some of the resources so saved may be used for greater aid from the Big Powers to the developing countries. Their own expenditure on the domestic manufacture and on the import of armament is deemed to be wholly necessary. It is an instance of the incapacity for self-examination which R.K. Laxman, cartoonist of *The Times of India,* pilloried when he depicted, at the time of the first World Conference on Poverty at Cancun, Mexico, in October 1981, a Third World leader telling the participants: "Ladies and Gentlemen, I have ordered a half-dozen five-star hotels. I invite you to hold your next conference in my capital."

Incidentally, Laxman and Vijayan illustrate the point that development communicators do not have to be long faced and preachy. They can make us at once laugh and learn.

NOTES

1. *Patriot* (p.5), 16 October 1987, New Delhi.
2. The Indian National Congress suffered a split in 1969 after Prime Minister Indira Gandhi secured the defeat of her party's candidate for the office of President of the Republic, by switching her support to an Independent candidate, V.V. Giri, who won. The majority faction of the Congress led by Indira Gandhi came to be known as Congress (Indira) or Congress (I) for short.

3. The Representation of the People (Amendment) Act which, on receiving the President's assent, became Act No.1 of 1989.
4. Quoted in Report of the Second Backward Classes Commission, First Part (p.25), Controller of Publications, Delhi. 1981.
5. The judgements cited in this paragraph are referred to by V.N. Shukla in *Constitution of India*, Eastern Book Co., Lucknow.
6. Report in *Patriot,* New Delhi, 28 December 1988.
7. Press Information Bureau news release, 12 June 1989.
8. Quoted by Verrier Elwin in Chapter II of *The Tribal People of India,* Publications Division, New Delhi, 1973.
9. *Inaugural speech by Congress President Shri Rajiv Gandhi* and The *Centenary Resolve* published by the All India Congress Committee (I), 24, Akbar Road, New Delhi. Price not stated.
10. Speech at 14th session of the Central Advisory Board of Education, New Delhi, 13 January 1948.
11. Speech while inaugurating the India branch of Union for the Study of the Great Religions, 29 May 1955.
12. Cited in article on 'Religious Pluralism and Social Conflict' by C.R. Prasad Rao and K. Radhakrishna Murthy in *Social Change,* journal of the Council for Social Development, June 1988.
13. Reproduced as an appendix in *Law of Hindu Religious and Charitable Endowments* by V.K. Varadachari (3rd edition), Eastern Book Co., 1985.
14. Report of the Second Press Commission, Vol. I (p. 25), New Delhi, 1982.
15. For a fuller account, see G.N.S. Raghavan, *PTI Story* (pp.168-169), published by Press Trust of India, New Delhi, 1987.
16. Quoted in *Organiser*, New Delhi, 18 May 1986.
17. *China's Betrayal of India* (p.27), Publications Division, New Delhi, 1962.
18. S. Gopal, *Jawaharhal Nehru: A Biography*, Vol. I. (p.356), Oxford University Press 1976.
19. S. Gopal, op. cit. Vol. II (p.262).
20. Ibid.
21. *Outside the Archives* (p.321), Sangam Books, 1984.
22. *Selected Works of Jawaharlal Nehru, Second Series* Vol. 2, pp. 503, 507.
23. *Harijan,* 12 January 1948.
24. *Harijan,* 28 September 1947.

Chapter III

DISPARITIES AND MASS POVERTY

Four decades and more after independence, the reality is a cruel mockery of the India of Gandhiji's dreams "in which there shall be no high class and low class of people". Disparities abound: between city and village; within a city, between its palaces and hovels; within villages, between landowners and the landless; and between men and women.

(i) Maruti: a Symbol

It is not only the pull of city lights but, and more so, the push of rural penury that accounts for the increasing proportion of the urban population from one Census to the next:

	Per cent of urban population
1921	11.2
1931	12.0
1941	13.9
1951	17.3
1961	18.0
1971	19.9
1981	23.7

A disproportionately high share of public resources is spent on civic services for the urban population, more especially in those parts of towns and cities where the well-to-do live. Jawaharlal Nehru, who served as chairman of the Allahabad Municipality for two years in the mid–1920's speaks in his autobiography of how the fashionable Civil Lines claimed a high share of public expenditure: "The poorer parts of the city are almost ignored. It has few good roads, and most of the narrow lanes are ill-lit and have no proper drainage or sanitation system. It puts up with all these disabilities patiently and seldom complains; and when it does complain, nothing much happens. Nearly all the Big Noises and Little Noises live in the Civil Lines."

The story of Delhi after independence has been much the same. The areas where Ministers, foreign diplomats, big business men and senior government officials live present a striking contrast to the crowded colonies of the lower middle class and the jhuggi slums in which the poorest, most of them immigrants from rural areas of many States, live.

When Gandhiji was asked to address the Asian Relations Conference convened by Jawaharlal Nehru in New Delhi in the early part of 1947, he told the participants bluntly: "You, friends, have not seen the real India." You are not meeting in conference in the midst of real india. Since then New Delhi has acquired more glitter.

The domestic lounges of its airport burst at the seams with expense-account air travellers. There has been a proliferation of multi-star hotels and multi-crore sports stadia. Privately owned or hired motor vehicles running on two wheels, three and four, choke city roads, guzzling petrol refined from imported crude oil paid for with borrowed foreign exchange. These vehicles pollute the atmosphere and cause an increasing number of road accidents claiming human lives and limbs. Those who have to rely on public transport suffer bestial crowding in buses, with women often having to suffer indecent harassment.

Conspicuous among the motor vehicles on the capital's roads is the Maruti car, symbolic of the increasingly elitist turn taken by India's planned development in the post-Nehru period. Maruti was the brainchild of the younger of Indira Gandhi's two sons. Sanjay Gandhi said that it would be wholly indigenous, and a low priced "people's car"--a contradiction in terms in a country as poor as India. There was no basis for the claim about indigenous manufacture, and the project should have faded out after Sanjay Gandhi's tragic death in June 1980 in the crash of a plane in which he and a friend were performing aerobatics. The project was nationalised instead.

Maruti Ltd., the company set up by Sanjay Gandhi, was taken over by the Central Government through an ordinance on 14 October 1989. The ordinance was soon approved by Parliament and replaced by The Maruti Ltd. (Acquisition and Transfer of Undertakings) Act, 1980. An agreement for collaboration, both financial and technical, was entered into by Maruti Udyog Ltd., as the public sector company was now known, with the Suzuki Motor Company of Japan in October 1982. The first vehicle rolled out of the assembly line in November 1983. Production has increased by leaps and bounds since then, hardly keeping pace with the increase in demand from the new rich. The output of passenger cars went up as follows:

	Production of Maruti passenger cars
1984	12,087
1985	48,635
1986	63,504
1987	90,909
Jan.-July 1988	51,299

The managing director of Maruti Udyog announced on 1 April 1989 that an expansion plan was being finalised for doubling the production from the present level of 100,000 vehicles of all types. The doubling, he said, would be accomplished over a period of 18 to 21 months after securing the government's approval. Meanwhile the equity shareholding by Suzuki which was 26% in the agreement signed in 1982--by an ironic coincidence on 2 October which marks Gandhiji's birth anniversary--was increased to 40% in 1987.

The public sector is thus making a substantial contribution to the increase in the number of personalised vehicles that are owned or hired by the well-to-do. According to the data with the Directorate of Transport, Delhi Administration, the growth was as follows:

Motor Vehicles on Delhi Roads

	1978	1983	1988
Private Cars	1,05,204	1,42,299	2,79,708
Motor Cycles/Scooters	2,82,338	4,88,307	9,78,698
Taxis	5,580	8,258	9,094
Auto-rickshaws,etc.	17,890	27,039	51,700
Total of personalised vehicles	4,11,012	6,65,903	13,19,200
Total no. of buses (Delhi Transport Corporation plus private bases including minis)	6,929	11,999	16,319
DTC buses (out of the above)	2,283		4,247

Personalised motor transport has thus more than trebled over a ten-year period, while buses which consume far less fuel per passenger, and whose number was grossly inadequate, have only slightly more than doubled. Elitism in road passenger transport makes a not inconsiderable contribution to the demand for petrol, at a time when the country is a net importer of crude oil.

Doubling of the production of Maruti cars is hardly in consonance with the call, in the document on 'The approach to the Seventh Five Year Plan (1985-90)' for "restraints on elitist consumption". Or with the remarks of the then Finance Secretary Gopi Arora on the need to hold down "import-intensive consumption items" (*Indian Express,* Delhi, 8 March 1989). The Mid-Term Appraisal of the Seventh Plan (p. 156) acknowledges: "Diesel consumption in road transport increased; so also motor gasoline due to increased personalised transport."

(a) Expense-Account High-Flyers: Another substantial contribution to the need for import of crude oil, and therefore to the borrowing of foreign exchange, is made by Indian Airlines. Instead of curbing air travel, the Government has allowed this public sector undertaking to keep on expanding its fleet of imported planes. A very large section of the air travelling class are those undertaking official journeys entailing no payment from their purse: the 'entitled' among officers of government departments, public sector undertakings and the numerous academic institutions and research organisations that are massively funded by the government. The bills are picked up by all those who pay taxes--including excise duties on matches, sugar, tea and beedis- -most of whom never fly. The air journeys, whether to inspect an office, attend a meeting or participate in a seminar (which could be on the theme of poverty alleviation) are often neatly dovetailed with attending to personal or domestic business. Among the free travellers are employees of the airlines themselves and members of their families.

Smaller in number but with a higher frequency of travel are Ministers, Central and State, and members of parliament. Expense-account air travellers from the private sector are the executives of firms, whose bills are met in the last analysis by the consumers of the company's products or services. Then there is the extensive travel by entitled officers of the Defence service. In addition, air travel by members of the families of Defence services officers is subsidised. Also subsidised is air travel by students (obviously not from poor families). It is only a very small fraction of the air-travelling public who pay for tickets wholly from their own pockets. They opt for air travel in case of extreme need, and are liable to find themselves crowded out by the hordes of free or subsidised travellers many of whom enjoy the additional privilege of access to reserved quotas of seats.

June 1989 saw Indian Airlines acquire the first of the A320 airbuses made by the multi-national Airbus Industrie. A contract has been signed the proposal 19 of these, and the government has cleared the proposal of Indian Airlines to purchase 12 more. The cost of these 31 aircraft is of the order of Rs. 60 crores, in foreign exchange, apiece.

An editiorial in the *Indian Express* of 13 June 1989 hailed the decision to buy 31 of the airbuses as "a sound decision". It said: "A320 is a highly sophisticated aircraft. Considerable improvement in air traffic systems and ground facilities will be needed...According to a scheme submitted by the National Airport Authority of India, revamping of air traffic systems in major airports alone will entail an investment of 300 crores.

The money has to be found." That this leading newspaper, a fierce critic of the Congress (I) and friendly to the then chief opposition party, the Janata Dal, should endorse the vast expenditure on air travel for the benefit of the ruling classes is significant. It shows that there is no basic difference between the main contenders for political power with regard to the elitist course of development.

Fast-flying jet aircraft are guzzlers of aviation fuel. The Seventh Plan document (Vol. II, p.129) says: "The main growth of petroleum consumption is in the middle distillates range comprising aviation turbine fuel, kerosene and diesel oil. But such skewed growth is not compatible with the refining capabilities. While with hydrocracker it may be possible to obtain from a suitable imported crude over 60% as middle distillates, the maximum yield from processing facility which is presently installed in most of our refineries is about 52%."

Oil production stood at 28.99 million tonnes in 1984-85, of which 20.14 million tonnes was offshore and 8.85 million tonnes onshore. Domestic oil production is expected to rise to 34.53 million tonnes by the terminal year (1989-90) of the Seventh Plan. Inclusive of more than 14 million tonnes of imported crude oil, the throughput in the oil refineries in the same year is expected to be 48.89, which will yield 45.47 million tonnes of petroleum products. The Plan document says: "The production of middle distillates in 1989-90 will be about 27.14 million tonnes as against the demand of 31.27 million tonnes. The gap of 7.20 million tonnes (out of which middle distillates account for 4.13 million tonnes) between demand and supply of petroleum products will be met through imports."

When they are not travelling by office cars, or flying, the privileged classes use air-conditioned trains. A journey may not really be necessary, but it is accomplished increasingly fast. Super-fast air-conditioned trains are the third mode, besides the Maruti car and imported aircraft, by which members of India's upper class are racing towards the promised 21st century.

A contract worth $20 million (over Rs. 60 crores) has been signed with British Rail Engineering Ltd. for the building of 42 railway coaches in England. These, says a news release of 31 January 1989 by the British Information Services in India, will form two new high-speed air-conditioned trains "for one of Indian Railways' most prestigious routes". A spokesman of BREL has described the contract as "the most significant railway coach export order to be secured by a Western European manufacturer in recent years." India's diversified dependence for inducting high technology for luxury travel includes French collaboration for building a 250 km. per hour super-fast train.

(b) Luxury Hotels: The earning of foreign exchange by catering for tourists from abroad is a justification advanced for the proliferation of multi-star hotels, both in the public sector and the private, over the last quarter century. Foreign exchange earning from tourists is also advanced as an argument in defence of the expansion of the Indian Airlines fleet. Soon, the Maruti project will be claiming credit for exporting some of its cars to Hungary and other countries. In each case, however, the foreign exchange argument is a fig leaf to cover the pampering of themselves by the ruling classes with the luxuries they taste when they visit affluent countries.

Enquiries made in the course of the present study, in respect of a cross-section of public and private sector five-star hotels, elicited the information that the revenue they earn in foreign exchange is generally around 30% and in no case exceeds 40%. The bulk of their revenue is in rupees, paid by expense-account executives in the two sectors, by officials of government departments who wine and dine along with visiting foreign delegations in luxury hotels, and by those Indians who have plenty of unaccounted money to spend. Some politicians in power have taken to holding press conferences in multi-star hotels, where they also host a meal, in order to ensure the presence of journalists in respectable strength. The taxpayer picks up the bill.

The Indian Tourism Development Corporation now runs 25 hotel units. At a meeting of the Consultative Committee of members of parliament attached to the Department of Tourism, on 9 May 1989 the Minister in charge, Shivraj Patil, said only 'a few' out of the 25 are in the five-star category. The majority, he said, were in the two to four-star categories catering for middle class tourists; special efforts were being made, according to him, for promoting domestic or budget tourism. This is a peculiar definition of the middle class as those who can afford to stay in hotels up to the four-star category.

The growth of facilities for the new rich of the country can be gauged from the following figures taken from the annual reports of the Ministry of Tourism and Civil Aviation:

Year	No. of approved hotels	Rooms
1970-71	177	9,657
1980-81	218	22,300
1982-83	425	N.A.
1984-85	470	32,692

In 1985, there were 253 new hotel projects which had been approved by the Department. They were to add 14,936, thus taking the total to 47,628 rooms.

The scale of investment on hotel building is staggering. When the Kanishka Hotel was constructured by ITDC in New Delhi in the mid-1980's, the cost per room--inclusive of the cost of the public areas: lounge, restaurant and shopping plaza--came to Rs. 4,50,000. The total cost of construction was about Rs. 13 crores. It is estimated that if Kanishka were to be constructed in 1990, the cost per room would come to between Rs. 13,00,000 and Rs. 14,00,00.

The latest hotel being built by Grover Leasing Ltd., in the private sector, opposite Centaur Hotel near Delhi airport is expected to cost about Rs. 30 crores.

(ii) Urban-Rural Disparities

The well-to-do and the poor were the two nations of whom Benjamin Disraeli, the 19th-century British statesman and novelist, wrote in *Sybil, or The Two Nations* in which he analysed Chartism, the first working class movement on a national scale in Britain. In the second half of the 20th century, these two nations have been present in almost all the newly free countries. The contrast between the two is conspicuous in India.

While the disparity between the rich and the poor is shocking enough in Indian cities and towns, the generality of the urban population is better off in comparision with the rural. Destitution, malnutrition and illiteracy prevail on a much larger scale in India's villages. In a written reply to a question in the Rajya Sabha on 10 August 1988, the then Minister of Planning, Madhavsinh Solanki, said that according to estimates compiled by the Central Statistical Organisation for 1970-71 (information for further years was not avilable), the per capita income in rural and urban areas was Rs. 499 and Rs. 1201 respectively. Since per capita data are averages, the maximum disparity will be even greater than these figures suggest.

The one indubitable achievement of the post-independence governments at the Centre and in the States has been an incerease in the expectation of life at birth, with a narrowing, and recent elimination, of the gap as between males and females. The figures are as follows :

Expectation of life at birth (years)[1]

	Males	Females	Persons
1941	32.09	31.37	N.A
1951	32.45	31.66	N.A
1961	41.89	40.55	N.A
1971	46.40	44.70	N.A
1980	54.1	54.7	54.4

The improvement owes mainly to two factors. One is the success of the campaigns to eradicate or control communicable diseases. The rich could not be afforded protection selectively against such diseases; the poor had to be protected as well. The most striking instance is malaria: "National Malaria Eradication Programme of India is the world's biggest health programme against a single communicable disease and continues to be the country's most comprehensive and multifaceted in public health activity. With the successful implementation of National Malaria Eradication Programme in 1958, the annual incidence of malaria was drastically reduced from 75 million to about 0.1 million in 1965."[2] Deaths due to malaria, which used to be of the order of 800,000 per year, were completely eliminated. Though there has been a resurgence of malaria since the mid-1970's the level of incidence has been brought down. Other communicable diseases which no longer take a heavy toll of life include tuberculosis, cholera and smallpox.

The second factor making for increased expectation of life is the avoidance after independence, through higher domestic production of foodgrains and imports whenever necessary, of large-scale deaths due to starvation such as occurred many times during British rule, the last occasion having been the Bengal Famine of 1943. It is another matter that widespread poverty results in malnutrition and deaths from diseases related thereto. Newspaper reports speak from time to time of starvation deaths in certain parts of the country, with the local authorities maintaining that the deaths were due to malnutrition or some specific disease.

(a) Mortality Indicators : There is a considerable disparity in the expectation of life at birth of the urban Indian and of the rural Indian. The following figures relating to 1982 speak for themselves.[3]

Indicators	Rural	Urban	Combined
Crude death rate	13.1	7.4	11.9
Infant mortality rate	113.7	65.2	104.8
Neo-Natal mortality rate	72.9	38.8	66.7
Post-Natal mortality rate	40.8	26.4	38.1
Peri-Natal mortality rate	57.7	33.1	53.2
Still birth rate	9.8	5.2	8.9

(b) Nutritional Status : The acuteness of rural poverty is reflected in low nutritional status, which in turn contributes to the depressing mortality picture.

Early in 1989, the National Institute of Nutrition, Hyderabad published the findings of surveys, conducted from 1975 to 1980 in ten States, of the mean intake of four categories of foods by the different economic strata of the urban population and by the rural population as a whole. The findings were as follows:[4]

MILK : As against the recommended daily intake of 150 g/cu (grams per head), the urban High Income Group consumed 424; Middle Income Group 251 (in both cases more than necessary); while the Low Income Group consumed 93, Industrial Labour 98, and Slum Dwellers 43. The rural population (all economic categories) consumed 70. Thus the rural consumption of milk was less than that of every urban category except Slum Dwellers.

FRUITS: As against the recommended daily intake of 30 g/cu, the urban HIG consumed 124; MIG 66; LIG 35; Industrial Labour 35 (in all the cases more than adequate) while urban Slum Dwellers consumed 26 and the rural population even less namely 15.

OIL AND FATS: As against the recommendned daily intake of 40 g/cu, only the urban HIG consumed more, namely 47. Consumption by MIG was 35, LIG 22, Industrial Labour 24, Slum Dwellers 12, and the rural population only 9.

SUGAR AND JAGGERY: As against the recommended daily intake of 30 g/cu, urban HIG consumed 34 and MIG 31 (more than adequate), while consumption by LIG was less at 28 and by Industrial Labour was optimum at 30. Urban Slum Dwellers' consumption was only 19, and that of the rural population even less, namely 18.

It will be seen that the rural per capita consumption of each of the four categories of foods fell short of the recommended daily intake.

(c) Drinking Water for Villagers: In contrast to the attention and resources lavished on the urban affluent is the neglect, over decades of planned development, of as basic a need as drinking water for those living in villages.

Of the 557,000 villages in the country (excluding Assam where the 1981 Census could not be held on account of disturbed conditions), as many as 1,61,722 were yet to be provided with safe drinking water facilities at the beginning of the Seventh Plan on 1 April 1985. Of these problem villages, the largest number (43,906) were in Uttar Pradesh, followed by Madhya Pradesh (14,714) and Orissa (14,443). A total of 98,333 problem villages are claimed to have been covered during the first three years of the 7th Plan, leaving a balance, as of April 1988, of more than 50,000 villages (inclusive of problem villages that have only been partially covered).[5]

It is a commentary on the sense of priorities of the Planning Commission and the Central Government that the Department of Rural Development could not secure the financial allocation of Rs. 510 crores it proposed for 1989-90 (as against Rs. 410 crores in 1988-89) for the National Drinking Water Mission including the Centrally sponsored Accelerated Rural Water Supply Programme (ARWSP). A working group recommended Rs. 440 crores, which was finally reduced to Rs. 410 crores by the Planning Commission. The Department requested the Planning Commission and the Ministry of Finance to reconsider the matter and allow an increase of Rs. 100 crores. The matter was also brought to the notice of the Adviser to Prime Minister on Technology Missions. But to no avail.

This was at about the same time that the then Prime Minister Rajiv Gandhi laid the foundation of a multi-crore sports stadium in East Delhi, scene of many deaths during 1988 from intestinal ailments variously described as cholera and gastro-enteritis, resulting from municipal failure to supply potable water. Though Indian performance in recent Olympics has been dismal, the construction of yet another stadium suggests that the ruling elite hope to secure for the country the distinction of hosting the Olympic Games sooner or later.

(d) Town and Rural Sanitation: If a part of the capital city can suffer from lack of municipal facilities, it is not surprising that India's 3,250 odd towns--and not only the villages--are neglected.

Gandhiji had given the name of Harijans (children of God) to the former untouchable castes who were condemned to scavenging and other unclean occupations. *Harijan* was the name of the weekly journal he founded in 1933 and in which he wrote most extensively. The first issue (11 February 1933) carried on the front page a free rendering into English, by Rabindranath Tagore, of a Bengali poem 'The Scavenger' by Satyendranath Datta.

Yet, more than forty years after independence, most of the Harijans who are engaged in the scavenging of dry latrines are still to be liberated from this nauseating occupation. The document on the Annual Plan 1987-88 tells us (on p.310, in Chapter 16 on 'Socio-Economic Programmes for Scheduled Castes and Scheduled Tribes') that the Central Government provides matching assistance to the States and Union territories "for schemes for the liberation of scavengers by converting dry latrines into waterborne latrines on the whole-town approach basis, including rehabilitation of liberated scavengers in alternate occupations. Till 1987-88, 25 towns in 11 States had been made scavenging- free. The provision during 1987-88 for the scheme was Rs. 9.50 crores."

There is also a rural sanitation programme which includes the construction of low-cost sanitary latrines. The *Annual Plan: 1988-89* document says on p. 380, in Chapter 24 on 'Minimum Needs Programme': "The centrally sponsored rural sanitation programme aims to supplement the efforts made under different Central and State sector programmes by providing sanitation facilities in the rural areas through construction of low-cost sanitary latrines for individual households so as to improve the quality of life in rural areas. During 1987-88, anticipated expenditure under the programme is Rs. 29.25 crores against an allocation of Rs. 30.16 crores. An outlay of Rs. 29.70 crores--Rs. 9.70 crores in the State sector and Rs. 20 crores in the Central sector--has been provided for 1988-89, with a target of constructing 2,10,000 latrines."

Yet another scheme which provides for the construction of sanitary latrines in rural areas is the National Rural Employment Programme (NREP), launched in October 1980 in replacement of the Food for Work programme. "The revised guidelines (for NREP) provide for earmarking of 25% of outlays for social forestry, 10% for works of direct benefit to Scheduled Castes and Scheduled Tribes, and Rs. 6 crores annually for construction of sanitary latrines." (Mid-Term Appraisal of Seventh Plan, p.38). It is stated on p.41 of the document that 59,533 rural latrines were constructed during 1986-87.

The launching of one scheme after another for the same purpose, often merely marking a change of name, may serve an immediate publicity purpose by creating a sensation of vigorous action for rural development. But it will be evident from the financial provisions made for rural water supply and for rural sanitation to serve the 600 million and more,who live in the villages that they are trifles compared with the hundreds of crores lavished on the manufacture of passenger cars, purchase of foreign passenger planes and construction of multi-star hotels.

(e) **Fair Price Shops:** Whether it is the opening and running of schools, health centres or fair price shops, it is easier to operate them to serve large numbers of people in urban centres than the rural population living in small and scattered habitations. The difficulties can be overcome only if the administration is highly motivated, and if the rural people are conscious of their rights and organise themselves to secure what they are entitled to. The public distribution system is a case in point.

It consists of about 347,000 fair price shops. About four-fifths of them are in rural areas. Yet the turn-over of the one-fifth of fair price shops in urban centres is greater, judging by the experience of the co-operative sector.

Figures of sales are available in respect of the consumer co-operative strores which account for 24% of the retail outlets in urban areas, and of the primary agricultural cooperative societies which run 29% of the retail outlets in the rural areas.

Sales by fair price shops in the cooperative sector in urban areas totalled Rs. 2300 crores in 1987-88, as against sales of only Rs. 2075 by the rural cooperative fair price shops[7] even though the latter are several times the number of the urban outlets.

Closer study needs to be made of the reasons for the lower off-take from the rural fair price shops. Is it because supplies are made of scarce commodities, like edible oils, on a lower scale to the rural outlets in the public distribution system? Or non-availability of the coarse grains which the rural poor prefer to rice and wheat? Or the sheer lack of purchasing power? An aggravating factor is unit-price difference between smaller and larger packs of the same commodity. The poor can afford to buy only small packs, while the well-to-do buy and store the larger packs which come cheaper per unit. Can there be a policy intervention to ensure that at least in the case of manufacturers and distributors in the public sector, the price per unit in a small pack is the same as in larger packs? Private sector companies could also be persuaded to adopt a similar policy.

The Department of Civil Suplies has given the following figures of offtake in lakh tonnes to claim that PDS has played an "effective role" in the drought year 1987-88.[8]

Year	Wheat	Rice	Imported edible oils	Kerosene
1984	28.62	56.22	7.75	57.31
1985	30.46	58.31	6.05	60.72
1986	41.15	72.30	7.26	64.39
1987	55.51	79.81	10.13	69.88
1988	72.22	84.37	8.99	74.93

However, in the absence of a break-up of this offtake from fair price shops as between the urban and rural ones, there is no telling whom the PDS helped during the drought years culminating in the severe drought of 1987-88. The Department should make it a rule to give the rural-urban break-up of the offtake of each commodity through fair price shops.

The increase in total retail sales of consumer goods handled in the urban areas, the annual report says, was from Rs. 1745 crores in 1986-87 to Rs. 2300 crores in 1987-88. The corresponding figures for rural areas are Rs. 1875 crores and Rs. 2075 crores. The higher urban growth rate would suggest that though the majority of the country's poor live in villages, urban dwellers benefit more from the public distribution system. Super Bazar in Delhi alone sold goods worth Rs. 87.5 crores during 1987-88. Though Delhi has one of the highest incomes per capita among the States and Union territories, it does have its quota of the poor. But the middle and upper classes, rather than the poor, form the bulk of the clientele of Super Bazar's three department stores, 117 branches and 63 mobile vans. Among the goods they sell are electric grinders, hot air fans and other domestic appliances of interest to the urban well-to-do.

An urban bias is evident in the scale of financial assistance to the States/Union territories under Centrally drawn up schemes to assist cooperative societies to strengthen the public distribution network.[9]

	(Rs. in lakhs)	
	1988-89	1989-90
Centrally sponsored scheme for development of consumer co-operatives in urban areas	75	175
Central sector scheme for distribution of consumer articles in rural areas (10% earmarked for tribal areas)	190	190

(f) Literacy: Multiple Inequalities : Disparities in the level of literacy are multi-faceted: as between the urban and rural population as a whole; between urban men and women and rural men and women; between the Scheduled Castes and Tribes and the rest of the country's population; and between men and women within the S.C. and S.T.

The terms in which the Census of India presents literacy figures makes a situation which is bad enough look worse, by including children in the age group 0-5 and treating them as 'illiterates'. Literacy at the 1981 Census for all ages was :

		(percentage)	
	Males	Females	Persons
Rural	40.79	17.96	29.65
Urban	65.83	47.82	57.40
Total	46.89	24.82	36.23

It will be seen that literacy among women of all ages is less than half the literacy rate among men in the rural areas, and a little over 70% of the male literacy rate in urban areas.

A more realistic approach is to exclude children in the age group of 0-5 from literacy calculations. This has been attempted in a Paper prepared by the Census organisation, and based on the 1981 Census data pertaining to 14 major States, namely Andhra Pradesh, Bihar, Gujarat, Haryana, Karnataka, Kerala, Madhya Pradesh, Maharashtra, Orissa, Punjab, Rajasthan, Tamil Nadu, Uttar Pradesh and West Bengal. The findings are as below :

Literacy rate % for age 5 years and above.[10]

	Males	Females	Persons
Rural	46.74	20.65	34.04
Urban	74.00	54.41	64.89
Total	53.48	28.47	41.44

The difference in literacy rates among the Scheduled Castes and Tribes, on the one hand, and the rest of India's population on the other is brought out in the following table.

There is a considerable disparity between the sexes over and above the overall disparity.

Literacy among S.C. and S.T. and rest of the population from 1961 to 1981.[11]

	Scheduled Castes		Scheduled Tribes		Rest	
Year	Total	Females	Total	Females	Total	Females
1961	10.27	3.29	8.53	3.16	27.86	16.59
1971	14.67	6.44	11.30	4.85	33.80	17.11
1981	21.38	10.93	16.35	8.04	41.22	29.51

It will be seen from these figures (which are for all ages) that exclusion of the S.C. and S.T. improves the total literacy figure at the 1981 Census from 36.23 to 41.22, and the literacy figure for females from 24.82 to 29.51.

The snail's pace of the improvement in literacy among the S.C. and S.T. shows the futility of offering free education and reservation of seats in higher educational institutions and in public employment without attacking the central problem of poverty among the S.C. and S.T.

(iii) Rural Disparities

Economic inequality within rural India is no less than the urban-rural disparity. A field survey was carried out in twelve villages of Madhya Pradesh during mid-1987 as part of the present study. It revealed a depressing picture of widespread poverty among the landless and those with small holdings, and the peristence of illiteracy and lack of access to health care.

(a) A Madhya Pradesh profile : A total of 168 persons were interviewed in eight villages of Vidisha district (Imblia, Karasia, Kotra, Mungod, Olinga, Pipalkhedi, Shakalkhedi and Suakheri) and four villages of Hoshangabad district (Biora, Pathrota, Rohna and Saheli). The attempt was primarily to study the living conditions and problems of the poor. But some who were relatively well off were also interviewed in order to obtain a comparative picture.

The classification of respondents as 'poor' was on the basis of a monthly household expenditure of less than Rs. 600 per month as reported by them, cross-checked with the reported figure of monthly household income. This cutoff point of Rs. 7200 per annum is higher than the rural poverty line defined as Rs. 6400 per annum per family for the purpose of the Seventh Plan (1985-90). However, the figure of Rs. 6400 is in relation to prices in the base year of the Plan. Since there had been a steady increase in the consumer price index for agricultural workers, it seemed realistic and necessary to reckon the poverty line somewhat higher (by 12.5%).

Of the total of 168 respondents (40 in the Hoshangabad villages and 128 in the Vidisha villages), 128 (76%) were poor and the rest well off. Males among the respondents totalled 136 and females 32. The distribution by sex among the poor was 107 males and 21 females and, among the well off, 29 males and 11 females.The social composition of the respondents was as follows:

Social Profile of Respondents

	Poor	Well off	Total number	per cent
Scheduled Castes	53	12	65	39
Scheduled Tribes	15	1	16	9
Other Backward classes	31	6	37	22
Others	29	21	50	30
Total	128	40	168	100

The preponderance of Scheduled Castes and Scheduled Tribes among the poor is apparent. The proportions, however, do not correspond to and are in excess of the district-wide percentage of Scheduled Castes (11.04 in Hoshangabad and 21.53 in Vidisha) and of Scheduled Tribes (7.17 in Hoshangabad and 4.68 in Vidisha).[12]

The survey showed that 63% of the poor families possessed no land. Those who had land up to four hectares (equivalent roughly to 10 acres) formed 31%. Their holdings ranged in size from marginal to semi-medium. Five per cent reported having land above four hectares. Among the well off, on the other hand, 47% possessed land above four hectares; 45% had land below that level; and 7% owned no land. The large landholders included one respondent in Shakalkhedi who owned 125 acres and another in Suakhedi with 80 acres. Four other respondents among the well off owned between 30 and 50 acres.

(b) Inequality in Land Holdings: This micro study in a dozen villages of Madhya Pradesh illustrated the skewed distribution of land holdings in the country as a whole:

Operational Holdings in India: 1980-81.[13]

(Figures in parentheses are percentages to total)

Size of holdings (hectares)	No. of holdings (Million)	Area of holdings (Million hectares)
MARGINAL (Below 1)	50.52 (56.5)	19.80 (12.2)
SMALL (1-2)	16.08 (18.0)	22.96 (14.1)
SEMI-MEDIUM (3-4)	12.51 (14.0)	34.56 (21.2)
MEDIUM (4-10)	8.09 (9.1)	48.34 (29.7)
LARGE (10 & above)	2.15 (2.4)	37.13 (22.8)
Total	89.35 (100)	162.79 (100)

Though an operational holding is not identical with ownership, the pattern of operational holdings indicates the actual access to oultivable land. According to the latest appraisal by the Planning Commission, "The number of marginal ownership holdings is much higher than the number of marginal operational holdings. This suggests that some of the marginal farmers who own land, lease it out to others for cultivating, and themselves work for wages on a full-time basis."[14]

The pattern is even more inequitable when a comparison is made of the ownership not only of land but of other assets such as buildings, livestock, implements, machinery, transport equipment and durable household assets. The first attempt to collect data on household assets and liabilities was through the All India Rural Debt and Investment Survey (AIRDIS) conducted by the Reserve Bank of India in 1961-62. The next attempt was by the National Sample Survey Organisation which conducted an All India Debt and Investment Survey in 1971-72. The results were worked out separately for four occupational classes, namely cultivators, agriculatural labourers, artisans and other non-cultivators. "Comparing the results of the 1961-62 and 1971-72 Surveys it is observed that the basic pattern of the asset holding has remained the same. The top 10% continues to enjoy a share of about 51% of the total, while the bottom 10% just 0.1%. There is thus no idication of any reduction in inequality."[15]

The Madhya Pradesh villages observed during this study exemplify the failure to carry through the laws for land redistribution, through the imposition of a ceiling on holdings, that were enacted more than three decades ago. On the basis of a 30-acre ceiling on land holdings, the potential surplus all over India had been estimated at one time at about 21 million acres. At a conference of State Revenue Ministers in New Delhi on 25 November 1986, the then Union Agriculture Minister, G.S. Dhillon, cited some relevant facts. A news release by the Press Information Bureau reported the Minister as saying that the 74.54 lakh acres of land declared surplus was much less than what had been estimated, and of this too, only 57.88 lakh acres or 77% had been taken into possession. The land actually distributed was only 43.36 lakh acres which was only 58.2% of the land declared surplus. The Minister said that the States had not taken effective measures for plugging loopholes in the laws, nor had they geared up the administrative machinery for unearthing concealed surplus land. He suggested that the bureaucracy should seek the help of organisations of rural poor to identify and to confer security of tenure on informal tenants.

(c) Unequal consumption levels : Sharp disparities in levels of income and consumption are reflected in the findings of household consumption conducted periodically by the National Sample Survey Organisation. They show only a marginal improvement in the share of consumption by the bottom 30% of the population, both rural and urban:

Distribution of Household Consumer Expenditure.[16]
(Percentages)

Category	1958-59	1961-62	1965-66	1970-71	1972-73	1977-78
RURAL						
Bottom 30%	13.1	14.7	15.1	15.4	15.4	15.0
Middle 40%	34.3	33.2	34.3	35.1	33.73	33.1
Top 30%	52.6	52.1	50.64	49.5	50.9	51.9
URBAN						
Bottom 30%	13.2	12.9	13.6	13.7	13.8	13.6
Middle 40%	31.7	31.4	31.9	31.8	31.9	32.4
Top 30%	55.1	55.7	54.5	54.5	54.3	54.0

The document on the Sixth Plan had the candour to admit: "The evidence suggests that the most than can be claimed is that there has been no perverse movement, no worsening of inequalities or in the incidence of poverty. In fact, in some respects a degree of progress had been achieved. But, on balance, the pace of movement is much slower than what is acceptable or possible within the framework of the plans, and a great degree of redistributive bias has to be built into our development effort."[17]

(iv) Definition Understates Poverty

Being a relative concept, the meaning of poverty varies from country to country. A household classified as 'poor' in the U.S.A. would be regarded in India as well-to-do. The differences in levels of economic development will justify the definition of poverty at a lower income level in India than in the affluent countries. But it will be futile for the ruling class of any country to bring down poverty statistically, or even define it out of existence, by prescribing an inhumanly low level of household income as the cut-off point. Poverty, like murder, will out.

(a) Quantifying a Concept : An early attempt to compute the household consumption expenditure necessary to provide the minimum necessary level of nutritional diet and to allow for a modest degree of items other than food was made by a Working Group set up by the Planning Commission in 1962. The Group came to the conclusion that the national minimum consumption expenditure per capita could not be less than Rs. 20 per month at 1960-61 prices. A household consisting of five persons would thus meed a minimum of Rs. 100 per month or Rs.1200 per annun.[18]

P.K. Basu[19] refers to a 'Srinivasan-Bardhan paper' on "Perspectives of Development: 1971-76--Implication of planning for a mininium level of living". This paper was prepared under the guidance of Pitambar Pant and issued by the Planning Commission in 1972. The study came to the conclusion that "half of the people live in abject poverty". It proposed a poverty line of Rs. 100 per month per family in terms of 1960-61 prices in the rural areas, and of Rs. 125 per family per month in the urban sector.

Subseqeuntly, in 1977, the Planning Commission appointed a Task Force on Minimum Needs and Effective Consumption Demand. This body defined the poor as those whose per capita consumption expenditure could not provide a per capita daily intake of 2400 calories in rural areas and 2100 in urban areas. The corresponding money value of consumption expenditure per capita per month for that level of calorie intake was computed at Rs. 49.09 in rural areas and Rs. 56.65 in urban areas at 1973-74 prices. Accepted by the Planning Commission and the Central Government, this definition of the poverty line has held the field till now.

(b) Official Map of Rural Penury : Applying the above definition of poverty, and based on data gathered during the National Sample Survey Organisation's quinquennial survey carried out in 1983-84, a State-wise picture of the rural incidence of poverty, in terms of the percentage of the population below the poverty line, was placed before Parliament on 2 March 1988.[20] A table[21] indicating also the urban incidence of poverty was subsequently prepared and is reproduced below. It will be seen that the three Hindi-speaking States of Bihar, Madhya Pradesh and Uttar Pradesh have the unhappy distinction, in that order, of holding the 'leading' positions in the poverty league, taking rural and urban poverty together.

PERCENTAGE OF POPULATION BELOW THE POVERTY LINE BY STATES SEPARATELY FOR RURAL AND URBAN AREAS : 1983-84 (PROVISIONAL)

Sl.No.	State	Rural	Urban	Combined
(1)	(2)	(3)	(4)	(5)
1.	Andhra Pradesh	38.7	29.5	36.4
2.	Assam	23.8	21.6	23.5
3.	Bihar	51.4	37.0	49.5
4.	Gujarat	27.6	17.3	24.3
5.	Haryana	15.2	16.9	15.6
6.	Himachal Pradesh	14.0	8.0	13.5
7.	Jammu & Kashmir	16.4	15.8	16.3
8.	Karnataka	37.5	29.2	35.0
9.	Kerala	26.1	30.1	26.8
10.	Madhya Pradesh	50.3	31.1	46.2
11.	Maharashtra	41.5	23.3	34.9
12.	Manipur	11.7	13.8	12.3
13.	Meghalaya	33.7	4.0	28.0
14.	Orissa	44.8	29.3	42.8
15.	Punjab	10.9	21.0	13.8
16.	Rajasthan	36.6	26.1	34.3
17.	Tamil Nadu	44.1	30.9	39.6
18.	Tripura	23.5	19.6	23.0
19.	Uttar Pradesh	46.5	40.3	45.3
20.	West Bengal	43.8	26.5	39.2
21.	Nagaland, Sikkim & all Union Territories	47.4	17.7	27.1
	All India	40.4	28.1	37.4

NOTE

(1) The above estimates are derived by using the poverty line of Rs. 49.09 per capita per month in 1973-74 prices corresponding to daily calorie requirement of 2400 per person in rural areas and the poverty line of Rs. 56.64 per capita per month corresponding to calorie requirement of 2100 in urban areas.

(2) For up-dating the poverty line for 1983-84, C.S.O. Private Consumption deflator has been used.

(3) These results are based on the provisional and quick tabulation of the NSS on household consumer expenditure of 38th Round (Jan. 1983 to Dec. 1983).

(4) The difference between the agregate all India private consumption expenditure estimated by Central Statistical Organisation in their National Accounts Statistics and that derived from the NSSO data has been pro rata adjusted among the different States and Union Territories in the absence of any information to allocate this difference among the States and Union Territories.

(5) The number of people below poverty line relates to the population as on 1st March 1984.

(c) No Indexing for Inflation : Depressing as the poverty figures are, they are under-statements. The truth about poverty is worse than the official map indicates. One reason is that the poverty line, urban and rural, is worked out on the basis of prices current in the base year of each Five Year Plan. The monetary definition remains unchanged during a Plan period. It is indexed for inflation only five years later, when the next Plan is drawn up.

Evaluation studies of the Integrated Rural Development Programme and other poverty alleviation measures estimate the income of beneficiary families at current prices. Since the erosion of money value caused by price rise is ignored, statistics of the number of families assisted to cross the poverty line get inflated. Thus, a family that is found, in the course of the Seventh Plan, to have crossed the rural poverty line defined at Rs. 6400 of annual household consumption expenditure, may in fact be as poor in terms of real income, as it was at the start of the Plan--or poorer even.

This point was brought out in the report on a study of the Integrated Rural Development Programme that was undertaken during 1983-84 by the Programme Evaluation Organisation of the Planning Commission. It was found during the study that about 26% of the families that had been assisted were 'ineligible' on a strict application of an annual household income of below Rs. 3500 as the cut-off point. Commenting on this, the Planning Commission's Adviser (Evaluation) said in the course of his Preface to the evaluation report: "Considering that after the adoption of this norm there was considerable price rise, the escalated value of an annual household income level of Rs. 3500 would have been appreciably higher even in 1981-82. Looked at in this light the aberration as to the misclassification of some 26% of the selected sample households, which the report points out were in the income bracket of above Rs. 3500, also assumes a somewhat different complexion than what may appear at first sight. This also suggests that there is a case for a suitable revision and also perhaps a measure of flexibility in the income norm to be adopted in future for the selection of beneficiaries and provision of benefits to them under IRDP."[22]

It was left to a simple newspaper reader to puncture the bubble of the Establishment economists' learned babble about Rs. 6400 as the rural poverty line. D.K. Chauhan of R.K.Puram, New Delhi, says in a Letter to the Editor carried by the *Indian Express,* Delhi, of 8 May 1989: "Anyone with a bit of humanitarian concern and common sense will be appalled at knowing the definition of the poverty line. How on earth do people coining such definition expect a family of five to survive on an income of Rs. 6400 per annum which comes to approximately Rs. 3.50 a person per day? Taking only food into account while defining poverty means that the aim is to just help a person not to die of sheer hunger. In that case, the 'poverty line' should be redefined as 'starvation line'." One is reminded of the words of Jesus in the New Testament (Matthew 11.25), addressing the Father: "Thou hast hid these things from the wise and prudent, and hast revealed them unto babes."

(d) Higher Household Size Ignored : It is understandable that the writer of the Letter to the Editor, quoted above, still carried in his mind the old impression that five is the average size of an Indian household. It is astonishing that the 'wise and prudent' experts inhabiting Yojana Bhavan, interviewed in the course of this study, were mostly unaware of the increase in the size of Indian families, both urban and rural, over the three decades from 1951 to 1981. The Census findings are as below:

Increase in Household Size

Census year	Rural	Urban	Total
1951	4.91	4.71	4.81
1961	5.20	4.96	5.16
1971	5.52	5.23	5.46
1981	5.59	5.45	5.55

It will be evident from the above figures that the rural poverty line of Rs. 6400 worked out for 1984-85, the base year of the Seventh Five Year Plan, needs to be increased by 12% on account of the reason only of increase in the average size of a rural household which now stands at 5.59 instead of the five assumed when the concept of the poverty line was first evolved in the early 1960's.

Allowing also for the erosion in the purchasing power of the rupee as the result of inflation, the rural poverty line of Rs. 6400 as of 1984-85, base year of the Seventh Plan, should now-- in 1989--be much higher at current prices, and not below Rs. 10,000 per year for a rural household.

(v) Alleviation Programmes: Limited Impact

The attention actually paid to the rural poor over the post-independence decades has been in inverse proportion to the intensity of rhetoric about Socialism and 'Garibi Hatao' ('Remove Poverty'). The eradication of poverty has yet to become the central aim of economic planning. There have only been feeble, less than half hearted efforts to alleviate poverty.

(a) Rural Inflation Rate : The movement of the Consumer Price Index for agricultural workers, with 1960-61 as the base at 100, has been as follows over the last 25 years:

CPI for agricultural workers [23]

1963-64	115
1964-65	149
1965-66	158
1966-67	190
1967-68	206
1968-69	185
1969-70	193
1970-71	192
1971-72	200
1972-73	225
1973-74	283
1974-75	368
1975-76	317
1976-77	302
1977-78	323
1978-79	317
1979-80	360
1980-81	409
1981-82	448
1982-83	481
1983-84	523
1984-85	525
1985-86	555
1986-87	578
1987-88	741
Jan.1989	739

The very existence of a Consumer Price Index for agricultural workers is not widely known, in contrast to the Wholesale Price Index and the CPI for industrial workers which are published regularly in newspapers and cited by economic analysts. The handy volume, *Statistical Outline of India,* brought out by the Tata House gives in the 1988 edition the Index Number of Wholesale Prices and the Index Number of Consumer Prices for industrial workers and for urban non-manual employees--but not the CPI for agricultural workers. And what of the annual Economic Survey compiled by the Economic Division of the Union Ministry of Finance and published by the Government of India? Neither the Survey for 1987-88 nor for 1988-89 carries the CPI for agricultural workers.

Another point to be noted is the working of the Matthew principle ('unto everyone that hath shall be given': Matt. 25:29). In the case of industrial labour, the Labour Bureau of the Central Government notes changes in the retail prices of a basket of goods and services which cover six consumption groups: (i) food; (ii) pan, supari, tobacco and intoxicants; (iii) fuel and light; (iv) housing; (v) clothing and bedding; and (vi) miscellaneous. In the case of agricultural labour, on the other hand, only four needs are taken into account, housing and pan-supari, tobacco-intoxicants being left out. Furthermore, the Government undertakes fresh inquiries into working class family income and expenditure patterns from time to time: "This Survey was conducted at 76 industrially important centres during 1981-82 to collect the necessary data for the construction of weighing diagrams required for the compilation of CPI numbers based on latest consumption pattern...The information on house rent collected at six monthly intervals is being used for the purpose of revising the house rent index which forms part of the CPI numbers for industrial workers."[24] There is no similar solicitude shown to agricultural workers, who are apparently expected to remain content with a pattern of consumption undiversified and unenriched over time.

(b) Token Laws on Minimum Wages and Working Conditions: Given this callousness towards the rural poor, it is not surprising that post-independence programmes of poverty alleviation have a long history but have made little difference.

The history of attempts at poverty alleviation begins as early as in 1948, when parliament passed the Minimum Wages Act. This legislation came into force from 15 March 1948. Forty years later it remains, in most parts of the country, more symbolic than operational.

The wages of landless agricultural labour and of workers in unorganised industries were very low when the Act was passed because: (i) the supply of unskilled labour was far in excess of the demand; and (ii) there was lack of awareness and of trade union organisation among rural workers. The legislation could have made a significant dent on rural poverty had there been a high level of commitment and efficiency on the part of the State and Union territory administrations at both the political and bureaucratic levels, backed by unionisation of rural labour by political parties whether in power or outside. Neither of these conditions having been fulfilled, the Minimum Wages Act has remained a token law.

Some State governments have themselves been violating the minimum wages law by paying workers less than the prescribed minimum rates. Newspapers of 31 January 1983 carried reports of a judgment by a division bench of the Supreme Court which directed the State of Rajasthan to pay each workman employed in the construction of the Madanganj-Harmara road in Ajmer district the prescribed minimum wage of Rs. 7 a day. The judgment was delivered on a petition moved by Sanjit Roy, director of a voluntary organisation known as the Social Work and Research Centre which operates in and around the village of Tilonia in Ajmer district.

The Rajasthan Government had argued during the hearing of the petition that the construction of the road in question was a famine relief work, and that those employed on it could be paid reduced wages under the Rajasthan Famine Relief Works (Exemption from Labour Laws) Act, 1964. Both Justice P.N. Bhagwati and Justice R.S. Pathak, who constituted the division bench, ruled that the 1964 Act of Rajasthan was unconstitutional and void since it violated article 14 (equality before the law) of the Constitution. Justice Bhagwati observed: "No work of utility and value can be allowed to be constructed on the blood and sweat of persons who are reduced to a state of helplessness on account of drought and scarcity conditions." Rejecting the State government's argument that the wages given to the workers were drawn from a limited fund, Justice Pathak said: "When the State employs workers for doing work needed on its development projects, it must find funds for such projects and ensure minimum wage to each worker."

Another judgment of the Supreme Court, delivered on 6 February 1984 in writ petition No. 5143 filed by workmen of slate pencil factories in the Mandsour district of Madhya Pradesh, shows up the indifference of the State administration to the enforcement of labour laws. Gone are the days of the 1950's and 1960's when the judiciary used to be blamed by politicians in power as an obstacle in the way of radical reforms, social and economic. The higher judiciary is now playing a dynamic role in the spirit of the Directive Principles of the Constitution, and has become a goad to the executive, pushing it towards action to promote social justice and human rights. In the slate pencil industries case, the division bench of the Supreme Court comprising Chief Justice Y.V. Chandrachud, Justice A.P. Sen and Justice A. Varadarajan said in its order:

"We expect that the State government, true to the affidavit of its Chief Inspector of Factories, will take all such measures as are necessary to protect the health of the workers who run the risk of contracting a disease called silicosis, which is an occupational hazard. We must impress upon the government that it is not enough, though necessary, to prosecute employers for breach of safety regulations which apply to these factories. Such prosecutions often result in the imposition of small fines which hardly constitute any deterrent. In appropriate cases, the government must consider whether the licences of factories which are found guilty of violation of the Factory Regulations, particularly the workers' safety regulations, should be revoked.

"We understand that compensation cases have been filed by the workers for the injuries suffered by them during the course of their employment. We are also informed that the legal representative of workers have filed compensation cases for the death of workers who were injured fatally during the course of employment. These and similar compensation cases shall be disposed of expeditiously."

In the course of a gathering of environment activists convened by the Gandhi Peace Foundation in New Delhi from 29 September to 1 October 1984, one of the participants, S. Chakrapani, said that even after the Supreme Court order of 6 February 1984, there was laxity on the part of the Madhya Pradesh government in the promulgation of rules under the Factories Act.

In the case of minimum wages, as of land redistribution, implementation has fallen far short of populist rhetoric. 'Garibi Hatao' was the principal plank on which, after the Congress split of 1969, the wing led by Indira Gandhi won the elections to the Lok Sabha in 1971 and the subsequent elections to State assemblies in 1972. But the 1948 legislation was remembered only when a Twenty-Point programme was drawn up in an effort to make palatable the internal emergency proclaimed by the Indira Gandhi government in June 1975. Enforcement of minimum wages was one of the 20 Points.[25] Another was the abolition of bonded labour. The Congress (Indira) was defeated in the general elections held early in 1977 but returned to power in 1980. Prime Minister Indira Gandhi announced a New 20-Point Programme on 14 January 1982. The State governments were advised "to draw up a programme of continuing publicity of the minimum rates of wages fixed or revised for agricultural workers, through various media and the field publicity organisation."[26] Following the assassination of Indira Gandhi on 31 October 1984, the new government formed by her son Rajiv Gandhi came out with a Revised

Twenty-Point Programme in 1986. Point No.6 is 'Special Programmes for Rural Labour'. It promised: "We shall:

> Enforce minimum wages for unorganised labour in agriculture and industry;
>
> Fully implement laws abolishing bonded labour;
>
> Involve voluntary agencies in programmes for the rehabilitation of bonded labour."[27]

As the Planning Commission acknowledges, "There is no allocation for the 20-Point Programme as such."[28] The outlay on the programme is derived from relevant Plan outlays. Another in the series of widely advertised schemes for the benefit of the rural poor was the Jawahar Rozgar Yojana, announced in the anticipated Lok Sabha election year 1989. The Jawahar Rozgar Yojana amalgamated, and augmented with an additional financial provision, the Integrated Rural Development Programme (which aims at promoting self-employment by assisting through subsidy and credit the creation of productive assets), the National Rural Employment Programme, and the Rural Landless Employment Guarantee Programme. This was an image-building exercise in renaming and freshly publicising the Government's programmes.

Meanwhile, an official review of the state of enforcement of the Minimum Wages Act, 1948, brings out the grim reality of governmental apathy. Under the 1948 Act, the Central Government was the 'appropriate authority' in respect of certain employments, and the State Governments in respect of others. The review recalls that it was "the statutory responsibility of the appropriate government to review the minimum wages at intervals not exceeding five years and revise them, if necessary."

So the position remained till the National Commission on Labour recommended that the period for review and revision should be reduced to three years. With this recommendation before them, the Labour Ministers of the States, at their 26th conference held in New Delhi on 19 July 1975, were compassionate enough to agree on reducing the period further to two years. Where variable dearness allowance was not a component in the minimum wage, they recommended, the States should revise the minimum wages within a period of two years. This was 27 years after the 1948 enactment, during which period the principle of compensation, at much shorter intervals, for increase in the cost of living had become a settled part of labour policy in respect of employees of the Central and State governments, in the public sector, and in the organised private sector.

The next landmark in the expression of solicitude for the unorganised rural and small-town proletariat was the decision taken at the 31st session of the Labour Ministers' Conference that "the minimum rates of wages may be reviewed and revised, if necessary, within a period not exceeding two years or on a rise of 50 points in the Consumer Price Index number, whichever is earlier." Thus for the first time--in July 1980--the concept of minimum wage revision was linked to a specified increase in the Consumer Price Index, though the deferment of revision till as much as 50 points was cruel and absurd.

Next, on 11 September 1981, a meeting of State Labour Ministers discussed the disparity in the minimum wages fixed for bidi workers in various States. They recommended that, in order to ensure that minimum wages were not such as to keep a worker's family below the poverty line, the minimum rate for employment in the bidi industry should be fixed between Rs.7 and Rs.8 per day. The Labour Ministers also recorded their view that, in view of the continual rise in the cost of living, "all State governments should introduce dearness allowance as a distinct element of minimum wages, linked to the Consumer Price Index, variable periodically or on the rise of every five points at a rate determined on the basis of the ratio between the minimum wages and the CPI number with reference to which it was fixed. Such of those State governments which found it difficult to introduce a dearness allowance formula should revise the minimum wage itself, with reference to the cost of living index, at least once every year."

This recommendation, in September 1981, of an annual review was an advance on the previous position. But it contrasts curiously with the decision taken by the Central Government earlier, in July 1981, that the dearness allowance of journalist and non-journalist employees of newspapers--who by no means constitute sweated labour--should be revised every quarter.

As regards the quantum of the minimum wage, the 36th Labour Ministers' Conference held on 29 May 1987 felt that, in view of the rise in the cost of living and in order to keep a worker's family above the poverty line as officially defined, the minimum rate should not be less than Rs.11 per day.

The slow rate of progress in the minimum wage scenario is in striking contrast to the gains made by the urban middle class occupants of the islands of well-being in the ocean of Indian poverty: Central government employees who have had the benefit of salary upgradation by four Pay Commissions is as many decades of independence, and who want all the perquisites (modelled after the private sector) available to public sector white-collar personnel, and vice versa; State government staff who want the same emoluments and dearness allowance as their Central government counterparts; college teachers who are solicitously looked after by the University Grants Commission; newspaper employees for whom there are periodic wage boards whose recommendations are often improved on by a generously disposed Central Government; and organised blue-collar workers in the large-scale sector of industry, both public and private, who are indistinguishable from the bourgeoisie in their aspiration for the good life perceived as the possession of colour television and access to English-medium education for their children as the key to an even better life.

These high wage earners enjoy perquisites that the minimum wage proletariat cannot dream of, such as medical expense reimbursement, leave with pay, leave travel concession, bonus, as well as pension and/or gratuity.

(c) Self-Employment: IRDP Loopholes: If the Integrated Rural Development Programme achieved nothing much else, it certainly gave a big fillip to the social science research industry. Dozens of research institutions, most of them supported by government funds, undertook painstaking studies to ascertain the nature and extent of the contribution made by the IRDP schemes of subsidy and credit for enabling families below the officially defined poverty line to enhance their income through the acquisition and use of productive assets.

As many as 27 research institutions conducted, in various parts of the country, during the nine-month period January-September 1987, studies to ascertain the results of the IRDP. A publication of the Department of Rural Development, presenting the findings of this concurrent evaluation, carries an 'executive summary' outlining the achievements as well as shortfalls of the programme. The positive features include:

(i) At the national level, 60% of the beneficiaries were selected in meetings of Gram Sabhas, and the rest by officials.

(ii) About 81% beneficiaries had found the assistance (subsidy and credit) sufficient for acquiring the asset.

(iii) In 72% cases, the assets were found in tact.

(iv) At the national level, 56% old beneficiaries had crossed the cut-off line of Rs.3500 and 13% old beneficiaries, the new poverty line of Rs.6400.

Among the areas of concern to which the publication draws attention are:

(i) In 19% cases, there was a difference of more than Rs.500 in the assessed and the recorded value of the asset created. This "indicates malpractices and leakages requiring investigation by the concerned authorities."

(ii) Working capital was required in 59% cases but it could not be provided in 24% cases.

(iii) Training was not imparted to beneficiaries in 30% cases out of the 34% cases requiring training.

(iv) In about 22% cases, no incremental income was generated by the assets.

These findings of studies based on samples of the intended beneficiaries are confirmed and illumined by the assessment of a retired senior official who was consulted in the course of this study. Shanti Pada Ganguly of the Indian Audit and Accounts Service, who was Financial Commissioner of Tripura at retirement, says:

"IRDP is designed in such a manner that its success lies in sincere and effective participation of three agencies, viz., banks, government agencies including panchayats, and the beneficiary. IRDP has failed to a large extend due to failures of all the three participants, as indicated below:

> **1. Banks:** (i) The concept that banking is now an instrument of national developmental efforts has not reached the lower echelon of banks, including rural banks. The result is that the IRDP beneficiaries are treated by them like other borrowers and not as beneficiaries of a development activity of which the banks themselves are participants. Instead of being of assistance to the IRDP beneficiaries, banks become instruments of harassment to the beneficiaries, where they have to make several rounds to get their dues in the shape of subsidy, inputs or loans.
>
> "(ii) Taking advantage of the simplicity and ignorance of rules and procedures of the beneficiaries, a class of touts has grown in the rural sector which acts as the go-between, with encouragement from the unscrupulous among bankers. Beneficiaries are often thus exploited by both the touts and the banks. The beneficiaries do not get the full assistance in the shape of subsidy, inputs or loans.
>
> (iii) The flow of inputs in the shape of loan, subsidy or material is rarely in time. This seriously affects income generation.
>
> (iv) When the assistance is in the form of materials, banks and government agencies connive in such a manner that the beneficiaries more often do not get it of full value. The balance goes to add to the volume of black money.
>
> (v) Banks insist on security before disbursement of loans, although the IRDP provides for security in the shape of assets created out of assistance only.
>
> (vi) Banks often try to recover dues without any reference to income generation.

2. Government agencies: (i) No survey is conducted which should be the basis of identification and selection of beneficiaries; as a result, identification is more on ad hoc rather than any scientific basis.

(ii) Because of (i) above, the selection of schemes for an individual beneficiary is faulty, without any reference to his ability and aptitude.

(iii) There is no monitoring either from the side of government agencies or the banks to find out whether the beneficiaries are able to generate enough income to take them beyond the poverty line.

(iv) There is no ongoing guidance or assistance to the beneficiaries to enable them to execute the schemes in a manner to generate stipulated income. Consequently income generation does not take place and the capital base is steadily eroded, leaving the beneficiary in a debt trap.

(v) Flow of funds to the implementing agencies is not need-based. More often the flow of funds takes place towards the later half of the financial year.

"**3. Beneficiaries:** (i) Because of their ignorance, the beneficiaries have no say in the schemes selected for them. The schemes are often unsuited to their circumstances and ability.

(ii) They fall victims of greed for easy money and become perpetual debtors."

(d) Wage Employment Fares Worse: If the promotion of self-employment under the IRDP has run into the inevitable pitfalls of a centrally planned and bureaucratically implemented scheme, the two programmes for promoting wage employment have fared worse. following are extracts from the Planning Commission's assessment:

"The National Rural Employment Programme was launched in October 1980, replacing the earlier Food for Work Programme... For ensuring the durability of assets created, the ratio of wage and non-wage expenditure is prescribed to be maintained at 50:50... Some studies evaluating the programme highlight some positive points such as prompt payment of wages... However, these studies brought out some areas of concern as well. It is revealed that employment being provided under the programme is for a very short duration, and cannot make an impact on the levels of living of the rural people. The wages paid under NREP are often lower than the market wage rates... Selection of the projects is not always made keeping in view the felt needs of the local people. there is no provision for the maintenance of the assets created. Under the social forestry programme the survival rate of saplings is very low, as the community is not involved...

"The Rural Landless Employment Guarantee Programee was launched during 1983-84 with the objective of improving and expanding employment opportunities for the rural landless labour with a view to providing guarantee of employment to at least one member of every landless household up to 100 days in a year, and creating durable assets for strengthening the rural infrastructure... However, for various administrative and financial reasons it has not been possible to implement the guarantee... A few sample studies have been carried out on the working of the programme. The studies have noted that in addition to stabilising the wage rates, the programme has been able to create durable community assets. However, some negative points too have been observed. The planning and preparation of a shelf of projects on the basis of an area approach was not done. The guarantee of 100 days of employment was not provided. Muster rolls had been manipulated by contractors implementing the scheme, and the wages paid were different form those documented."[29]

(vi) Poverty and Population Growth

Poverty breeds large families, because a pair of hands bring in more than it takes to keep a mouth fed at bare subsistence level. Failure to recognise and act on this truth has led to an enormous waste of public funds on the population control programme--euphemistically called 'family welfare programme' after a bad odour was given to family planning by the strong-arm methods employed by the younger son of the then Prime Minister, Indira Gandhi, during the internal emergency of 1975-76.

Expenditure on family Welfare[30]

Year	Rs. Crores
1974-75	68.6
1775-76	89.4
1976-77	172.8
1977-78	97.0
1978-79	110.4
1979-80	121.8
1980-81	146.4
1981-82	192.2
1982-83	294.6
1983-84	392.1
1984-85	428.9
1985-86	574.5
1986-87	623.2

And the results achieved by these massive outlays? They are negative in terms of population control even if the outlays on related health schemes have contributed to a welcome reduction in pregnancy-related deaths of women and in infant mortality.

The Seventh Plan had assumed that the population growth during 1981-86 would have been 2.1%, and that it would decline to 1.9% in 1986-91. The observed reality has been different.

Vital Rates: 1981-85[31]

(per thousand population)

	Estimated	Observed
Birth Rate	33.2	34.6
Death rate	12.2	12.4
Growth rate	21.0	22.2

The corelation between satisfactory economic status, which elitist planning has failed to achieve for the majority, and lower fertility rate is evident from the following data:

Fertility by Socio-Economic Levels (1978: all-India)[32]

	Rural	Urban
Educational Level		
Illiterate (General Fertility Rate)	140.4	117.2
Literate (General Fertility Rate)	111.1	88.9
Economic level		
Per capita monthly expenditure		
Below Rs.50 (General marital fertility rate)	190.8	183.0
Rs.51-Rs.100	150.6	147.2
Rs.101 and above	106.9	87.9

(General Fertility Rate is the number of live births per 1000 women in the reproductive age-group 15-49 in a given year. General marital fertility rate is the number of live births per 1000 married women in the reproductive age-group 15-49 in a given year.)

There are numerous factors which affect fertility. The Planning Commission points out: "Fertility behaviour dependents on much more than access to family planning services. Nearly half the decline in fertility levels that took place between 1961 and 1981 were due to other factors, most notably a rise in the age at marriage. Fertility rates themselves are influenced by factors like female literacy and female employment."[33] Several of these factors are in turn linked to the economic.

In a study of the *Geography of Hunger*,[34] Josue de Castro offered a physiological and psychological explanation, based on experiments upon animals, for the association of high fertility with malnutrition: "In its sexual effects, chronic hunger operates quite differently from acute starvation. Starvation is known to diminish libido. Groups of people subject to malnutrition, on the other hand, appear to be sexually stimulated. The psychological effect of chronic hunger is to make sex important enough to compensate emotionally for the shrunken physiological appetite." Lord Boyd Orr wrote in his foreword to this book: "Birth rate is high among the ill fed and lowest among the well fed--where indeed it falls to or below the replacement level in spite of an ever-decreasing death rate. A high protein intake leads to a high percentage of cases of sterility. The birth rate falls as the consumption of protein-rich food, e.g. meat, eggs and milk, increases. As these are the expensive foods, consumption is proportionate to wealth. There are, of course, economic and cultural factors apart from diet which affect birth rate. There is, however, little doubt that the only really effective method of birth control is to improve the diet."

An elitist pattern of development has permitted only feeble attempts to alleviate poverty instead of the all-out effort to eradicate poverty and illiteracy which should have been at the core of the Five Year Plans. As a result, the absolute size of population rise is now greater than before the family planning programme was launched. In the 1970's, a talking point supplied to government publicity officials to exhort people to limit family size was that India was every year adding an Australia-- i.e., about 14 million people--to the population. Many years and several thousands of crores of rupees later, the then Planning Minister, Madhavsingh Solanki, told the parliamentary consultative committee attached to his Ministry on 11 May 1989: "We are adding 17 million persons every year to our population."

(vii) Goodbye to Temperance

Weaning the poor from the liquor habit which perpetuated their poverty, and made it more acute, was an important part of the Constructive Programme which Gandhiji drew up in February 1922. This item of the programme read: "To organise the temperance campaign amongst the people addicted to the drink habit by house-to-house visits, and to rely more upon appeal to the drinker in his home than upon picketing."

Foremost among Gandhiji's lieutenants in the cause of Prohibition was C. Rajagopalachari, popularly known as Rajaji. The picketing organised by him 1930 in various district of Madras Presidency was so effective that there was a steep fall in sale of liquor vending licences.

Rajaji would present incessantly in his writings and speeches, vividly and with pathos, the misery caused by the drink habit to the poor man, his wife and children.

The main reason why Gandhiji supported the acceptance of office in the provinces of British India in 1937, following the elections held that year, was that it would enable the implementation of some items of the Constructive Programme such as promotion of Khadi and village industries, and Prohibition. In Madras, Rajaji became Prime Minister (that was the designation in those days of provincial autonomy, when there was no Prime Minister in Delhi). He implemented Prohibition in several districts, starting with his home district of Salem, and introduced a sales tax to offset the loss of excise revenue.

After independence, sales tax has stayed and has become a major source of revenue for the States. But, over the years, Prohibition has been virtually scrapped everywhere except in Gandhiji's home State of Gujarat. The consequences for the poor have been wholly adverse. S. Guhan[35] points out that alcoholism among the poor is an important cause of poverty: "Liquor revenues of the order of Rs. 3000 crores in India (1988-89) suggest that consumption may be of the order of Rs.12,000 to 15,000 crores, assuming a general tax incidence of 20 to 25 per cent. This is as high as five per cent of national income. Some studies indicate that liquor accounts for a particularly high proportion in the consumption of manual labourers and, among them, those belonging to the Scheduled Castes and Tribes. Besides the other deprivations it involves, drink particularly affects the welfare of women and children. Effective total prohibition may not be feasible but several measures are possible for reducing the availability and consumption of liquor... Prohibition also raises the moral-philosophical issue of whether it is legitimate for the State to interfere with 'consumer sovereignty'. It is instructive that the Constitution of India (Article 47) while calling upon the State to bring about prohibition, places this obligation in the context of its duty 'to raise the level of nutrition and the standard of living and to improve public health'. Our founding fathers appear to have recognised in this case that the positive side of the coin of freedom can surface only if its negative side is turned down."

The liquor lobby has emerged as a powerful factor influencing political parties and governments, even as excise revenue has become a major source of revenue. Not the Congress which keeps invoking the name of Gandhiji, but the Christian church in Mizoram took a stand against the growing drink habit in that State when elections were held there in January 1989. "The church, whose support had once ensured that his (Laldenga's) insurgency was kept alive, came out against him. Concerned about the influence of alcohol on the younger generation, it wanted the government to shut down all liquor shops. But Chief Minister Laldenga refused to clamp down on the lucrative Rs. 12-crore-a year liquor trade."[36]

The early Plan documents used to discuss Prohibition as one of the programmes of social welfare. On 31 March 1956 the Lok Sabha passed a non-official resolution, accepted by the government, which said: "This House is of opinion that Prohibition should be regarded as an integral part of the Second Five Year Plan and recommends that the Planning Commission should formulate the necessary programme to bring about nationwide Prohibition speedily and effectively."

Referring to the report of the Prohibition Enquiry Committee which had recommended the setting up of a standing central committee to review the progress in implementation and to make a report once a year to the National Development Council, the Planning Commission said in the Second Plan document: "We are in agreement with these recommendations." The State governments were advised to reduce progressively the number of liquor shops both in rural and urban areas,increase the number of dry days, and gradually reduce the permitted strength of distilled liquor. The only rider was that foreigners resident in or visiting India should not be inconvenienced , and that the ways of life of India's tribal communities (who are accustomed to using homebrewn beverages of low alcoholic content) should not be interfered with.

The addiction of State governments to excise revenue from liquor increased steadily over the years, with a corresponding decrease of interest in Prohibition. The Sixth Plan (1980-85) did have a paragraph (p.434) on Prohibition, but it marked the abnegation of government's responsibility, which mass communication was asked to take over: "Excessive consumption of narcotics, alcoholic drinks and addictive drugs is delecterious to health and causes physical and mental damage besides economic ruin to many poor families. Their use would have to be curbed and discouraged through sustained propaganda and community education. Mass media would have to be fully utilised for propagating knowledge about the ill effects of addiction of various types and promotion of temperance."

The document on the Seventh Plan, which marks the culmination of the western-oriented modernisation and elitisation of the development process, makes no mention at all of temperance. There is a reference only to 'drug addiction' (p. 317 of Vol. II).

(viii) Poverty and the Flesh Trade

The successive Plan documents are as reticent on the subject of prostitution as of prohibition. The Sixth Plan had a paragraph (p.425), in the

Chapter on Women and Development, which said that advisory committees would be set up for monitoring the implementation of "various social legislations such as Anti-Dowry Act, Child Marriage Restraint Act, Indian Succession Act, etc." There was no mention of the Suppression of Immoral Traffic in Women and Girls Act, 1956, which had been amended in 1978. In the Chapter on Social Welfare, there is a mere glancing reference (p. 430) to "immoral traffic in girls and women", as one of the problems of social defence for tackling which the Central government extended financial support to the States.

For the draftsmen of the Seventh Plan, prostitution is (Vol. II: p. 317) one among a miscellany of problems allotted to the voluntary sector: "It has been well established that blindness, leprosy, tuberculosis, polio, accidents, drug addiction and prostitution afflict vast numbers of our population... Voluntary agencies, educational institutions and training centres would be involved and aided to take up various activities for promoting preventive measures in a planned and coordinated manner. Production of films, documentaries, literature and other forms of mass communication and employment of non-formal channels of communication by these agencies and institutions would be fully supported."

It is astonishing that there should be such inanity on the part of the Planning Commission fifteen years after the Committee on the Status of Women in India drew pointed attention, in its report,[37] to the economic roots of prostitution, in most cases, in poverty.

Quoting Gandhiji's remark that "Man is primarily responsible for the existence of these unfortunate members of society", the Committee described prostitution as "the worst form of women's exploitation and inequality". The central recommendation made in the report is: "Women and girls who do not wish to continue in this profession, but are compelled to do so for economic reasons, should be rescued and engaged in remunerative work."

The pitiful inadequacy of efforts by those in authority to rescue the victims of the flesh trade is brought out by the figure of 'protection homes and district shelters'[38] Their number throughout India as on 31 December 1985 was 120. And their capacity was limited to taking care of 6,158 inmates. The number of cases reported from 1976 to 1982, under the Suppression of Immoral Traffic in Women and Girls Act, ranged from 13,924 to 16, 150.[39] But these figures mean little. The collusion of corrupt elements in the police with pimps and brothel keepers, as with bootleggers engaged in illicit distillation of liquor, is well known.

Voluntary prostitution, as by call girls of the middle and upper classes who, as the Committee says, pursue "the cult of consumption", is the business of those who choose to engage in it. Involuntary prostitution, on the other hand, whether resulting from hereditary and pseudo-religious practices indirectly arising from poverty, or due directly to poverty, is a shame on society. That the government and the planners should evade the problem of prostitution is an index of the decline of values in public life.

NOTES

1. *Health Information of India* (p.51), Directorate General of Health Services, New Delhi, 1986, and *Year Book 1986-87* (p. 2), Department of Family welfare, New Delhi.
2. *Annual Report 1988-89* (p.25), *Ministry of Health and Family Welfare*, New Delhi.
3. *Health Information of India* (p. 43)
4. *Nutrition News*, Hyderabad, Vol. 10, No. 1.
5. *Annual Report 1988-89, Department of Rural Development*, New Delhi, Annexure XXXVII.
6. *ibid.*, Annexure XXXII.
7. *Annual Report 1988-89* (p. 70), *Department of Civil Supplies*, New Delhi.
8. *ibid.*
9. *ibid.*
10. *Women in India: A Statistical Profile 1988* (p. 63), Department of Women and Child Development, New Delhi.
11. *ibid.*, p. 65.
12. *Report of the Commissioner of Scheduled Castes & Scheduled Tribes*, 1979-80.
13. *Statistical Outline of India* (p.62), Tata Services Ltd., Bombay, 1988.
14. *Mid-Term Appraisal of Seventh Five Year Plan* (pp. 29-31), Planning Commission, New Delhi.
15. *Poverty: Concept and Measurement* (p. 17), Central Statistical Organisation, New Delhi, January 1981.
16. *Sixth Five Year Plan 1980-85* (p. 16), Planning Commission, New Delhi, 1981.
17. *ibid.*, p. 9.
18. Stated by Ajit Kumar Panja, Union Minister of State for Planning, in written reply to a question in the Lok Sabha on 26 February 1986.

19. Secretary, Ministry of Programme Implementation, in a paper presented in his personal capacity at a National Seminar on Poverty Alleviation held in New Delhi on 20-21 December 1988.
20. By the then Union Minister of State for Planning, B.S. Engti, in a written reply to a question in the Lok Sabha.
21. *Health Information of India 1986* (p. 267).
22. *Evaluation Report on IRDP* (p. iv), Programme Evaluation Organisation, Planning Commission, New Delhi, May 1985.
23. *Indian Labour Gazette*, Union Ministry of Labour, New Delhi.
24. Annual Report 1988-89: Vol. I (p.51), Ministry of Labour, New Delhi.
25. *Minimum Wages for Agricultural Labour*, Directorate of Advertising & Vusual Publicity, Ministry of Information & Broadcasting, July 1982. (55,000 copies of the pamphlet were printed in English for free distribution.)
26. *ibid.*
27. *The Twenty-Point Programme: 1986*. Directorate of Advertising & Visual Publicity, August 1986. (3,00,000 copies of the pamphlet were printed in English for free distribution.)
28. *Annual Plan 1988-89* (p. 369), Planning Commission, New Delhi, 1988.
29. *Mid-Term Appraisal of the Seventh Plan* (pp.38-43).
30. *Family Welfare Year Book 1986-87* (p.306)
31. Mid-Term Appraisal of the Seventh Plan (p.195)
32. *Family Welfare Year Book 1986-87* (pp.101-101)
33. *Mid-Term Appraisal of the Seventh Plan* (p. 196)
34. Victor Gollancz, 1955.
35. Senior Fellow, Madras Institute of Development studies, in a paper presented at the National Seminar on Poverty Alleviation, New Delhi, December 1988.
36. *India Today* (p. 44), 15 February 1989.
37. *Towards Equality*, Department of Social Welfare, New Delhi, December 1974.
38. Table 6.16 on p.162 of *Women in India: a Statistical Profile*, Department of Women and Child Development, Ministry of Human Resource Development, New Delhi.
39. *ibid.* (p.142)

PART 2

As Development, So Communication

As elitist pattern of development has been accompanied by a lopsided growth of education, with widespread illiteracy continuing alongside a vast expansion of institutions of higher learning for the children of the privileged. The mass media of communication cater for the needs of information and entertainment of the urban middle and upper classes and the land-owning and other well-to-do in rural areas. Advertising of luxury goods and services is a prominent feature of elitist communication, promoting a self-regarding consumerist culture unsuited to a country where poverty is widespread. There has been steady growth of an information bureaucracy that publicises the achievements and intentions of the government at the Centre and in the States, but contributes little to enabling the under-privileged to secure a better share of the gains of development.

Chapter IV

EDUCATION: BETRAYAL OF ARTICLE 45

Education is the most organised, direct and potent form of consciousness-raising. Its role in development is crucial. It was for this reason that the founding fathers wrote into the Constitution: "The State shall endeavour to provide, within a period of ten years from the commencement of this Constitution, for free and compulsory education for all children until they complete the age of fourteen years." But this Article (No.45) forms part of the Directive Principles of State Policy, which are only morally binding on the State and are not legally enforceable like the Fundamental Rights.

For breaking the vicious circle of poverty and illiteracy the attack has primarily to be on poverty. This is because the poor need to put to work every available pair of hands, even of children, whether to attend to family chores, domestic or economic, or to earn a wage by employment outside the home. In the meanwhile, if the ten-year target set by the Consitution was to be realised, millions of boys and girls from poor homes would have had to be physically removed from the natal environment of poverty and squalor and put into free residential shcools. Additionally, compensation would be payable to the parents, in fairness, for the loss of income from family labour thus caused by the State. This was not obviously feasible, nor is it today. The alternative was to make a determined effort to eradicate poverty at the earliest while taking steps to make schooling relevant to the rural environment and offering incentives to the poor for sending their children to school. This was entirely feasible but, as seen in the preceding Chapter, the pattern of development became elitist and urban-oriented. While it is not surprising that universal elementary education was not achieved by 1960, it speaks for the callousness of the ruling classes that parliament has not even bothered to amend Article 45 to set a new target date.

According to a projection made in the Office of the Census Commissioner, at the pace of progress between 1971 and 1981 and allowing for the likley increase in population, the period required for achieving a literacy rate of 85% will be:

100 to 115 years	In five States (Andhra Pradesh, Madhya Pradesh, Meghalaya, Rajasthan and Uttar Pradesh);
50 to 99 years	In 13 States and Union Territories (Bihar, Gujarat, Haryana, Jammu & Kashmir, Karnataka, Manipur, Orissa, Punjab, Tamil Nadu, West Bengal, Arunachal Pradesh, Chandigarh, and Dadra & Nagar Haveli); and
15 to 49 years	In 12 States and Union Territories (Himachal Pradesh, Kerala, Maharashtra,Nagaland,Sikkim, Tripura, Andaman & Nicobar Islands, Delhi, Goa Daman & Diu, Lakshadweep, Mizoram and Pondicherry).

Statistics of the increased number of schools and their proximity to rural habitations are impressive enough. According to Dr. P.L. Malhotra of the National Council of Educational Research and Training, of the 9,79,065 rural habitations, 5,02,806 (51.36%) habitations covering 80.34% of the rural population had primary schools/sections in 1986. And 94.60% of the rural population were served by primary school/section located within the habitation or up to a walking distance of one km. What were the factors which militated against utilisation of this available facility? To quote Dr. Malhotra himself (from a paper presented at the National Seminar on Poverty Alleviation in New Delhi, December 1988): "Some of the steps to be taken are: providing education with the content directly relevant to the material welfare and increased productivity of the poor which could, in part, offset the opportunity cost to the family adopting flexible school calender synchronised with agricultural and other occupational activities of the target groups; subsidising instructional materials and distributing them free to the needy to lessen the direct cost of education to the target groups; and providing other incentives like mid-day meals, free uniforms and scholarships to the poor while they are being educated."

Even if the curriculum is made relevant to the rural environment, how can a single teacher attract and hold the attention of chidlren in four or five classes? In 1986, as many as 1,48,033 (27.97%) primary schools were single-teacher schools. In the same year, 1,71,389 (32.38%) primary schools had only two teachers. Such has been the priority accorded to elementary education over three and a half decades of planned development. On the other hand, there has been no lack of funds for the highly subsidised advanced education of children of the ruling classes, large numbers of whom end up by migrating to more lucrative pastures outside India. A Press Information Bureau release of 1 April 1988 gave the findings of a study regarding brain drain of B.Tech. graduates of the Indian Institute of Technology, Bombay, who passed out from 1973 to 1977. It was found that out of 1,262 graduates, 39.4% went abroad. Of these, only 8.6% had returned. Of the 38.8% who stayed back abroad, 82.6% were in the U.S.A./Canada, 7.8% in West Asia and 9.5% in other countries.

(i) Rural Girl Drop-outs : Among the depressing findings during the survey of some Madhya Pradesh villages that was conducted as part of this study was the high rate of rural girl drop-outs even at the primary stage of education.

A statement furnished by the single teacher in charge of the primary school at Suakheri (in Vidisha district) revealed the following picture of attendance by boys and girls in classes I to V from 1983-84 to 1987-88:

		I	II	III	IV	V
1983-84	B	10	20	13	12	5
	G	5	5	2	3	2
1984-85	B	14	20	12	11	11
	G	7	4	3	2	2
1985-86	B	22	18	18	12	9
	G	14	8	1	3	2
1986-87	B	20	22	22	13	11
	G	8	15	10	–	3
1987-88	B	10	22	18	21	10
	G	13	9	13	8	–

Much the same pattern emerged form the figures furnished by the teacher in charge of the primary school at village Kotra in the same district. The situation at the high school stage is infinitely worse. The following figures were given by the principal of the Government High School at Pipalkhedi:

	Class IX		Class X	
	Boys	Girls	Boys	Girls
1985-86	8		-	-
1986-87	59	1	22	-
1987-88	35	1	36	2

The situation on the ground observed in the Madhya Pradesh villages confirmed and vividly illustrated such macro statistical data as that the majority of non-enrolled children of the elementary school going age in the country as a whole are either girls or belong to the most disadvantaged social groups; that at the 1981 Census Madhya Pradesh had a rural female literacy rate (all ages) of less than 10%; and that 70% of the illiterate adults in the country are women.

(ii) Abandonment of UEE as Goal : It is sad to find, in this context, that the 'National Perspective Plan for Women: 1988-2000 A.D.' implicitly gives up the objective of universal elementary education for women. This report (1988) of a core group set up by the Department of Women and Child Development says (p. 173): "The success of all development plans and programmes including those relating to education, small family norm, health and nutrition etc. depends upon the active involvement and participation of women. Human resource development necessitates equipping women and girls with information, knowledge and skills to facilitate their active and equal involvement and participation in the nation's development programme and activities. *Formal education as the path to human development is both costly and a long term process*. Thus, in a developing country like India it is critical to harness mass media and other forms of communication, including traditional folk forms of entertainment." (Emphasis added.)

The mass media in a country like the U.S.A., where illiteracy is marginal, do run some programmes (*Sesame Street* is an often cited example among TV serials) of adult literacy and social education. These are for the benefit of immigrant labour and of the poor among blacks. Here in India illiteracy is not marginal but is, along with poverty, the central problem. To suggest that mass communication can be a substitute for formal education is astonishingly naive. It is on a par with the government disowning its responsibility for enforcing Prohibition or for ending involuntary prostitution and, as in the Seventh Plan document, calling upon communicators and voluntary workers to take up these causes.

The defeatism of the National Perspective Plan for Women is of a piece with the earlier abandonment, carefully disguised by verbal jugglery, of the goal of universal and compulsory education in the much trumpeted National Policy on Education. The text of this document was got printed by the Department of Education, Ministry of Human Resource Development, in 1986. But it is unpriced, and therefore not easily accessible. It says (p.12), under the heading 'A Resolve': "The New Education Policy will give the highest priority to solving the problem of children dropping out of school and will adopt an array of meticulously formulated strategies based on micro planning and applied at the grass-roots level all over the country, to ensure children's retention at school. This wll be fully coordinated with the network of non-formal education. It shall be ensured that all children who attain the age of about 11 years by 1990 will have had five years of schooling, *or its equivalent through the non-formal stream*. Likewise, by 1995 all children will be provided free and compulsory education up to 14 years of age." (Emphasis added.) To see through the hypocrisy of this policy, it is only necessary to raise the question whether the members of the Council of Ministers at the Centre and the members of parliament, who endorsed the policy, will be content to let their children receive the non-formal equivalent of formal schooling.

(iii) The Navodaya Extravaganza: While failing to secure the universalisation of elementary education and even abandoning it as a goal, the government has been implementing an expensive scheme for opening a model 'Navodaya Vidyalaya' in every district of the country, residential and run on the pattern of the highly exclusive 'public schools' of which the Doon School is the best known. Everything from board and lodging to tuition, uniform, books and stationery, is free for every student irrespective of the level of parental income. The direct expenditure on students per head was estimated in mid-1988 at about Rs. 350 per month.

The Navodaya schools start from Class VI. Admission is on the basis of a talent test. But there is reservation of seats for the Scheduled Castes and Scheduled Tribes. This is supposed to reconcile the claims of equity with the claims of excellence. Considering that non-enrolment and drop-out is highest among the S.C. and S.T. (exceptions like the S.T. of Mizoram excepted), it is clear that only the children of those Harijan and tribal families who can afford to send their sons and daughters to school and keep them there till Class V can benefit from the reservation policy.

It is claimed that applications for taking the admission examination are entertained only if the student is from a rural area. It has been further claimed by the Director of the Navodaya Vidalaya Sanghatan, K.S.

Sarma, that a large proportion of Navodaya students are from poor homes. He said in the course of an interview with a correspondent of *Patriot* (24 January 1989): "When the scheme was announced there was a lot of criticism that, willy nilly, the rural rich will corner the seats. I can emphatically tell you this is not so. Out of the 209 schools, it has been found that more than 40% of the children's parents have an annual income of less than Rs. 6,000."

This figure of annual income is below the rural poverty line of Rs. 6,400 at the price level of 1984-85, the base year of the Seventh Plan, and far below the poverty line if it is indexed for inflation. Is it believable that children from rural families living below the poverty line go to school for full five years, and are moreover able to secure admission through a competitive test on the basis of merit? (The figure of 40% is higher than the combined reservation for S.C. and S.T. students.)

The socio-economic profile of a cross-section of students of a Navodaya school was sought to be ascertained in the course of the present study. Sixteen children--ten boys and six girls-- studying in the Navodaya school at Cancon in Goa were interviewed informally. It transpired that 11 out of the 16 had a television set at home; 14 homes had radio; two had cars; five had a cycle or scooter; and 15 homes took a daily newspaper. Three said that they lived in towns, and seven near towns.

According to the school records, the occupation and annual income level of the head of the family (the father in all cases except one--a woman labourer) of the 16 children were as follows:

Teacher	5	Rs. 12,000 to Rs. 24,000
Shopkeeper*	4	8,000 to 24,000
Engineer	2	36,000
Bank manager	1	40,000
Coolie	1	2,000
Fisherman	1	6,000
Labourer (woman)	1**	1,200
Taxi driver	1	12,000

*One of the girls, daughter of a shopkeeper with a reported income of Rs. 8000, said that they had a VCR at home.

**Only the women labourer's daughter said that they did not get a newspaper at h. ne.

The socio-economic profile of a cross-section of students of a nearby non-Navodya school was also studied. This was the Popular High School run by a Christian organisation at Margao, an urban centre. Nine out of the ten students interviewed had TV at home; all ten had radio; and one a car. The father's occupation in four cases was shopkeeping; teaching, in the case of three; and the father of one student was a doctor. The profile was thus of a somewhat higher but not markedly different socio-economic class.

Conversation with some of the teachers at the Navodaya school revealed that, according to their information, 25% of the students were urban. About 40% were stated to be girls--much higher than the national average of 16% among the 5,800 students admitted to Navodaya schools in 1986-87. (According to an official of the Navodaya Vidyalaya Samiti, not many rural girls studied up to the fifth standard, and parents--specially in the Hindi belt--were reluctant to send their daughters to a residential school.)

The teachers of the Navodaya school at Cancon also said that most of the children were from middle class homes, only seven or eight out of the total of up to 80 per class being from poor families, and a similar number affluent. It was found that the children from an urban backgroud did better, though rural children whose parents were teachers did well too. As for the quota reserved for the Scheduled Castes, one or two did well in their studies (like the coolie's son) but many might have to be relegated after the eighth standard despite special attention being paid to them.

It was learnt that many schools conduct special coaching for their students for the Navodaya entrance examinations. Some other schools, on the other hand, do not wish to lose their bright students for fear of a fall in the school results. The overall impression was of the Navodaya scheme being a boon for the small-town and rural middle class who would like their children to become upwardly mobile.

As part of the Navodaya scheme there is an inter-regional migration of a section of its students, from and to the Hindi belt. Twenty per cent of students from each school are to go to another language region after class VII. The children in the 'host' school are prepared for this by being taught the language of the guests. The Navodaya scheme is claimed, for this reason, to be conducive to national integration. At what cost is the question. The Lok Sabha was informed in reply to a question on 26 November 1987 that a provision of Rs. 59 crores had been made for setting up Navodaya Vidalayas in the revised estimates of the budget for 1987-88. It was also stated that the governments of Tamil Nadu, Assam and West Bengal had reservations about the medium of instruction under the Navodaya scheme (which is Hindi along with English). Other States and

Union Territories were, however, offering land and buildings for the establishment of Navodaya Vidyalayas in their districts.

The money lavished on the Navodaya scheme has drawn criticism on the ground that it increases the disparity between a few good, well-endowed schools and the many which lack a blackboard, decent accommodation and the necessary teacher strength. Coaching intitutions for the Navodaya entrance examination have come up in Madhya Pradesh on the model of coaching classes for the IAS and allied services competitive examination. A teacher working with the voluntary educational group known as Eklavya, in Madhya Pradesh, said: "You take the child from the reality of the village life and put him in a special school where he is cut off from his social ethos--with television and other amenities. Will this child want to return to the village? Obviously only the village elite can afford to pay the fees for the Navodaya coaching classes that have been opened. We talk of equal opportunity. On the other hand we equip one school so well while the others lack the minimum facilities. Is this fair?"

Navodaya is likely to acclerate the brain drain already in process from the villages to urban centres, and eventually add to the brain drain from urban India to the West.

Chapter V
MISUSE OF ELECTRONIC MEDIA

With less than a fifth of the population literate at the beginning of the First Plan, and considering that attainment of universal literacy was bound to be a long haul, immediate intervention through non-formal education was necessary in order to inform and mobilise the people for broad-based national development.

(i) Radio: Lost Opportunity

Non-formal education could have been undertaken through inter-personal communication as well as through the literacy-free among the mass media. The scope for promoting social consciousness through inter-personal communication was severely limited by the lack of committed cadres (discussed in Chapter II: i). Among the carriers of impersonal or mediated communication, film was a costly and cumbrous medium, while television and video cassettes were yet to arrive. Radio was at that time the most potent of the instruments available for social education on a mass scale.

(a) Lenin on Role of Radio : Born within a year of each other, Gandhi and Lenin, who led two very different kinds of revolution in the twentieth century, both recognised the potency of radio as a means of mass communication.

Gandhi attached importance to the cultivation of moral strength by the individual rather than the indoctrination of men in the mass. He made a statement, brief but significant, about radio: "This is a miraculous power. I see Shakti, the miraculous power of God."[1]

Lenin who believed in central planning by the State, envisaged the possibilities of radio communication more systematically. In a letter to Joseph Stalin, he wrote in 1922: "Appended are two reports, the first from an expert in electricity about radio telegraph and telephone communication; and the second from a prominent specialist and inventor in radio engineering. These reports show that it is technically quite feasible to broadcast human speech over any distance by wireless. Furthermore, it is also possible to use many hundreds of stations that could broadcast speeches, reports and lectures delivered in Moscow to many hundreds of places throughout the Republic, situated hundreds and, under certain conditions, thousands of versts (a 'verst' is a Russian measure of distance equivalent to 1.067 kilometers) away from Moscow. I think from the standpoint of propaganda and agitation, specially for those masses of the population who are illiterate, and also for broadcasting lectures, it is absolutely necessary for us to carry out this plan." Lenin hailed radio as a "newspaper without paper" and "without distances". He offered talented inventors and engineers all-out assistance and encouragement for further innovations in radio technology. He regarded the matter as of "immense importance, for with a loudspeaker with the receiver which has been developed in such a way that it will be easy for us to produce hundreds of receivers, all Russia will be able to hear a newspaper read in Moscow."[2] Within the democratic structure of free India radio could have been developed as a truly mass medium. But it was not assigned a role comparable in importance to what Lenin envisaged for it in a centralised, single-party system.

(b) No Reorientation after Freedom : Unlike those who were to step into his shoes in the office of Prime Minister, Nehru was too big to need or want to use the medium of broadcasting for building up his own image. Replying to a debate on External Publicity in the Constituent Assembly which functioned as the provisional parliament of India, he said on 15 March 1948: "My own view of the set-up for broadcasting is that we should approximate, as far as possible, to the British model, the British Broadcasting Corporation; that is to say, it would be better if we had a semi-autonomous corporation under the government, of course with the policy controlled by the government, otherwise being not conducted as a government department but as a semi-autonomous corporation. Now, I do not think that is immediately feasible. I have merely mentioned this to the House. I think we should aim at that, even though we may have many difficulties. In fact in most matters we should aim at the same semi-autonomous corporation, the policy and other things being distantly controlled by the government but the Government or government departments not interfering in their day-to-day activities." Jawaharlal Nehru's impulses were liberal but he did not always act on them. Until Nehru's death in 1964, nothing was done to make All India Radio autonomous. Thereafter, AIR was reduced, in its programmes of news and current affairs, to a mouthpiece and propaganda organ of the Prime Minister and the political party for the time being in power at the Centre.

If in Jawaharlal Nehru's time there was no political misuse of the medium, there was no commercialisation of it either. This was a significant contribution, though of a negative rather than positive character.

Nehru's attitude to commercial advertising was in the tradition of the great practitioners of educative journalism--or development communication as we would call it today. Annie Besant, after she acquired the *Madras Standard* and ran it as the daily *New India* from 1914, wrote to a friend that the first thing she did was to "clear off all the coarse advertisements".

Gandhiji excluded advertisements altogether from his journals. He was against the multiplication of wants (as distinct from needs), and expressed the wish in the course of an article in *Young India* in October 1919 that "there were, for each province, only one advertising medium--not a newspaper--containing innocent, unvarnished notices of things useful for the public."

In *The Discovery of India,* written in 1944 during his last spell of detention, Nehru said: "The advertiser is one of the symbols of our age with his continuous and raucous attempts to delude us and dull our powers of perception and induce us to buy unnecessary and even harmful products." In an address to the All India Newspaper Editors' Conference at Allahabad on 16 February 1946 he said: "The quality of advertisements apprearing in some newspapers sometimes pains me. I appeal to the editors that they should exercise a strict censorship over advertisements so that undesirable advertisements are not accepted."

Referring to commercial advertisements carried by Radio Ceylon and other foreign broadcasting systems, Nehru said in 1963: "Personally I react strongly if an advertisement comes through radio. My reaction is never to encourage that advertiser. What does he mean by interfering with my peace of mind? It angers me when it suddenly comes in; it upsets me. But that is not the reaction of most others, I suppose. Otherwise why should advertisers advertise?"[3]

Although Nehru preserved All India Radio from misuse for political and commercial advertising, there was no radical reorientation of the medium. During the nearly 17 years of his prime ministership, radio continued to play its old role of providing entertainment and information of interest to the urban middle and affluent classes who alone could afford the luxury, in the pre-transistor age, of owning a radio set. Radio was not turned into an instrument for promoting broad-based development. District level stations could have been established, in order to provide folk entertainment and to disseminate among the rural poor, through free access to radio sets at public places, information relevant to the improvement of their condition such as laws on land redistribution, tenancy reform or minimum wages, and programmes like those for adult education, community development and the empowerment of panchayats to draw up and implement development programmes to meet local needs.

(c) Top-Level Expansion, Urban Bias : The pattern of expansion of All India Radio continued to be what it had been prior to independence.

It was in Bombay that the first radio station was established, in the private sector, by the Indian Broadcasting Company in 1927. Inaugurating it, the British Viceroy, Lord Irwin, said: "India offers special opportunities for the development of broadcasting. Its distances and wide spaces alone make it a promising field. In India's remote villages there are many who, after the day's work is done, find time hang heavily enough on their hands, and there must be *many officials and others whose duties carry them into out-of-the-way places where they crave for the company of their friends* and the solace of human companionship. There are of course, in many households, those whom social custom debars from taking part in recreation outside their own homes. To all those and many more, broadcasting will be a blessing and a boon of real value." The words emphasised in this passage and spoken more than six decades ago apply with even greater force today to the role of Doordarshan as a forger of solidarity among the middle and upper classes that rule the country, bringing accustomed entertainment and familiar faces and voices to members of the civil, police, para-military and Defence services posted in various parts of the country, not to speak of the geographically mobile middle and upper echelons of private and public sector enterprises.

The second radio station was opened by the Indian Broadcasting Company in Calcutta on 26 August 1927, and the third by the Madras Corporation in 1930. Brought under the control of the Government of India as the Indian Broadcasting Service from 1 April 1930, the broadcasting system grew over the years with the opening of new stations as follows.[4]

10 Septemeber 1935: 'Akashvani' station at Mysore, capital of the princely State of that name.

1 January 1936: Delhi station of the Indian State Broadcasting Service, redesignated from 8 June 1936 as All India Radio.

2 April 1937: Lucknow station.

1 May 1939: Baroda station: foundation stone laid.

16 May 1939: Trichinopoly station.

1 December 1947: Jammu station.

26 January 1948: Patna station.

28 January 1948: Cuttack station.

1 July 1948: Gauhati station.

16 July 1948: Nagpur station.

12 October 1948: Vijayawada station.

21 October 1948: Srinagar station.

1 February 1949: Allahabad station.

4 March 1949: Ahmedabad station.

16 May 1949: Jullundur station..

8 January 1950: Dharwar station.

1 April 1950 : All India Radio takes over the broadcasting stations of the former princely States at Trivandrum, Mysore, Hyderabad and Aurangabad.
14 May 1950: Kozhikode station.
2 October 1953: Poona station.
13 April 1954: AIR takes over the station at Srinagar.
16 December 1954: Jammu station is taken over by AIR.
4 January 1955: Rajkot station.
9 April 1955: Jaipur station.
22 May 1955: Indore station.
16 June 1955: Simla station.
2 November 1955: Bangalore station.
31 October 1956 : Bhopal station.
27 July 1957: Ranchi station.
January 1963: Kohima station.
June 1963: Port Blair station.
August 1963 : Imphal station.
6 March 1966 : Pasighat station.
November 1966: Mathura station.
November 1966: Aizawl station in Mizoram.
November 1967: Pondicherry station.
25 June 1971 : Station at Leh, in Ladakh.
11 August 1972: Silchar station.
September 1974: Station at Tawang, in Arunachal Pradesh.
2 February 1976: Darbhanga station.
8 May 1976 : Rohtak station.
1 August 1976 : Chattarpur station in Madhya Pradesh.
11 December 1976 : Mangalore station.
26 December 1976 : Ambikapur station.
22 January 1977 : Jagdalpur station.

This chronology of the first fifty years of broadcasting in India shows that when the expansion of stations was resumed after the interruption caused by World War II, the pattern was the establishment of stations at each State capital, followed by stations at other big urban centres within a State. Everywhere, the nature of the programmes--both music and spoken-word--have been predominantly such as to appeal, and be intelligible, to the middle and upper classes living in urban centres, and not to the rural masses whether tribal or non-tribal. An exception is the time applied, particularly by stations in the north-eastern region that were established after the hostilities of 1962, to news bulletins and talks in tribal dialects.

According to a fact sheet prepared by the Audience Research Unit giving the position as of 31 December 1987, the Home Service--excluding Vividh Bharati--consists of music to the extent of 38.43%, news 22.38% and spoken word 39.19%. The music programmes comprise, to the extent of 64.01%, three categories which are of interest almost exclusively to the middle and upper classes: classical music (28.41%); light music (21.41%) and devotional music (14.19%). Film music, which is of very wide appeal, accounts for 19.37%. Western music occupies 4.81% of total music time, and folk music 11.81%.

Out of the total time of spoken word programmes, those categorised as 'educational' occupied 29.69%. The distribution as between target audiences was: rural 12.68%; school/university 7.86%; women 3.84%; industrial workers 3.25%; and children 2.06%. As against the rural-interest spoken word programmes accounting for 12.68%, talks and discussions on current affiars, in language that only the educated can follow, claimed as much as 26.87% of total spoken word time.

A medium of communication can, after all, address itself only to the audience actually available to it. AIR's ability to contribute to rural development in general and in particular to promote awareness of anti-poverty programmes, adult education and health is strictly limited by the fact that only a fifth of the total number of radio receiving sets in the country, estimated at 80 million in 1987, are in the rural areas.[5]

(d) Tokenism: School Broadcasts.--A token contribution to development used to be made by some AIR stations even in the pre-independence period. Rural programmes began to be broadcast from Delhi in June 1936. School broadcasts were inaugurated in October 1938, and broadcasts for colleges from Madras station in November 1939.

Programmes for schools are now produced and broadcast by 44 stations, and relayed by thirty other stations. Fifty per cent of the programmes are meant for primary schools. It is instructive to compare the number of schools in the country with the number and distribution of school radio sets State-wise.

Number of schools in the country[6]

	1950-51	1980-81	1984-85 (Estimates)
Primary	2,09,671	4,85,538	5,50,000
Middle	13,596	1,167,447	1,40,000
High/Higher Secondary	7,288	51,549	60,000
TOTAL	2,30,555	6,53,579	7,50,000

The total number of schools with radio sets was 1,16,975 as on 1 January 1983, as against the likley total of about 7,00,000 schools of different categories. No figures were available in the Directorate-General of AIR of the the distribution of the schools with radio sets as between urban and rural areas. As will be seen from the following figures of State-wise distribution of the school radio sets, there is considerable disparity between need on the basis of a State's population and the availability of radio sets in schools.

State-wise distribution of school radio sets

Andhra Pradesh	10,500
Assam	5,400
Bihar	4,000
Gujarat	20,230
Haryana	2,190
Himachal Pradesh	456
Jammu & Kashmir	1,381
Karnataka	1,817
Kerala	6,200
Maharashtra	10,143
Madhya Pradesh	1,500
Meghalaya	132
Orissa	900
Punjab	2,100
Rajasthan	2,102
Tamil Nadu	36,111
Uttar Pradesh	3,775
West Bengal	5,022
Other States & Union Territories which furnished data	2,616

Uttar Pradesh, the most populous of the States, had only 3,775 school radio sets, and Bihar, the second most populous, only 4,000. In contrast, Gujarat ranking tenth in population strength had 20,230. The reasons are worth investigating. Is insufficiency of reach of radio stations originating or relaying programmes in the local language among the reasons? Or that the programmes are not interesting and/or in language difficult for school children to follow? In addition to the urban-rural distribution of schools having radio sets, the break-up of such schools as between primary, middle and secondary needs to be ascertained. It has been the experience of those involved in school broadcasting that secondary schools have little use for broadcasts, though broadcasts for primary schools are generally well received, specially in single-teacher schools where they at least give the teacher some relief. On the other hand, secondary schools have little use for broadcasts, though they are now syllabus-related, since it is all that the teachers can do to take the students through the prescribed text-books. Moreover, coordination of the school time-table--specially when the same class is divided into different sections--and that of the AIR station is next to impossible. Broadcasts can be recorded and played at the right time, but this will entail cost which only the better-endowed schools can afford, and effort which only highly motivated teachers will undertake. Even the maintenance of a transistor radio receiver is a problem since each replacement of two to three batteries will cost about Rs. 20. This raises the crucial question: how many of the one lakh odd school radio sets are in working order, and actually being utilised?

As regards intelligibility and interest, perusal of a programme guide on radio broadcasts during 1988-89 for classes VIII, IX and X, brought out in Telugu for radio-equipped schools served by the Vijayawada, Hyderabad, Cuddapah and Visakhapatnam stations, suggests that the programmes can be followed by school teachers, not students.

(e) Tips for Farmers, Not Farm-hands : The first major experiment, after independence, in the use of radio for rural development was the Farm Forum project launched by the Pune station on 19 February 1956 in implementation of a programme drawn up by All India Radio with the assistance of UNESCO. Subsequently similar broadcasts were undertaken by other stations.

As pointed out by Mehra Masani, who retired as Deputy Director General of AIR after a long and distinguished career in broadcasting, the project was modelled on the Farm Radio Forums of Canada.[7] Members of listening groups of 15 to 20 persons were expected to discuss the information and suggestions contained in the programme and to decide on a plan of action. Mehra Masani says: "After the first flush of enthusiasm the collective listening has dwindled...No one knows how many forums are active. The reasons for the failure are not far to seek. AIR lacked the resources...The machinery for carrying the reactions of the forums to the programme planners was weak. In Canada the forums were the joint responsibility of the Canadian Broadcasting Corporation, the Canadian Broadcasting Federation of Agriculture and the Canadian Association for Adult Education. While the broadcasts were the responsibility of the broadcasting organisation, the other two provided the money for running offices to look after the forums. Unfortunately AIR could not afford anything like this organisation. Without a close contact between the radio stations and the forums, their success was only partial at best...It is the farmers in the age group 30-50 with a middle-school level of education who are most keen on listening to radio programmes which would help them to improve their productivity and thus their standard of living. The poor and illiterate farmer fails to derive any benefit from the broadcasts."

Apart from the forums, AIR stations broadcast tips for farmers every day on agricultural operations relevant to the season, and on weather conditions. The rural programmes also convey information on new and high-yielding varieties of seeds and how to utilise them to best advantage. There is no doubt that such information has benefited many farmers. A widely quoted instance is of a new variety of rice which was popularised by radio stations in Tamil Nadu and therefore came to be known as 'radio rice'. But there is little in these programmes for the landless agricultural labourer or the village artisan. To quote Mehra Masani's summing up: "As the greater part of AIR's audience today belongs to the same classes and sections of society from which it was drawn twenty-five years ago, the programme pattern has also remained the same...This confirms that at no time after India became independent has an attempt been made to recast the broadcasting service to cater for the under-privileged listener. The majority of programmes continue to be directed to the educated and semi-educated in cities."[8]

(f) Abandonment of Community Listening : Had community listening not been given up as a Centrally assisted scheme in 1969, it might have retained its under-privileged rural listeners while those who could afford their own receiving sets began to listen indoors. The composition and size of the audience for community listening might have led to the broadcast of more information of relevance and interest to the rural poor. Unfortunately, a number of factors led to the decline of community listening.

Started in 1954-55 as a Centrally sponsored scheme entailing 50% subsidy to the States on the initial cost of the receiving set and ancillaries, it ran into the organisational problem of replacing wet batteries. Substitution by transistorised sets was not practicable either, because of the shortage of battery cells at that time. Secondly, a Committee on Broadcasting and Information Media (popularly known as the Chanda Committee), formed by the Government in 1964, recommended in its report (April 1966) the discontinuance of community listening since the authorities in many States had failed to organise and operate the scheme satisfactorily. The Committee recommended that listening in rural areas should move from the community set to the village home through the supply of one-band receivers at a low price by adopting correct industrial and fiscal policies. Thirdly, the general elections of 1967 resulted in the formation of non-Congress governments in several States. They did not like the proliferation of Centrally sponsored schemes, which they saw as resulting in the distortion of locally relevant priorities by the bait of Central financial assistance. At a meeting of the National Development Council in 1969 the baby of community listening was thrown out along with the bathwater of excessive centralism. It was decided to discontinue the 50% Central subsidy for installing community listening sets. An exception was made for political reasons in the case of Jammu & Kashmir where the scheme continues to be handled by All India Radio, even as the installation and maintenance of community viewing TV sets in the valley is looked after by Doordarshan.

At the peak of the functioning of the community listening scheme the number of CL receivers was estimated at about 90,000. Had the scheme been continued and expanded, and the problem of maintenance logistics been solved, instead of taking the easy and lazy course of scrapping the scheme, the relevance of radio for the rural poor might have increased. Revival of the scheme country-wide has not been considered, on the specious argument that 'everybody' has a transistor. This is an instance of the urban picture being mistaken for the all-India scene. The spectacle of the farmer carrying a transistor set to his field is confined to areas like Punjab, Haryana, western Uttar Pradesh and coastal Andhra where there has been a Green Revolution. Very few own radio sets in the rural areas of eastern Uttar Pradesh, Bihar, Orissa or Telangana. The landless living below the poverty line certainly do not.

(g) AIR Goes Commerical : On 3 October 1957 AIR introduced a service known as Vividh Bharati, full of film music (to the extent of 60%) besides other light music, interspersed with news bulletins, short plays, etc. This was done in order to counter the pull of Radio Ceylon which was broadcasting Indian film music. Though radio listenership went up by leaps and bounds with the broadcast of the Vividh Bharati service by more and more stations, creating an audience of tempting size for the commercial advertiser, it was out of the question for AIR to go commercial as long as Nehru was alive. Commercials were introduced on 1 November 1967, within two years of Indira Gandhi becoming Prime Minister. Unlike Nehru, his successors felt the need to project their image through the medium of radio, and subsequently television, and to disseminate news selected and slanted to present in favourable light the party in power at the Centre. This public relations effort was undertaken as a counter to the Press. Several newspapers with a large circulation criticised Indira Gandhi's policies from a conservative standpoint, as at the time of the nationalisation of banks and abolition of princes' privy purses. This was in 1969, when she adopted a populist platform to mount her campaign against the older guard who controlled the Congress. Some other newspapers were critical of the government from a radical standpoint.

They carried news--of rural poverty and exploitation, corruption in the administration, and the like--which was unflattering to the government. The Press had been critical in similar fashion, both from the Right and the Left, in Nehru's time too, but he did not mind.

The easiest way to stimulate the purchase of radio sets and widen the exposure through radio to the Prime Minister and to news about the government's achievements and intentions was to provide more and more of popular film music. The purchase of radio sets was further encouraged by abolishing, in August 1980, the requirement of paying a licence fee in respect of one-band and two-band receivers. The production of radio receiving sets has gone up steeply and stood in 1989 at 8 million, as estimated by the Department of Electronics.

The abolition of licence fee for single-band and two-band radio sets has meant forgoing the greater part of the substantial revenue from broadcast receiver licences, which had been increasing over the years as follows:

Revenue from Radio Licences

	(Rs. crores)
1974-75	19.83
1975-76	26.93
1976-77	27.54
1977-78	28.96
1978-79	26.11
1979-80	36.46

According to the annual report of the Ministry of Information & Broadcasting for 1987-88, there were 29 commercial broadcasting centres. Ten per cent of the total broadcasting time from these centres is allotted to advertisements. From April 1982, the primary channels of AIR stations are also carrying commercials. In reply to a question in the Rajya Sabha on 15 March 1982, the then Minister of I & B, Vasant Sathe, outlined the following phased programme: from 1 April 1982, commercials would be broadcast before and after the national news bulletins in English and Hindi, both in the morning and evening; thereafter, these would be extended to slots before and after national news bulletins in regional languages, regional news bulletin, women's and rural programmes, and in between popular light music programmes. AIR's income from commercial advertising has increased steeply over the years.

AIR's Income from Commercials

	(Rs. crores)
1980-81	12.23
1982-83	15.51
1983-84	16.07
1984-85	15.69
1985-86	19.82
1986-87	24.00
April-Oct.1987	14.86

Commercial advertising on AIR reflects the change of life-style, imitative of the West, among the middle and upper classes. A popular commercial jingle used to be, "Mummy, Mummy, Modern Bread!" Children in the majority of Indian families neither eat packaged and branded bread, nor do they 'mummy' their mothers. However, since radio sets are within the reach also of the lower middle class and of industrial labour, the products advertised are not as expensive as the goods and services advertised by Doordarshan.

(h) Local Stations Lack Resources: There is a long history of recommendations made to the Government for establishing district-level radio stations for local broadcasting in support of the development process.

The Chanda Committee said in its report (1966) that local- interest programmes must be broadcast over low-power transmitters located at the headquarters of each of India's (then) 400 districts. Each station would serve one or two million people. This would ensure that the programmes would be relevant to the specific problems of people in comparatively small areas. The local station should be allowed to modify or add to centrally planned messages about development, with appropriate local inputs. News should be locally prepared. Operators of small-town radio stations in the U.S.A., Australia and elsewhere had found, the Committee pointed out, that comprehensive local news coverage is the single most attractive programme which makes listeners forsake the national networks in favour of their local station. Village folk are interested in district developments and the activities of the Taluka Panchayat Samiti, and not in those of the remote State legislative assemblies and the even remoter Lok Sabha and Rajya Sabha. They want news of the work of co-operatives, about rural industries, irrigation rates, the construction of village roads, a new bus service, problems of landholders and agricultural labourers, and all those things that affect their lives. A local station can collect such news from district officials, panchayats, social workers, teachers, traders and others, and also give timely warning of flooding of roads, breakdowns in the bus service, and so forth. Local broadcasting alone could ensure coordination with district authorities and with extension services.

The document on the Fourth Plan (1969-74) wanted the correction of information imbalance in the country. Though it did not specifically suggest local radio stations, they would have been the appropriate means of realising the objective which the Plan document set out in these words: "In the spread of information facilities, the imbalance in favour of urban concentrations and prosperous areas continues...There is need for a deliberate attempt to inform the people in the rural areas, and in particular those in backward regions, about the specific schemes in agriculture, forestry, road construction, marketing, the supply of credit and other inputs, so that the benefits of these programmes are more widely spread. Even in a single region or homogeneous area, there will be more than a single audience to be approached. These will have to be identified and reached."

Next came the report in February 1978 of the Working Group on Autonomy for Akashvani and Doordarshan, appointed by the Janata Government in August 1977 with B.G. Verghese as chairman. It ably summed up the principles of social education through the electronic media: "Instructional broadcasting presupposes specific small audiences in terms of age (for example, school broadcasts) and in terms of agro-climatic and socio-cultural variables including language. Decentralised and participative development from below sugests the need for decentralised messages through local radio and television. We would envisage the Station as something more than a single studio-transmission complex, distant and seeminlgy exclusive, or even inaccessible to the people it is intended to serve. Instead, we envisage at the local level a small and relatively simply equipped 'mother station' with a cluster around it of small recording units and programming facilities which will help bring broadcasting to the people and the people to broadcasting. This consideration applies both to radio and television."

Nothing was done in pursuance of this recommendation. It was only in the document on the Sixth Plan (1980-85) that local broadcasting was envisaged for the first time. The Plan included a "pilot scheme for local radio broadcasting...radio stations with low power transmitters for local areas to augment the development-oriented programmes for such regions. The pilot scheme visualises location of such stations in areas with large population of Scheduled Castes and Scheduled Tribes."

This seemed to hold out the promise of a revolution in Indian broadcasting. The 'working instructions' for local radio stations issued from the Directorate-General of AIR in New Delhi left little to be desired. The circular incorporated the approach to local broadcasting recommended by the Chanda Committee and by the Verghese Working Group.

However, as will be seen presently from the experience of the Nagercoil station in Tamil Nadu--the first to come up out of the half dozen local stations provided for in the Sixth Plan--the resources made available for local broadcasting are too little for achieving the intended purpose.

The 'working instructions' document reads as follows:

"Local Radio is a new concept in broadcasting in India. Each of the stations, serving a small area, will be basically a utility service and reach right into the heart of the community which will use the microphone to reflect and enrich its life and artistic expression. What distinguishes local radio from the regional network will be its down-to-earth, intimate and uninhibited approach. Programmes will be area-specific. They will be flexible and spontaneous, enable the station to function as the mouthpiece of the local community. It will demolish the division between the broadcaster and the audience. Local authorities, police, emergency services, adult educationists, schools, transporters, farm scientists, entertainers will all look up to the local radio for a sustained community service. Its accent will be on handling the local problems extensively, local news and views and local talent, and it will be available to a broad spectrum of the local people. Comprising predominantly field-based programmes, it will adopt a down-to-earth character and establish a two-way communication system between the listeners and the extension agencies of various government departments. Local events and functions, games and sports, exhibitions and fairs, meetings and debates, cultural or literary, will find ample coverage. Its 'access' programme will provide opportunities to distinct groups in the community to present their own programmes affording scope for the articulation of local talent and views. It will organise a number of 'helpline' services to the listeners--in employment, education, housing, law, and even family problems. The local aspirations will find fulfilment through the local radio.

"Working Instructions:

(1) Flexibility in programming being the main characteristic of local radio, the station may take the Fixed Point Chart as a broad guideline and make deviations as and when required. Directorate may be approached only when changes involving staff and funds are made. There will be no need to refer to the headquarters for effecting changes in the Fixed Point Chart. Instead of preparation of quarterly schedules the station may prepare fortnighly plans.

(2) The station's main emphasis may be field-based programmes. It must be the objective to cover every village in the district by turn. Inadequacy of staff for Outside Broadcasts could be overcome by casual bookings. The station may use cassette recorders which could be replenished by local purchases.

(3) The station may devote broadcast effort mainly to programmes of farming, rural development, health, family welfare and education. The agencies engaged in these fields may be tapped for supply of materials, scripts and recordings. Programmes of education could be supplemented by obtaining recordings from neighbouring stations in the State and from the Directorate of Transcription and Programme Exchange Services.

(4) Programmes may be presented in the local dialect/language by engaging, if required, casual comperes who may present the programmes in a breezy, chatty conversational style.

(5) The station may make provision for programmes of special audience like women, children, youth, labour, farmers etc. and groups, associations, organisations engaged in their welfare may be encouraged to produce and present programmes.

(6) The station may relay one news bulletin in the local language originating from Delhi, and another from the State capital. Stations situated in the Hindi zone may take one Central Hindi news bulletin. No other news bulletin is compulsory nor recommended.

(7) The station will not relay any programmes from Delhi/State capital except the broadcast of the President and Prime Minister. Mandatory relays will not apply to local radio stations.

(8) The stations will be free to indent programmes from other stations and use them at their discretion, keeping in view listeners' interest in such programmes."

The circular goes on to deal with the question of payments ("The scale of fee payable to unauditioned artists will be on par with the fee scale for Yuva Vani artists. Station will be free to fix the fee at any point within the fee range."); travelling and daily allowance ("The stations may make, in addition, payment towards TA/DA if the distance from the headquarters is 8 kms. and above. TA will be only second class rail fare, and DA at a flat rate of Rs. 25 per day. No fee will be payable for escorts of women artists or children."); and advisory committees ("The station may have an informal advisory panel. It may comprise important persons representing different interests like education, agriculture, extension services, panchayats, cooperation, small industries, health and hygiene, women, youth and social welfare and cultural organisations. No consultancy fee is payable.")

There is a lack of realism in the stipulation that no travelling or daily allowance may be paid to the escorts of women or children who participate in programmes. Surely this is no way to promote the participation of rural women. The staffing pattern for the district-level stations has no provision for a news unit, whereas the broadcast of news of local interest is a major factor in the service expected of a local station. The Nagercoil station, with a 1 KW transmitter that can cover only part of the Kanyakumari district of Tamil Nadu, went on the air from 30 October 1984 with a single transmission in the evening (6 p.m. to 9 p.m.). Headed by an Assistant Station Director with the requisite engineering and administrative staff, on the programme side it had a Farm Radio Officer (a post sanctioned but unfilled during the entire first year of the station's working); two Programme Executives; and two announcers besides a tape librarian and a production assistant. The station has one vehicle only. No wonder that outdoor recordings formed a small part of the programmes. The station could put out only a fortnightly 10-minute bulletin of local news.

The plus points of the station's performance are brought out in a paper prepared by the first Assistant Station Director of the Nagercoil station, K. Anjaneyulu, for his principals. (A summary of the paper has been published in an Amercian journal devoted to development communication.[9]) Following are some points from the paper:

"The 'wandering mike' captures "the joys and sorrows of people of different walks of life, like a wandering mendicant, a toiling labourer in a tea estate, an agricultural labourer, a worker in a cashew-nut factory, a domestic maid, etc.

"A myth centering round a tmple here, the history of a church or mosque there ...or the latest details pertaining to two rival groups of fishermen concerning their fishing rights sanctioned by tradition--all these are put across.

"If there is a public grievance about the drainage facility, it is presented along with the reply from the concerned municipal commissioner. Problems faced by the public in obtaining essential commodities from fair price shops are taken to the concerned civil supplies officer and his replies together with information on remedial steps are presented to the listeners."

Though the picture drawn is rosy, the paper also says: "The norms of staff requirements on the programme side based on the total hours of transmission, normally practised, should undergo drastic rethinking when it concerns a local radio station. A major percentage of programmes originated by a local radio station is (*sic*) field-based. This requires extensive field work involving adequate infrastructural facilities." It would be more accurate to say that a major percentage of programmes originated by a local radio *should be* field-based. This is brought out in a study of the Nagercoil experiment conducted in October 1985, after a year of its working. Carried out by the audience research wing of All India Radio, the study presents the following findings and suggestions:

(i) An analysis of the programmes over a period of three months showed that they were more or less on the same pattern as other stations, with the highest proportion being claimed by music: film, devotional, light classical and folk.

(ii) Talks formed 57.1% of the programmes for women, and 50% of the Farm & Home programmes (which occupied only 4.1% of broadcast time, presumbaly because no Farm Radio Officer was in position). The programmes for industrial workers consisted entirely of talks.

(iii) Almost all programmes were studio-recorded.

(iv) Manpower was insufficient and there were no OB recording facilities.

(v) The highest listening by radio owners (the other stations they could hear being Radio Sri Lanka, Tirunelveli and Tiruchi) was between 6 a.m. and 8.a.m. and 8.p.m. to 10 p.m. The study recommended the introduction of a morning transmission also, and extension of the evening transmission till 10.30 p.m.

(vi) Officials of the development departments feared that they might be violating the code of conduct if they spoke frankly on radio. It was recommended that the Ministry of I & B should arrange for high-level clearance by the State government, of participation by officials.

(viii) Local news should be broadcast for a duration of 15 minutes daily. For this purpose there should be a news unit with a correspondent and a news editor.

(i) Kota: a Foreign-Aided Exception : An exception to the rule of AIR's local stations lacking the resources necessary for playing their expected role is Kota. This station has a Development Broadcasting Unit (DBU) which is funded, under a four-year project, by the Asia-Pacific Institute for Broadcast Development (AIBD) with its headquarters at Kuala Lumpur and by the Ryerson International Development Centre, Canada. The resources available enable the production of researched, participative and field-based programmes.

In contrast to the staffing pattern at the Nagercoil station, Kota's DBU alone has four programme executives. They visit the villages in the 50-km. radius covered by Kota station, talk to the people and ascertain their problems and interests. The 20-minute programmes are made with the collaboration of the villagers, and the language employed is the locally spoken Haroti--not standard Hindi (Rajasthan, where Kota is located, is classified as a 'Hindi-speaking State').

The weekly programmes of DBU began to be broadcast from 7 January 1988 at the peak listening time of 7.20 a.m., before the farmers leave for their fields. The series is under the title 'Nai Kiran' ('New Ray of Light'). Since a one-shot broadcast may be missed by several even among radio-owners, and since many may not possess a radio set, each programme is recorded on tape and the cassettes are supplied to the workers of the official development agencies as well as to voluntary workers and non-governmental organisations who express interest. They play the cassettes for groups of villagers at any time convenient.

Among the 38 DBU programmes broadcast from Kota station till the end of September 1988 are several which helped to bring about desirable change, on the ground, among the rural communities in interaction with whom the programmes were made.

For example, the people of Naigon village were suffering from guinea worm infection. They attributed it to the water from hand pumps, and therefore switched over completely to using the village well. A DBU producer talked to the villagers as well as the doctors of the health department. It was found on inspection by a specialist that it was actually the well water in which the worms were breeding. This was explained to the villagers, and the well was sealed for disinfection. With treatment of the worm wounds organised by the health authorities, the village was soon relieved of the affliction.

Another DBU programme was aimed at promoting cleanliness in the village of Sorgia--to serve as a model for other neighbouring villages. Prizes were announced for a 'clean child' contest, and the prize-giving ceremony was followed by films and talks on hygiene and sanitation. Households were invited to participate next in a cleanliness contest, and the winners awarded prizes.

The objective of another programme, which took the final form of a community drama, was to encourage the enrolment of children in schools instead of utilising them as child labour. The expenditure incurred on the programme was nearly Rs. 10,000, but it had an impact on school enrolment.

An indicator of audience interest in these programmes is the large number of letters received by the Kota station from village listeners. Ms. Roberta Borg, the project coordinator who was interviewed in the course of this study, said that though the villagers are largely illiterate, they took the trouble to have their messages--stating a problem or requesting advice--written out for them by others. This was a measure of the interest evoked by the DBU programmes.

The experiment in development broadcasting at Kota should induce All India Radio to endow each local radio station with adequate resources, of personnel and finance. Particularly important is the example set by Kota of supplementing the broadcast of programmes promotive of rural development with audio cassettes for utilisation in the non-broadcast mode. The problem of access to radio for the rural poor can be met best by a combination of the community listening facility with audio cassettes for use by village level development workers, both in the official and the voluntary sector.

(j) **No Access for Rural Poor:** The study of one year of the Nagercoil station's working suffered from the defect common to most studies carried our by AIR's audience research wing, namely that it was confined to radio-owning homes. No attempt was made to ascertain what proportion of the population, rural and urban, has access to radio listening.

While the Nagercoil station broadcasts on medium wave, almost all the district-level radio stations proposed for the Eighth Plan will employ Frequency Modulation. This is because of the congestion of the medium wave spectrum. And FM radio receiving sets made in India now cost more than ten times the price of a MW transistor set. The rural poor will therefore have even less access to local radio than they now have to regional stations.

If middle and upper class listeners are alone going to be available for local stations, they will be different from the regional stations only to the extent that they offer opportunities to local singers and talkers drawn from the same privileged section of the population. The contribution of such 'local' radio stations to development can only be nominal.

Unless there is a policy decision to provide access to local radio for the rural poor, through a revival of the community listening facility as well as providing opportunity to them to voice their needs and views, the expenditure on setting up district-level stations will have no social justification. The so-called local stations may end up by having their spare transmission capacity utilised for relaying the National Channel.

(ii) Doordarshan: a Communication Aberration

A variety of forces were at work in the 1950's to bring television to India. Businessmen, politicians in power, and civil servants who went abroad and saw television in the U.S.A. and elsewhere wanted to have similar entertainment at home. Multi-national corporations in the field of television saw in India a big potential market. UNESCO was interested too, dominated as its secretariat was by experts and officials from the industrialised and media-saturated countries of the West with their own ethno-centric notions of development and of communication. A committee formed by UNESCO came up with 'norms' by which to measure the sufficiency or insufficiency of mass communication facilities in developing countries. As an 'immediate target', the group recommended that every developing country should aim at providing for every 100 of its inhabitants ten copies of daily newspapers, five radio receivers, two cinema seats and two television receivers. This was a simplistic and quantitative approach. The 'UNESCO norms', as they came to be known, considered the mass media in terms of growth in their size and not the relevance of their content, or their accessibility, to the common people in developing countries. A commendable feature of the formula, however, was the one pertaining to daily newspaper copies, which implied vigorous efforts to promote literacy and purchasing power among the masses in the newly free and developing countries.

(a) Educational Beginning : Anyone looking at Doordarshan today will find it hard to believe that television was introduced in India in 1959 with an educational and developmental intent. Jawaharlal Nehru was prime minister at the time, and he would not have countenanced the expenditure of rupee and foreign exchange resources on introducing television as a medium primarily of entertainment as in the affluent countries. Television was therefore canvassed on the grounds of education and development.

A transmitter was offered for sale at a reduced price to the Government of India by Philips (India) after they had demonstrated the use of television at an industrial exhibition in New Delhi. It was decided to use it for an experimental service, to see what television could contribute to community development and to education. UNESCO made a grant of $ 20,000 for the purpose, and the U.S. government helped by providing some equipment.

The service from the experimental TV station at Delhi began on 15 September 1959, with a range of about 40 km. around the capital. Programmes of rural social education were telecast twice a week for about 180 teleclubs formed for viewing and discussion. UNESCO provided the funds for the community viewing sets as well as for a study in 1961 which indicated that the programmes had made some impact. A service for schools was started on an experimental basis in 1961 and was in 1965 made part of the curriculum of higher secondary schools run by the Delhi Administration.

It was in 1965--when Indira Gandhi was Minister of I & B in the Lal Bahadur Shastri Cabinet--that a daily service of one hour's duration, of general interest comprising entertainment and information for those who could afford to buy their own TV receiving sets, was started. Since then television has been expanded as a means of Entertainment (much of it coarse) and Information (with the news part of it selective and angled), merely token obeisance being paid to Education and Development. The growth of the television system has been impressive, but only among the upper and middle classes and a section of the urban working class. It is not meant for, and does not reach, the country's poor.

(b) Pluses and Minuses of SITE : A late flicker of the educational and developmental impulse of Indian television was the agreement entered into by the government with the National Aeronautics and Space Administration of the U.S.A. for a Satellite Instructional Television Experiment (SITE). Before SITE became operational from 1 August 1975, terrestrial stations telecasting programmes of entertainment and information for the urban well-to-do had come up at Bombay, on 2 October 1972 in mocking commemoration of Gandhiji's birthday; at Amritsar on 29 September 1973 (to wean the affluent from viewing Pakistan's television programmes); and at Srinagar on 6 November 1973 (also as a counter to Pakistan TV).

In contrast to the terrestrial stations which had gone bourgeois in their orientation, SITE concerned itself not only with the production of rural-interest television programmes and their transmission, but also their wide-scale social consumption. Direct reception sets with 24-inch screens were installed in 2,330 villages in backward districts of six States with programmes in four languages: Oriya for Orissa; Hindi for the States of Bihar, Rajasthan and Madhya Pradesh; Telugu for Andhra Pradesh; and Kannada for Karnataka. SITE utilised ATS-6, which was made available and put into geostationary orbit by NASA. The Indian Space Research Organisation (ISRO) was responsible for all technical operations of the ground segment, including the maintenance of the direct reception sets. Doordarshan was responsible for the software.

There was a morning transmission of one and a half hours for school children, with programmes of 22 1/2 minutes each in the four languages. The programmes covered science education, biographies of great Indians, health education, current affairs and entertainment. The evening transmission of two and a half hours was intended for the rural adult population (though children turned up in the evening too and accounted for well over a third of the audience). It carried news; entertainment programmes, many of which served also to portray the unity underlying India's cultural diversity; and instructional programmes on agricultural improvement, animal husbandry, health, hygiene and nutrition, and family planning. A news bulletin formed part of a half-hour 'national segment'in Hindi, which was telecast in all the six districts.

While the experiment was an unqualified success in terms of hardware and technical operations, SITE was only a qualified success as an exercise in social education for the rural population. Software presented a more varied and continuous challenge during SITE than the installation and operation of hardware. The main reason for the limited social impact of SITE was that there were only three base production centres (BPCs) to make the bulk of the programmes for villages with varied agro-economic and cultural backgrounds, many of them more than a thousand kilometres apart. Area-specific programmes were therefore minimal. And it is a truth apparent to common sense that decentralised and area-specific programmes, employing local speech and depicting the local agro-economic and human landscape, are necessary in any attempt to persuade people to change their attitudes and practices, whether in agriculture and hygiene or-- and even more so--in family planning.

(c) Lost Lesson of Pij : The common sense view on the need for area-specificity and the employment of local speech in development communication has been borne out by the findings of a research study undertaken by ISRO. It entailed holistic studies by anthropologists in seven villages: one each in the six clusters served by the satellite and, in addition, one village--Dadusar--served by a terrestrial transmitter at Pij in the Kheda district of Gujarat. The Pij experiment was undertaken by a group of socially concerned space scientists of ISRO. The transmission comprised the half-hour national programme of SITE in Hindi, telecast through rediffusion, and a half-hour Gujarati programme prepared at Ahmedabad under the auspices of ISRO. In several of these Gujarati programmes, the Charautari dialect prevalent in Kheda district, instead of standard middle-class Gujarati, was employed. The programmes themselves were research-based, and dealt with the felt needs and interests of the audience. About 500 community viewing sets were installed in 355 villages of Kheda district. Several villages thus had more than one set. This was a densification of viewing perhaps higher than even in Kashmir Valley--the other island of television relevant and accessible to the rural population.

The social anthropologists who lived for about a year and a half in the seven villages, for data collection and continuous observation, found:

> "The linguistic profile of these villages shows a higher use of dialects than the standard language of the region...None of the languages spoken in the villages were used on TV except in Dadusar where Charautari was utilised to some extent. Furthermore, the use of English-sounding technical names(in programmes on agriculture and animal husbandry) compounded the problem...If the programmes were entertaining enough in terms of songs and dances, language did not become a barrier. Due to this reason, recreational programmes of other clusters were viewed with enthusiasm in all the

> villages...The Hindi common news was almost ineffective in all villages...The problem of lip synchronisation affected the credibility of the TV medium to an extent (in Andhra Pradesh and Karnataka which used one video and two audio channels.)"

In other words, the most effective communication during the Satellite Instructional Television Experiment was achieved not via satellite but through a low-power, local, terrestrial station which interacted with the community round it and dealt with local problems in local speech.

The need for communication to be localised and participatory if it is to play a developmental role was realised by the more perceptive among Western scholars of communication like Wilbur Schramm. He was the leader of a team of experts who were invited by the Indian government in 1963 to advise on the development of information infrastructure. It was on the recommendation of this team that the Indian Institute of Mass Communication was established in New Delhi in August 1965. On a visit to the Institute in 1977, Wilbur Schramm said in the course of a remarkably candid address to the faculty and stduents:

> "There is a confession that I have to make. It is about the book that I published, *Mass Media and National Development,* in 1964. Actually it was written in 1962. I want to confess now some of the things I did not see then, some of the things I would do differently today if I were to write this book all over again...
>
> "Number one: the concept of what mass communications can accomplish by themselves has been almost completely revised. The bullet theory, that you can shoot a message into a person and he falls over, that it has a predominant effect, died simply because it was found that people did not fall over. They would brush away some of these information bullets; they would catch it in their hand, or eat it like chocolate candy. This was not like an electric current flowing through a wire on any thing like that. The receiver was as active as the sender. That is, we got away from the idea that the audience was passive, and we got away from the idea that we could do things with him by putting some information into him without doing anything else.
>
> "Secondly, the trickle-down theory. The idea of trickle-down development is something of which I would be less proud now than in my book in 1962. But that was how the pattern looked in 1962, when the great experts in the

capital city, the government, the universities would go on radio or the television and talk to the village people about how to be healthier, more prosperous or how to have small families. Well, it simply does not look any more that way. What we have found out in these last 15 years, rather painfully, is that important as communication from top to bottom is, more important is communication at the bottom--that is, communication between the people at the same level.

"Activity at the village level is the only means, I would say, of effective village change and whereas communication has to travel down, it has got to travel up and, much more important, it has got to travel round at the village level. People have to work together and discuss together; they have got to make their changes together. Only when communication can build itself into the social structure, is it going to show any real hope of extensive results. Only when media channels can mix with inter-personal channels, and with the organisation in the village, are you going to have the kind of development that you will like. In other words, the idea of big media, of talk-down communication, is something which is not going to work."[10]

The Indian government did not listen to the older and wiser Schramm. Had the SITE experience been properly analysed and understood, it would have pointed to the conclusion that television to be effective in a developmental role would have to be localised and the community would have to be provided with access; that district-level television is much too expensive in the circumstances of India; and that local radio continued to be the best option for developmental mass communication in the broadcast mode (as distinct from audio or video cassettes).

Instead, more Doordarshan Kendras were opened in the cities to cater for the urban middle and upper classes for whom televsion is basically a one-time, wholesale investment in film enertainment; it obviates the need to travel to cinema halls and queue up for buying tickets. Lured by the entertainment it offers, large numbers of the urban working class, too, are acquiring a television set whether or not they can truly afford it in the context of other needs like health care and children's education.

The four pre-SITE TV centres were followed by Kendras at Calcutta (August 1975); Madras (August 1975); Lucknow (November 1975); Jaipur (March 1977); Bangalore (November 1981); Trivandrum (November 1982); Guwahati (November 1982); and Ahmedabad (November 1983). In addition to these twelve centres, there are six more that are usually listed separately because they have the distinction of making some programmes of rural interest and social education on the SITE pattern. The centres are at Hyderabad (Andhra Pradesh), Nagpur (Maharashtra), Cuttack (Orissa), Ranchi (Bihar), Gorakhpur (Uttar Pradesh), and Rajkot (Gujarat). The programmes prepared in the respective languages are of the duration of about half-an-hour per day. They are brought to Delhi and uplinked to INSAT on a time-sharing basis for community viewing by rural audiences. But the size of the rural population thus served is very small. The total number of community viewing sets throughout the country--located in schools, panchayat ghars and elsewhere--as of June 1988 was a mere 30,834. The distribution was as follows:

Community TV Sets[11]

State/Centre	*Number*
Andhra Pradesh	930
Bihar	993
Delhi	1074
Gujarat	4503
Madhya Pradesh	412
Maharashtra	6919
Orissa	694
Punjab	514
Rajasthan	1799
Uttar Pradesh	4064
Calcutta	309
Madras	8042
Srinagar	581
TOTAL	30834

(d) Asian Games and Delhi-Centrism

The introduction of television in Indonesia was on the occasion of the Fourth Asian Games which opened at Jakarta in August 1962. In India, the Ninth Asian Games held in New Delhi marked the introduction of the more expensive mode of programme- making and transmission in colour.

Mehra Masani recalls: "In Iran, the Shah introduced colour TV to cover the coronation of Empress Farah. In Uganda, Idi Amin brought in colour TV at a cost of $6 million to cover a meeting of the Organisation of African Unity and also to cover his most recent wedding in 1975. In Thailand it was introduced in a great hurry to cover a beauty competition. We, not to be outdone, started on colour TV in a hurry to relay the Asian Games."[12]

Two dozen low power relay transmitters were imported from the U.S.A. This took to more than 40 the total number of transmitters, including those which were relaying the regional Kendras then in operation. Software presented no problem during the course of Asiad, from 19 November to 4 December 1982. Performing talent did not have to be spotted, trained and rehearsed by Doordarshan's producers. The performers were there, fully trained. And the language of their performing art was the universal language of body movement, obviating the need for dubbing or sub-titling. The camera had only to be focussed properly on the performers.

The software situation would be different after Asiad. This might have been among the reasons for the Government of India deciding on 6 December 1982 to appoint a Working Group "to prepare a software plan for Doordarshan, taking into ocnsideration the main objectives of television of assisting in the process of social and economic development in the country and to act as an effective medium for providing information, education and entertainment." Dr P.C. Joshi of the Institute of Economic Growth, Delhi, was the chairman of the Working Group and the present writer was among its members.

The Working Group was agreed in its approach to Doordarshan's programmes promotive of national integration that they should be national in content but local in language. A paper on the 'Uses and Dangers of Networking', considered and broadly endorsed by the Group, said:

"Networking via satellite can be an aid to programmes conducive to national integration. This communication technology can also be counter-productive if unimaginatively used.

"Occasions like the Republic Day parade in the capital, or the Independence Day rally at Red Fort, are visually spectacular and it is a heartwarming experience for people in widely separated parts of the country to be able to view them simultaneously. However, even the impact of the Republic Day parade shown on television will be enhanced if the commentary from Delhi, in Hindi or English, is overlaid from time to time with translation in the local language...

"The prevailing concept of a 'national programme' is to put together a number of regional programmes which are largely unintelligible to viewers outside the region concerned. A recent example is the presentation of 'Pinnal Kolattam' on 4 November (Diwali Day) 1983. The words of the song sung by the women while performing this traditional Tamil dance conveyed fine humanistic sentiments--but only to those who know Tamil; to the rest of the viewers in the country, the words were gibberish. Discreet, unobtrusive and brief sound overlays, to explain the words of the Tamil song in the other Indian languages, would have enabled intelligent appreciation of the programme instead of its appealing only to the eye."

Even as the Working Group was discussing suggestions on these lines, including the overriding need for area specificity in programmes that seek to promote development, the Government announced a Special Plan for TV expansion by setting up more low power transmitters to relay programmes from Delhi. This seemed to pre-empt the Working Group's formulation of a software plan and to render it redundant. However, the Group did not despair but presented its recommendations in a report[13] notable for its plain speaking. Here are some extracts:

"No wonder that a member of our Group has characterised the Special Plan for TV expansion, to take the Delhi Kendra's programmes of meretricious entertainment and government publicity to the middle and upper classes all over urban India as the greatest communication aberration in the history of the Third World. Given the disparity in access, and the lack of relevance of the software of Doordarshan to the harsh living conditions of the common people, it seems ironical that television should be claimed--as it has been by a widely quoted Amercian writer--as a medium which retribalises humankind..If Doordarshan, with its foreign social comedy serials and Indian feature films projecting the aping of Western life styles, is promoting a process of universal tribalisation, it is by inducting sons and daughters of TV viewers and the moneyed Indian upper crust comprising businessmen and politicians, civil servants and academics, and every other category of the privileged into the international fraternity of rock and roll, jive and disco. The international elite of the developed and developing countries do indeed consitute one tribe irrespective of their skin colour and geographical location.

"In order to correct the aberration of Delhi-centrism, and to restore Doordarshan's orginal purpose of promoting social education and development, we recommend that each transmitter of Doordarshan's network should be provided with the facility of making and telecasting locally orginated programmes, as well as programmes from the nearest major Kendra in the linguistic region (either obtained on videotape or at a later stage by relay through microwave or satellite), besides relaying progrmmes from Delhi.

"Implementation of this recommendation will help to transform a forest of relay transmitters into a large complex of TV Kendras that are required in a vast and lingustically diverse country to provide programmes of national, regional and local interest...

"If the locally comprehensible telecast of nationally integrative programmes should lead to a diminution in the telecast time occupied by the 'National' Programme it need not cause any concern. On the contrary, those who make Doordarshan's policy should be happy if a nationally integrative programme fulfils its objective more effectively by employing local speech. This understanding implies an acceptance of the proposition that vision has not abolished the need for words, that the eye has not rendered the mind redundant.

"Even para-dubbing will be of limited assistance to those among rural viewers who are familiar only with the local dialectal form of an Indian language. We have therefore suggested that, at community viewing centres, the custodian should further promote comprehension by furnishing explanation in the local dialect."

Far from acting on the recommendations of the Working Group, the government has been expanding the number of relay transmitters linked exclusively with Delhi. They numbered 195 as on 31 December 1988. On the other hand, not one new programme production centre had been commissioned after the last of the 18 Kendras listed earlier, in section (ii) (c), came up at Cuttack on 11 March 1985. The Seventh Five Year Plan had provided for 30 centres, additional to the 18, to be equipped with studio facilities. In a written reply to a question in the Rajya Sabha on 29 July 1988, the Minister of Information & Broadcasting, H.K.L. Bhagat, listed the thirty centres: Agartala, Aizawl, Allahabad, Bareilly, Bhopal, Bhubaneswar, Chandigarh, Daltonganj, Dibrugarh, Gangtok, Gulbarga, Capital of Haryana, Imphal, Itanagar, Jammu, Kohima, Madurai, Muzaffarpur, Panaji, Patna, Pondicherry, Port Blair, Pune, Raipur, Shillong, Shimla, Silchar, Siliguri, Tura and Vijayawada. The achievement was zero at the end of August 1989.

(iii) Advertising: Political and Commercial

The reason for hardware racing ahead of software is that the pretence of Doordarshan serving to promote broad-based development has been dropped. Along with radio it is being utilised unabashedly as an instrument of political advertising of the party in power at the Centre and in particular of the Prime Minister, and of commercial advertising. The latter helps to augment the resources available to the government to expand the Delhi-centric TV network as an instrument for political image-building.

The misuse of Doordarshan is more blatant than of All India Radio because television is the more potent medium.

Manipulation of the Centrally operated electronic media for partisan political purpose would have been difficult it the electoral system had been based on proportional representation, in which case there would have been coalition governments at the Centre much of time. The electoral system has contributed to the emergence of a scenario of development and of communication in India which combines the worst features of early capitalism and of totalitarian regimes. Whereas decades of the growth of trade unionism in Western Europe and the U.S.A. have resulted in social security schemes like unemployment insurance and old age pension which have given 20th-century capitalism a human face, the living conditions of India's toiling masses are those of early capitalism and feudal serfdom. Yet the advertising of luxury goods and services for the top crust of society in the Indian mass media is exactly as in the affluent West. Such advertising adds insult to the injury of the poor. To cap this, the use made of Indian radio and television for political propaganda closely resembles the use of the official media in one-party regimes, whether communist or plain militarist.

(a) News: Emergency and After: The official communication media are yet to recover from their gross abuse during the internal emergency which Prime Minister Indira Gandhi, without benefit of discussion and approval of the proposal by her Cabinet, got the President to proclaim in June 1975. The Press was brought under rigorous censorship, and the country's news agencies were amalgamated into a single governmentally sponsored 'Samachar' through threats and pressure. The news bulletins of All India Radio became a string of reports of what the Prime Minister had said that day at this official meeting or that public gathering. Television extensively publicised not only the Prime Minister but her second son Sanjay Gandhi who emerged as a powerful extra-constitutional authority.

Led to think by her own propaganda organs and intelligence agencies that the people were happy with what had been done during the emergency, Indira Gandhi called elections, in March 1977, which she lost. The new government formed by the Janata party dismantled the apparatus of censorship. A document was compiled on the misuse of mass media during the internal emergency.[14]

But it is in the nature of all governments to want to hide unflattering information. When the Communications Minister in the Janata government, Brijlal Verma, was held in quarantine at Delhi's Palam airport because he returned from a foreign tour without the requisite injection against yellow fever, the then Health Minister, Raj Narain, was upset. He called the officer of the Press Information Bureau attached to the Health

Ministry and asked him how the news came to be published. The officer pointed out, with respect, that it was his (Raj Narain's) government that had lifted Press consorship, and that he (the officer) was powerless now to black out any information.

After the fall of the Janata government due to internal dissension, the Congress led by Indira Gandhi returned to power in the elections held in January 1980. It seemed as if the Congress (I) had been chastened by experience and would not again manipulate the official media. A letter was issued by the Ministry of Information & Broadcasting to the heads of the media unit on 2 July 1980 which was in the nature of a signal that a return to the ways of the emergency period was not desired or expected. Initially classified as 'Confidential', this letter setting out policy guidelines for the official media was placed before the Lok Sabha on 12 August 1980 and before the Rajya Sabha on 16 March 1981. Though by no means a charter of professional autonomy, the letter was a step in that direction. It said:

> "The Government is committed towards the establishement of an egalitarian society and to promote social and economic justice for all in the country. The official media units have to play a vital role in the context of over-all development strategies and programmes of the Government. The various processes of thinking, planning and execution of publicity programmes have to be tuned to the efforts in these directions. People have to be mobilised towards the goals set by the Government and public support mustered for the programmes. The official media have, therefore, an obligation to provide information and build up motivation in support of such programmems and policies. It is in this context that the activities of the media should become an input in the nation building tasks. They must strengthen the confidence of the people, promote the concept of self-reliance and encourage forces of unity and national harmony.
>
> "2. All this has to be done by the official media with a certain degree of creativity, originality and ingenuity so that the official media remain credible as well as interesting to all sections of the society and specially the youth of the country.
>
> "3. The Government have in this context carefully considered and approved the following guidelines for assisting the various official media units in their functioning:

(i) Media Units should give effective coverage to Government's programmes, policies and achievements. Particular attention should be given to programmes and dissemination of information relating to developmental activities in all their facets including, for example, extension work in Agriculture, Education, Health and Family Welfare and Science and Technology.

(ii) Media Units should devise and present suitable programmes relating to youth, including information regarding opportunities for and generation of employment in various fields.

(iii) Vigorous steps should be taken by the official media units to serve the rural population, minority communities, women, children, illiterates as well as other weaker and vulnerable sections of the society.

(iv) Each media unit should try to encourage both individual as well as collective effort by the handicapped such as blind, deaf, dumb and other disabled persons as well as institutions doing service to this section of society. Media Units should also try to propagate the good work that is being done to eradicate social evils such as untouchability, narrow parochial attitudes and loyalties, inequalities and exploitation. Steps taken by the Government in this regard should be highlighted.

(v) Dissemination of information, news and comments in Akashvani and Doordarshan and Films Division should be done in a fair, objective and balanced manner including contrasting points of view, with emphasis on events and developments. Reference to personalities may be made primarily for providing human interest.

(vi) Media Units should adopt a professional approach in their activities. They should strive for creating audience interest and to meet their needs and expectations by talking about what is on the ground, having stories of local interest in a realistic manner by adopting actual field-based coverage. The Media Units should, instead of limiting themselves mostly to what the Government is planning to do, identify and highlight successful examples of group and individual efforts in developmental activities and towards solutions of local problems. Problems and issues should also be covered from the public point of view without any hesitation in bringing out healthy criticism.

(vii) Media units, and particularly Akashvani and Doordarshan, should endeavour to put out news and features which are investigative and in depth. There should be a greater attempt in diversification of coverage in terms of personalities being brought in for participation, places of origination of news, and sources being relied upon.

(viii) Media Units should have a constant dialogue among themselves and establish effective horizontal linkages to support and supplement one another's programme and resources.

(ix) Each media unit should have adequate systems for continuous evaluation and re-assessment of its performance in the context of its specific objectives, resources and schedules."

The hope of the official media being given a credible and constructive role to play in the total flow of communication in the country was strengthened when, on 28 November 1980 the Ministry of Information & Broadcasting constituted a Media Advisory Committee "to advise on various matters relating to policies and programmes relating to the media units under its administrative control." Chairman of the Committee was G. Parthasarathi, former journalist, diplomat and educationist. The members included distinguished practitioners of communication in the widest sense in the non-official sector, as well as some with experience of work in the governmental media. They were: E. Elkazi, Mulk Raj Anand, Basu Bhattacharya, E.V. Chitnis, N.L. Chowla, K.S. Duggal, B.V. Karanth, P.V. Krishnamurthy, K. Kurian, V.K. Narayana Menon, Sumati Mutatkar, N. Bhaskara Rao, and Fatima Zakaria.

The terms of reference were wide. The Committee was to advise the Government on:

(a) Structural changes in the different media organisations under the Ministry of I & B, and if necessary, in the Ministry itself to bring about greater professional efficiency and improvement in the quality of performance of the media in response to wide-ranging national requirements and aspirations;

(b) Measures to be taken at the national, state, regional and local levels to associate the people more directly in the planning and initiation of innovative programmes in the different media organisations under the jurisdiction of the Ministry of I & B, through creative participation and inter-communication so as to enrich their cultural identity and promote national integration;

(c) Determining priorities in different areas of media development and providing adequate infrastructural support and strengthening the capacity of the media to reach out to all sections of the people;

(d) The mode and mechanics of coordination amongst various media groups under the Ministry of I & B and of cooperation between the Central and State media organisations with a view to maximising the impact of communication support for developmental efforts; and

(e) Any other matter referred to the Committee by the Government for advice."

(b) Exemplary Guidelines, Blatant Violation: The Media Advisory Committee formulated a statement of news policy for the broadcast media. This document elaborated, and took much further forward in the direction of professionalism and credibility, the policy guidelines issued earlier by the Ministry of I & B for the official media.

The news policy suggested by the Media Advisory Committee was approved by the Ministry of I & B and issued to All India Radio and Doordarshan on 4 May 1982. The document was placed before the Lok Sabha in reply to an unstarred question on 13 July 1982. It said:

"There has to be a clear understanding of the difference between news and views. The reporting of news has to be factual, accurate and objective and only such views as make news should find a place in news broadcasts. There can be no editorialising in broadcast news.

"Each news story should be judged strictly on the basis of its news value.

"In the selection of news received from wide ranging sources and in news editing, AIR and Doordarshan should be guided by the highest possible professional standards. While newsworthiness will determine the selection of news, its treatment and presentation should be directly related to the speical characteristics and potential of each medium as well as the target audiences.

"Apart from treating news factually and objectively AIR and Doordarshan should provide, where necessary, a background to the events and happenings in order that listeners in any part of the country are able to place such events and happenings in proper perspective.

"The broadcast news should satisfy the highest criteria of accuracy and responsibility. AIR & Doordarshan cannot indulge in speculative stories of the type which appear in certain journals. They should develop their own sources for the verification of events.

"In a developing country like ours, a special function of broadcasting should be the coverage of development: its significance, achievements and problems. Development news covers a wide range of activities--economic, technological, social and cultural. It should not be confined to mere statements and plans but explain their significance. For this purpose news gathering operations of AIR and Doordarshan should be expanded and properly dispersed. In other words, the news gathering apparatus should make a deliberate effort to explore new areas of development and nation building news. People's participation in such activities should be duly highlighted as also significant work being done by voluntary agencies. Thereby the broadcast media should not only supplement the work normally undertaken by the news agencies but put out well backgrounded stories on their own.

"With the limitation of time, the vast audiences reached and the presentational demands, AIR and Doordarshan cannot be expected to follow the pattern of news coverage followed by the newspapers. The range and scope of news gathering and selection will have to be suited to the media.

"The style and method of news reporting should reinforce the fundamental principles including territorial integrity, national integration, secularism, maintenance of public order and upholding the dignity and prestige of Parliament, State legislatures and the judiciary.

"Ministerial statements on policy matters, particularly those of the Prime Minister, are important in as much as they enable the people to understand national policies. Similarly implementation of government programmes should be given proper place in the news. The focus should be on information rather than on individuals. It is also necessary that views critical of official policies and the manner of their implementation should find adequate time.

"In reporting on political controversies the broadcast media should be guided by objectivity and fair play. Due representation of differing viewpoints should be the aim. If a variety of viewpoints cannot be projected in the same bulletin, the balance should be achieved within a reasonable period of time.

"In the choice of international events the objective should be to keep the people informed of world developments. A special effort should be made to give proper background of events. In the selection of news, greater attention should be given to events in developing countries, particularly our neighbours. Apart from strictly pruning and editing the copy from the world agencies which have an overload of news from advanced countries and also a subtle bias, it would be desirable for AIR to use copy from the Nonaligned News Pool and other third world agencies on news merits. What is most essential is for AIR to increase the number of its foreign correspondents and carefully select their location and area of news coverage so that we can project a view of world developments as seen by India and other non-aligned developing countries. AIR and Doordarshan should aim at creating informed public opinion on international events and developments. In preparing programmes in news and current affairs, the national interest must be kept in mind. The national policy of peace and peaceful co-existence, non-alignment, friendship with all countries, support for people fighting for independence and freedom and the struggle against racism and racial descrimination and for an international order based on justice and equality should be highlighted. This does not exclude the reporting of any significant criticism of Government's foreign policy, either in the content or in its implementation.

"The primary purpose of the current affairs programmes should be to enlighten the people on various aspects of political, economic, social and cultural developments. The treatment of the subject should be comprehensive, projecting different viewpoints. It should aim at providing adequate background for a proper understanding and interpretation of events and issues.

"The current affairs programmes should be broadbased in the selection of topics and participants. The interests of various sections of the people should be taken into account. The formats should be innovative and suited to the medium. There is scope for experimentation in this respect.

"Internal evaluation of news and current affairs programmes after their broadcast should be a regular exercise on a daily basis. A panel of outside experts for news and current affairs in a particular language should be considered.

"The characteristics and potential reach of the broadcast media necessitate the drafting of news items in spoken style. The language should be addressed to the ear, unlike the printed word in a newspaper or journal which is meant to be read.

"The constraint of time also calls for precision and brevity. The differences in the level of comprehension of listeners are yet another factor to be taken into account. Simplicity and clarity are essential. Reporters and those who give talks should aim at easy communication with the people, and not parade their literacy skills. AIR and Doordarshan should develop their own idiom and style.

"There should be provision for evaluation from time to time of the language of the bulletins. There has to be a much greater emphasis on specialisation and training of the news personnel within AIR and Doordarshan. A style book in each language should be prepared without delay.

"The implementation of these policies and norms will depend upon the professional capacity of the people who run the news and current affairs programmes. The choice of personnel is most important. A professional must have had training in news work. He should be able to choose items well and to rewrite the stories to suit the medium. Professional training and appreciation of the role of the media in a democratic society will give him the confidence to take the right decisions."

This exemplary statement of news policy for the broadcast media was cited and warmly commended by the Working Group on Doordarshan in the report it gave early in 1984. The Working Group said: "Like the letter incorporating Policy Guidelines, the statement of news policy is informed by an enlightened and liberal approach which acknowledges the need for programmes of news and current affairs in the government-run electronic media, in a developing and democratic country, to reflect the progress and problems of the country's development and the diversity of political opinion."

Soon, however, the hopes raised by the issue of the Policy Guidelines and the formation of the Media Advisory Committee were frustrated. Misuse of the official media in the post-Nehru years has been in direct proportion to the degree of acrimony in public life. Mishandling of problems in Assam and Punjab led to a revival of the politics of confrontation and violence-prone agitation, and with it the misuse of the official media. When the Punjab crisis culminated in the assassination of Indira Gandhi on 31 October 1984, Doordarshan's prolonged display of the slain Prime Minister's body on the television screen made its own contribution to the fury let loose on Sikhs in Delhi during the ensuing days by anti-social elements. The hopes created by the conciliatory policy of accords pursued in the beginning by the new government headed by Rajiv Gandhi also proved short-lived. With the exit of V.P.Singh from the government on the issue of kick-backs received by Indians on Defence purchases from abroad, the ferocity and bitterness of political controversy attained new dimensions--and with it the manipulation of the electronic media.

The former Minister of Information & Broadcasting, H.K.L. Bhagat, had the effrontery to claim repeatedly that All India Radio and Doordarshan were adhering to the guidelines formulated by the Media Advisory Committee. The Committee itself is in hibernation, not having held a meeting for years. Misuse of the official media is among the issues which the non-Congress parties, under-represented in parliament over the years on account of our electoral system, have taken to the streets. This has resulted in the use of police force, and disruption of normal life which is detrimental to the development process.

(c) Meretricious Entertainment : Both political and commercial advertising aim at maximising audience size. The megalomania of the politician in power coincides with the commerical advertiser's lusting after expansion of the market for his product or service. Both want maximum exposure. Neither has qualms about the means employed for achieving it. They do not hesitate to appeal to the lowest denominator of popular taste in order to attract listeners and viewers. The mutually reinforcing combination of political and commercial advertising accounts for the vulgarisation of much of the entertainment offered by Doordarshan and of the advertisements carried by it.

Commenting on the heavy reliance of Doordarshan on the screeing of films and film-based programmes, the report of the Working Group on Doordarshan Software said:

> "Even worse than the third-rate feature films screened in full are the compilations from such films, many of which are a concentrated offering of love duets accompanied by obscene gestures and scenes of imbecile hero chasing imbecile heroine round bushes or down a city street, teasing and harassing and finally winning her. The compilers of Chitrahaar and similar song-and-dance sequences appear to think that it promotes national integration if they show, from different regions of India, a man and woman rolling over each other down a grassy slope, or allegedly 'folk' dancers swinging hip and bosom.
>
> "Unlike a pornographic book or journal read in privacy by an individual, or a lewd or sadistic film viewed by a person in the anonymity of the crowd in a darkened cinema hall, a film screened on television is often

> watched by three generations of a family. To watch these lewd scenes in a family group is highly embarrassing. It is unfortunate that most of the feature films and song-and-dance sequences telecast by Doordarshan reduce to repulsive public exhibition so private and precious an experience as the man-woman relationship. The objection is to vulgarity, and not to so-called permissiveness which has always existed in every society and entails relationships not sanctioned by a society's mores, specially the mores of the middle class which tends to be more prudish and hypocritical compared to working people or the very rich."

Nothing daunted, Doordarshan has gone on to offer its viewers more of the same fare. The Working Group's advice against sexist advertising has been similarly disregarded. The Working Group quoted with approval the remarks made on the subject by the Second Press Commission (on p.22 of its report). Noting that there had been an increasing tendency to exploit sex appeal, the Press Commission had said: "The exploitation of the female form in commercial advertising promotes the notion of women as sex objects and runs contrary to the news items and articles which many newspapers carry in support of treating women as equals and respecting their personality as individuals endowed with as much human worth as males. It is a pity that all the rhetoric in the country during and since the observance of 1975 as International Women's Year has had so little effect on advertisers and advertising agencies, and for that matter on editors and publishers." The Working Group commented wryly: "And, we may add, on those who direct Doordarshan at the level of the Kendra, the Directorate-General and the Government."

(d) Stoking the Fires of Consumerism : Besides vulgarising popular taste, Doordarshan is through its advertising promoting the self-regarding culture of consumerism. This culture desensitises the privileged members of the middle and upper classes to the mass poverty round them. It is antithetical to the socialism which was written into the Preamble of the Constitution in 1976 and which all political parties are now compelled to pay allegiance to--even if as hypocritically as the Congress (I).

Following are some quotations from Indira Gandhi on the adverse ethical consequences of promoting consumerism. Addressing a joint conference of officers of the Central Bureau of Investigation and of State anti-corruption agencies in New Delhi on 23 March 1981, she named the promotion of consumerism by the mass media first among the factors making for corruption: "The constant emphasis of the media on material goods, the vision of the comforts enjoyed in advanced societies, proliferation of regulations, the pressure of inflation, the breakdown of religious and ethical constraints, a general rise in permissiveness--all these contribute to increase in corruption."

In the course of the Raul Prebisch Lecture at Belgrade on 3 June 1983, Indira Gandhi spoke of the continuance of colonial education systems perpetuating the psychology of imitation, and said: "Educated persons view progress and development in terms of the level of goods and services they can command, and not the inherent self-reliant strength generated.in the economy. Transnational advertising arouses new desires which distort economic priorities, and lures people into artificial consumption patterns." Domestic advertising does the same.

Returning to the theme during her address to the United Nations General Assembly in New York on 28 September 1983, Indira Gandhi said: "In this age of instant globe-encircling information technology, the media dazzle eyes, and fill ears, with images and reports of affluence. Even the modest expectations of our peoples are far beyond our present means."

Unfortunately there was a mismatch between these perceptions of Indira Gandhi and her practice. It was during her prime ministership that TV commercials were inaugurated on 1 January 1976. Over the years, advertising has become a money-spinner as will be evident from the following figures:

Revenue from Doordarshan's Commercial Service.[15]

Year	(Gross, in Rs. crores)
1976-77	.77
1977-78	2.07
1978-79	4.97
1979-80	6.16
1980-81	8.08
1981-82	11.27
1982-83	15.89
1983-84	19.79
1984-85	31.43
1985-86	60.20
1986-87	98.31
1987-88	136
1988-89 (up to July)	54.14

Even in the case of the Press, which does not have its hand in the taxpayers' pocket and must pay its way through circulation and advertising revenue, the Second Press Commission had observed: "It was recognised that classified advertisements relating to employment, matrimony, housing and the like serve a useful function but a considerable part of display advertising was prodigal...The glossy magazines and the glossiest of advertisements in the Press--of jeans and soft drinks, cigarettes and cosmetics, air travel or entertainment in five-star hotels (not a few of them in the public sector)--are directed at the newly affluent and their children. We are of the view that the Press must address itself to the question of what contribution it is making to the strengthening of the moral fabric of society, and discouragement of the trend towards conspicuous and excessive consumption which a developing country can ill afford."

Citing these remarks with approval, the Working Group on Doordarshan Software said: "If privately published newspapers should address themsleves to the propriety of promoting consumerism in a developing country, surely Doordarshan which is subsidised by the taxpayers (including the millions who pay excise duties on matches, bidies and kerosene but have no access to television) also should...The social effects of commercials have to be considered. The advertising on Doordarshan is overwhelmingly of consumer goods and services which should, in the Indian context, be classified as luxuries."

Instead of Doordarshan relying less on advertisement revenue and more on licence fees on TV receiving sets, the opposite has been the case. While the price of the poor man's post-card has been trebled over the years, the annual licence fee for a telelvision set remained unchanged at Rs. 50 and was altogether abolished soon after the Working Group turned in its report. It is noteworthy that among the reliefs announced by the Union Finance Minister on 27 April 1989, in the higher imposts proposed in the Budget for 1989-90, were those relating to excise duties on TV receiving sets.

Whatever the moral cost to society, the purpose both of the political and commerical advertisers has been served by the entertainment and advertising policies pursued by Doordarshan. The number of TV receivers in the country rose from 6,76,615 licensed sets in 1977 to an estimated 132,56,000 in 1987. The level of increasing demand can be inferred from the following figures of the production of TV receiving sets in the country as estimated by the Department of Electronics:

(figures in millions)

	1986	1987	1988
B & W	2.15	3.20	4.40
Colour	0.85	1.10	1.30
Total	3.00	4.30	5.70

(e) **Sustained Plea for Autonomy : Requisite for the utilisation of the publicly owned electronic media for broad-based development is their** liberation from direct and day-to-day control by the Minister of Information & Broadcasting and his or her official minions. Equally necessary is the decentralisation of their operations so that they can become locally relevant and serviceable.

Advocacy of autonomy for the official media has a long history. It dates from the report given in April 1966 by a Committee on Broadcasting and Information Media, popularly known as the Chanda Committee. This committee was appointed when Indira Gandhi was Minister of Information & Broadcasting in the government headed by Lal Bahadur Shastri.

In those days of innocence, when political life had not become fiercely acrimonious, autonomy was advocated by the Chanda Committee on grounds of free play for creativity rather than of insulating radio and television and short films from misuse for partisan political purposes.

"It is not possible in the Indian context," the Chanda Committee's report said, "for a creative medium like broacasting to flourish under a regime of departmental rules and regulations. It is only by an institutional change that AIR can be liberated from the present rigid financial and administrative procedures of government." The Committee accordingly recommended the constitution of separate corporations for Akashvani and for Doordarshan, with the freedom to evolve their own methods of recruitment, scales of pay and conditions of service according to needs, and to devise a financial and accounting system appropriate to their creative activity.

The Cabinet considered this recommendation in December 1969. The date is significant. It was after the split in the Congress party from which Indira Gandhi emerged as leader, on a populist plank, of the majority faction. The government informed the Lok Sabha in April 1970 that "it was agreed that the present is not an opportune time to consider the conversion of the All India Radio into an autonomous corporation."

Came 1975 and the emergency. The All India Radio Code, formulated in 1967 and amended in March 1970, on both occasions with the Cabinet's approval, was scrapped--without the matter going to the Cabinet. The Code said, inter alia, that broadcasts on All India Radio would not permit "attack on a political party by name" or "hostile criticism of any State". The scrapping of the Code was decided at a meeting taken by the MInister of Information & Broadcasting, V.C. Shukla, who said that if the Prime Minister approved the action, it would not be necessary to go to the Cabinet. The Prime Minister noted on 4 May 1976: "The guidelines given to the broadcasters are now obsolete. Hence the Code should lapse. But I do not think that it is necessary to formally inform Parliament." Thus, though the Code had earlier been placed before parliament, the matter did not go either to the Cabinet or to parliament. This is recalled in the White Paper on Misuse of the Mass Media.

Voted to power in a surge of popular revulsion against the excesses committed by the authorities during the emergency, the Janata Party could have decided straightway to implement the recommendation of the Chanda Committee to liberate the publicly owned media from departmental control. L.K. Advani, who was Minister of Information & Broadcasting in the Janata government headed by Morarji Desai, has acknowledged that it was a mistake to have appointed another committee, with George Verghese as chairman--the Working Group on Autonomy for Akashvani and Doordarshan--instead of acting on the Chanda Committee's recommendation.

To the credit of the Verghese Group, it completed its work most expeditiously. Appointed on 17 August 1977, the Working Group turned in its unanimous report in February 1978. In addition to statutory autonomy for All India Radio, the Verghese Group envisaged the licensing, by the proposed National Broadcast Trust, of certain non-governmental institutions to set up local low-power stations: "In the first instance we would recommend that such broadcast franchise be limited to educational institutions, whether these be universities and colleges, Indian Institutes of Technology, agricultural universities and research stations, medical colleges, or other approved institutions which have an educational, extension or cultural orientation."

The Verghese Group did not stop with recommending a line of action. It gave the government the draft of the legislation necessary for giving effect to its recommendations, in the form of an Akash Bharati Bill, 1978, complete with a Statement of Objects and Reasons and a Financial Memoradum and a Memorandum regarding Delegated Legislation. Such workmanlike performance is rare on the part of committees formed bv the Government. However, following the break-up of the Janata Party,the Congress (Indira) was voted back to power and the Verghese Report was ignored.

Against this background, the Working Group on Software for Doordarshan did not repeat the plea for statutory autonomy. It suggested a restructuring of the I & B Ministry's secretariat to enable the Minister to receive policy advice from communication professionals rather than general administrators, and the formation of a National Doordarshan Council as a guardian of Doordarshan's functional and professional autonomy.

The first suggestion was put forward in the chapter on Information, in these words: "The I & B Ministry is structured on conventional lines with its officers 'dealing with' attached offices such as Doordarshan. The senior officers of the Ministry are drawn mostly from the Indian Administrative Service and allied services. They keep moving from one

Central Ministry to another, or between the Centre and the States and public undertakings. The year 1983 saw the exit of all three of the I & B Ministry's senior officers dealing with Doordarshan before completing even two years in the Ministry: the Secretary, who came from chairmanship of the Madhya Pradesh State Electricity Board and left to become Secretary of the Coal Department; Joint Secretary (Broadcasting), who was earlier Commissioner of a Division in Maharashtra and returned to that State as Managing Director of the State Finance Corporation; and Deputy Secretary (TV), who also came from district administration and left for a training course abroad. It is hardly to be expected that the problems of Doordarshan and its news wing can be appreciated and resolved by such birds of passage.

"Senior officials of a Ministry are expected to tender policy advice to the Minister, who in a democracy like ours is necessarily a generalist with a tenure of uncertain duration depending on the vicissitudes of politics and elections. We do not regard it as a satisfactory arrangement in a sensitive Ministry like I & B that the Minister should have to rely for policy advice on other generalists who serve in the ministry for brief periods.

"This is also the view of the Second Press Commission which submitted its report in April 1982. It noted that the running of the Central Information Service by the Ministry of I & B has not been satisfactory. Recruitment to the two levels of direct entry into the Servive was held in abeyance for nearly ten years during which a reorganisation of the Service was 'under consideration' in the Ministry.

"We endorse the recommendation of the Second Press Commission that the Ministry of I & B should be restructured on the lines of the Railway Board, with an Information Board comprising professional heads of media units, including Doordarshan, to tender policy advice to the Minister and with the secretariat of the Ministry attending only to financial and administrative matters."

The National Doordarshan Council envisaged by the Software Group was to include, among others, six to eight non-officials with an outstanding record of knowledge and experience in one or more of the areas of formal and non-formal education, the arts and literature, news and current affairs, conscientisation and mobilisation of women, agriculture and rural development, industry, science and technology, the organising of self-employed producers and workers in agriculture and industry, communication research and advertising, and sports. Three roles were seen for the Council, which was to meet at least each quarter under the presidentship of the Minister of I & B: "(i) as a body that rewiews and guides the organisation's performance; (ii) as a guardian of Doordarshan's functional and professional autonomy; and (iii) as a counterpart of the Press

Council for examining complaints of inaccuracy or bias in the reporting of news and comment on current affairs."

NOTES

1. Report in **The Hindustan Times**, New Delhi, 13 November 1947, quoted by P.C. Joshi in an article on 'Role of Local Radio' in **Communicator**, quarterly journal of the Indian Institute of Mass Communication, New Delhi, March, 1989.
2. Quoted by P.C. Joshi in an article on 'Culture, Communication and Social Change' in **Communicator**, October 1988.
3. At a seminar in New Delhi, jointly organised by the Press Institute of India and the India International Centre, on 17 February 1963.
4. **Fifty Years of Broadcasting,** All India Radio, New Delhi, 1978.
5. Sunil Misra, Director, Audience Research, All India Radio, placed the figure of radio sets in the country at not less than 80 million in a paper presented at a seminar in Bangalore on 11 July 1987.
6. **Second Five Year Plan**, Vol. II, p. 258.
7. **Broadcasting and the People** (pp. 109-110), National Book Trust, New Delhi, 1985.
8. *ibid.*, p. 52.
9. K. Anjaneyulu on 'Local Radio in India' in **Development Communication Report** (1989/1) published quarterly by the Clearinghouse on Development Communication, Arlington, Va., U.S.A.
10. 'Communication and Development: A Revaluation', **Communicator,** April 1977.
11. **Television in India** (p.12), Audience Research Unit, Doordarshan, New Delhi, October 1988.
12. **Broadcasting and the People,** p.46.
13. **An Indian Personality for Television**, Publications Division, New Delhi, March 1985.
14. **White Paper on Misuse of Mass Media,** Controller of Publications, Delhi, 1977.
15. **Television in India** (p. 34), October 1988.

Chapater VI

OTHER OFFICIAL MEDIA

Unlike radio and television which are Central government monopolies, other communication media are available to State governments also. But whether it is the short film (newsreel and documentary), print material or the traditional modes of communication, the primary aim of the State governments, too, is to publicise their achievements and intentions rather than to take relevant information to the rural poor as a weapon with which to overcome their poverty.

A typical State government journal is like a counterpart, in print, of a Doordarshan news bulletin--with the Chief Minister occupying the centre of the stage in place of the Prime Minister.

Urban and middle class bias is the other great limitation of development communication in the official sector. Even when, instead of publicising the government's achievements, an attempt is made to give practical guidance in the form of do's and dont's, the rural poor are most often beyond the offical communicator's mental horizeon. A DAVP folder, advising the expectant mother and her family on getting ready for the baby, recommends a perambulator and mosquito net among other things.

(i) Short Films: Urban and Centralised

The short films screened compulsorily in cinema houses throughout the country are close to, even if not quite, a Central government monopoly. The Films Division of the I & B Ministry with its headquarters in Bombay is a huge film production organisation that turns out every year about 125 documentaries and featurettes every year besides about 25 news magazines. These are released in dubbed versions in each of the dozen major languages of the country, multiple prints being made in each language for quick release in the theatrical circuit and supply to the field publicity units for non-theatrical screening. The Films Division also releases some short films made by the State governments, if they are found suitable politically and otherwise.

The annual report of the I & B Ministry for 1987-88 says: "Under the compulsory exhibition scheme, over 12,866 public cinema halls in India screen the Films Division's documentary films and news magazines in each show. It is estimated that about 100 million people see them in a week."

Urban bias renders many of FD's motivational films unsuitable for rural viewers, whether in fixed or mobile cinema theatres or in free screenings by field publicity units. A documentary on family planning, for instance, shows a father of six children standing pensively, smoking a cigarette, while the kids pester him for school fees and pocket money. When such a film is screened in a vaillage, the audience is likely to regard the father not as the harassed head of an unduly large family but as a rather lucky urbanite, draped in several yards of white clothing, who can afford cigarettes in contrast to the beedi or cheroot of the villager. Again, the depiction of over-crowded tenement-houses or suburban trains in the metropolises is unlikley to impress the villager as a warning against unchecked population growth. He is free of such problems.

Contralised production is the other great limitation of FD documentaries. They are made for all India, and addressed to no group of Indians in particular. A film made in one part of rural India may not evoke audience identification in another region. This writer once met a group of extension workers engaged in fertiliser promotion in the State of Andhra Pradesh. When asked whether they had audio-visual vans for screening films on the subject, they said yes, but the films were made in locations in Maharashtra and therefore did not click with Andhra Pradesh farmers. Maharashtra and Andhra Pradesh are not widely separated parts of the Indian Union but are adjoining States.

The language of the commentaries in the documentaries is often difficult for rural audiences to follow. The short films are dubbed in the correct literary form of the major languages of India, whereas villagers use the locally prevalent variant of a language. Hindi, for instance, is spoken in many distinctive forms such as Garhwali, Haryanvi, Rajasthani, Braj Bhasha and Chattisgarhi.

(ii) Printed Give-aways

Both the Central and State governments are lavish in the production of printed publicity material, much of it designed to project the image of the political leader for the time being in power. The Central government's Directorate of Advertising and Visual Publicity is a case in point. Presented in this section are the findings of an analysis made, in the course of the present study, of DAVP's budget for 1988-89, the print jobs undertaken by it, and the working of its mass mailing unit.

Of DAVP's budget (revised estimates) of Rs. 13.33 crores (Plan and non-Plan taken together), the largest allocation was for display and classified advertising in newspapers. It claimed Rs. 7.67 crores. Printed publicity comes next with an allocation of Rs. 80 lakhs. The greater part of 'distribution expenses', for which there is a provision of Rs. 30 lakhs, is on account of the mailing of print publicity material--pamphlets, folders, posters, the annual calender, etc. Also attributable to print publcity is about Rs. 10 lakhs, as charges for the hiring of casual labour by the distribution wing, out of the provision of Rs. 15 lakhs under 'other charges'. The total expenditure attributable to print publicity would therefore be Rs. 1.15 crores. Exhibitions account for Rs. 57 lakhs, radio spots for Rs. 40 lakhs and outdoor publicity (hoardings, cinema slides etc.) to Rs. 30 lakhs.

The print material brought out by DAVP is entirely for free distribution. It is divided into two categories: those items whose printing and distribution costs are met out of I & B Ministry's budget (Rs. 80 lakhs during 1988-89) and jobs undertaken on behalf of client ministries such as Health and Family Welfare (the biggest client), Income-tax, Customs, Handicrafts and Handlooms.

Speeches and statements by the Prime Minister account for more than 90% of the expenditure incurred on print publicity out of the I & B Ministry's budget. Among the nine print jobs executed during the three months from October to December 1988 the only items other than Prime Minister Rajiv Gandhi's speeches were a poster of Jawaharlal Nehru, a folder on Jawaharlal Nehru, and a booklet entitled 'Indira Gandhi: what she stood for' (with a combined print order of 200,00 in English and Hindi). The Prime Minister's speeches are usually brought out only in English and Hindi, with a print order of 60,000 and 40,000 respectively. The burden on the taxpayer would be much higher if they were published and distributed in all the other major Indian languages. Distribution costs have gone up considerably with the increase of the minimum rate for book-post from 50 paise to one rupee.

The targets for distribution of a given pamphlet or other item of print publicity are chosen, in the case of I & B Ministry titles, from out of the various categories in the list compiled by DAVP for mass mailing. Client ministries determine the targets in the case of material sponsored by them. The total number of addresses maintained in the mass mailing unit is about 15 lakhs, including about two lakh panchayats. The other categories include schools, cooperative societies, libraries, field publicity officers of the Central government, State governments' District Information Officers, and Block Development Officers. In practice five to ten copies of an I & B Ministry title go to categories like libraries, FPOs, DIOs and BDOs.

Since DAVP brings out print publicity literature--counting titles in each language separately--at the rate of almost one per working day, namely 225 in a year, there is a considerable strain on the distribution wing of DAVP--and a corresponding bonanza for the paper and printing trades. Given below is the normal pattern of production and distribution of the Prime Minister's speeches:

DAVP's Normal Pace

Subject	Date of speech	Date of Printing	Print order
1. Indira Gandhi's passion for India	19 Nov.1987	March 1988	60,000
2. Satyamurti as a dedicated patriot (Hindi)	21 Dec.1987	May 1988	40,100
3.Youth and national development (Hindi)	18 Jan.1988	May 1988	40,100
4.Transformation of Indian engineering industry	19 April 1988	Sept.1988	60,100
5.India's transformation into an industrial economy	7 June 1988	Sept.1988	60,100

During the election year of 1989 a spectacularly fast pace was achieved in putting out Prime Minister Rajiv Gandhi's speeches and statements. It entailed higher expenditure both on printing (by about 50%) and on distribution (by up to 75%, for hiring the extra casual labour needed to handle more copies per day.) Following is an illustrative list of the speedily handled print material:

DAVP's Pace during 1989

Subject	Date of speech	Date of printing	Date of distribution in Delhi*
1. New Initiatives (Lok Sabha speech on 'Punjab Package', global peace, etc.)	3 March 1989	March 1989	
2. Transforming the rural scene	25 March 1989	April 1989	
3. Thakkar Commission Report	10 April 1989	April 1989	22April 1989
4. Jawahar Rozgar Yojana	28 April 1989	April 1989	3May 1989
5. Panchayati Raj	5 May 1989	May 1989	19 May 1989
6. Successful launch of AGNI	22 May 1989	May 1989	1 July 1989
7. Towards a responsive and representative municipal administration	5 June 1989	June 1989	1 July 1989
8. Role of Media in projecting nation's growth	7 June 1989	June 1989	1 July 1989

***Given in this column are the dates on which the present writer received the pamphlets by book-post in Delhi.**

While massive expenditure is thus incurred on publicity for the Prime Minister through the free distriution of unpriced pamphlets, many Central Government reports giving information of great interest to students of current affairs are not put on sale and are therefore difficult to get at. Among the documents consulted in the course of this study which belong to the unpriced category are: Annual Reports of the various Central Ministries and departments; Approach to the Seventh Plan; Seventh Plan: Mid-Term Appraisal; Annual Plan: 1988-89; Women in India: a Statistical Profile 1988; National Perspective Plan for Women 1988-2000 A.D.; and National Policy on Education. A university teacher or student may not even become aware of the existence of these documents unles he comes across a reference in a newspaper report. After that he will find it difficult, specially at places outside Delhi and the State capitals where there may be no libraries on the free-mailing list of the government, to consult a copy unless he has a friend in a senior government position who can secure it for him. Not to place on sale official documents of public interest amounts to denial of information to the public.

(iii) Field Publicity

The central field publicity organisation is associated chiefly with the free screening of films. When the film van arrives, word usually goes round the village that the 'cinema babu' has come. His visit is generally welcome. A film show offers villagers a diversion from their daily grind.

It matters little whether they understand the commentary or get the message of the film. They are in the same position as those TV viewers who cannot follow a foreign sitcom or Shapespeare play but will not miss a minute of it. Images moving on the screen have for many a compelling fascination independent of meaning.

Another respect in which field publicity resembles Doordarshan is that the government makes similar grandiose claims regarding both, as great contributors to social education and development in rural India. In a mixture of deception and self-deception, every time a low power transmitter is installed in some remote part of the country to relay Delhi's telecasts, the Press Information Bureau solemnly announces the size of the population, urban and rural, that it will 'serve'. A press release of 16 September 1985 was headlined: 'Four more TV transmitters for tribal areas'. As if Doordarshan's network programmes are either comprehensible or relevant to the tribal people. The annual report of the Ministry of I & B for 1987-88 says: "Doordarshan has grown into one of the biggest networks in the world. Through its 238 transmitters, television has brought within its reach an estimated 72% of our population." The report says of the Directorate of Field Publicity: "It is the biggest rural-oriented publicty network in the country. It is the organisation that puts its men and material face-to-face with the people, reaches village panchayats in an informal manner, interprets the Government's policies and people's programmes in the people's own language/dialect and organises programmes keeping in view the area, audience and the occasion."

(a) Information Extension : The fact is that, most of the time, field publicity units screen centrally produced films and distribute centrally prepared print material which are not area specific. But it is true that field publicity, as an agency for information extension, tries to reach the rural population--or as much of it as 237 field units can reach, out of the five hundred million and more of India's rural population. Secondly, field publicity adds the dimension of inter-personal communication to the media material that it uses. A dedicated and imaginative field publicity officer can, through his remarks, supplement the message of a film and relate it to local circumstances.

Unlike the impersonal media discussed so far, the personnel of field publicity--like those of its sister organisation, the Song & Drama Division--come into face-to-face contact with their audience. The information extension work of field publicity, though it relies considerably on the materials of mass communication, entails inter-personal communication too. Since knowledge of the local language is essential for this purpose, an attempt was made in the early 1970's to recruit local personnel to work as Field Publicity Officers--and for that matter also for work as projector operators, drivers and cleaners--in the units located in tribal-inhabited border areas.

Between a quarter and a third of field publicity units have, over the years, been categorised as 'border' units. In their case the Directorate of Field Publicity had been authorised to make direct recruitment of Field Publicity Officers, instead of the posts having necessarily to be filled by members of the Central Information Service. Though this was intendned to facilitate the recruitment of persons knowing the local languages of the border areas, in practice the Directorate recruited as Border FPOs persons from Punjab, the Hindi-speaking States and West Bengal. They met the essential requirement of knowledge of "a border language". Posted at places like Mokokchung in Nagaland, Tawang in Arunachal Pradesh and Aizawl in Mizoram, they were totally ineffective as communicators and, moreover, became home-sick in the unaccustomed environment. So did the other staff of the field publicity units sent from outside to work in the north-east.

(b) Experiments in Localisation: For the first time in the early 1970's, the Directorate of Field Publicity conducted the recruitment of Naga graduates to work as FPOs in Nagaland, of Arunachalis to work in

Arunachal Pradesh, and of Mizos to work in and around Mizoram. In Kashmir Valley, similarly, a conscious attempt was made to recruit suitable persons from the majority (Muslim) community as FPOs and as part-time publicity assistants. There was, as was to be expected, a striking improvement in rapport and communication with audiences.

Localisation of personnel was not enough. It was necessary also to adapt the broad national messages to the local conditions and give information material a local flavour. This was attempted through the production of area-specific calendars, pamphlets and posters.

The most spectacular improvement in communication was achieved through localised films. Till then, field publicity units all over the country used to be supplied with prints, obtained without charge from the Films Division, of almost all documentaries and newsreels without prior screening to determine where a particular short film would be useful and of interest, and where it would be wasted. With the introduction of a system of pre-viewing before placing indents on a much reduced scale on the Films Division, that organisation responded readily to the request for production of area-specific films for utilisation by field publicity units. A reference is made to this by the Working Group on Doordarshan Software in its report (p. 43):

> "We have referred already to the Pij experiment in localised TV. Another and earlier instance is the production by the Films Division, at the instance of the Field Publicity Directorate, in the early' seventies, of a series of area-specific documentaries of about an hour's duration each, with commentary in the local dialect or language, for utilisation in the border areas. The aim of these films, which were based on conducted tours of small groups of people from border areas to places of historical, cultural and development interest in different parts of the country, was to enable people in the border areas to see the rest of India through the eyes of their own kith and kin. The first in the series of such films was 'Mizo Memoirs', of 60 minutes duration and with commentary in Lushai. Its screening in Mizoram evoked, we were told, enthusiastic response and repeated applause from the audience--quite different from the reaction to the usual run of Films Division documentaries which are made for audiences in all parts of India and no part in particular. Similar was the experience with localised films, designed to promote national integration, which were made for and screened in Arunachal Pradesh, Nagaland, the Kashmir Valley and the Lakshadweep Islands."

(iv) Use of Traditional Modes

The First Plan had suggested that development messages should be "carried into every home in the language and symbols of the people...with the assitance of creative writers and artists which has to be specially enlisted." What can be closer to the 'language and symbols of the people' than such traditional modes of communication as the songs of the bauls in Bengal, the Tatwalu sung by minstrels in Andhra, Jatra and Nautanki, Bhajan and Qawwali, Tamasha and Yakshagana, Ottam Thullal and Villupattu, Harikatha and Burrakatha--all combining ethics with aesthetics, education with entertainment?

The singing of patriotic songs, and the staging of anti-imperialist plays even if disguised by parallels from earlier Indian history, played an important part in mobilising nationalist sentiment during the freedom struggle. The communists in the Andhra region employed Burrakatha, the locally popular form of stylised and dramatic narration, in the 1940's to put across their messages. But in the context of the Five Year Plans the emphasis has been on expansion of the mass media in imitation of Western communication models. Utilisation of the traditional forms of communication in rural areas has been confined to occasional performances by departmental troupes of the Centre's Song & Drama Division and its State counterparts, or by private professional parties screened and registered by these government agencies. They have no doubt done commendable work. It is heart-warming to read in the I & B Ministry annual report for 1987-88 that the Song & Drama Division "organised cultural rallies in Punjab where masses joined the artistes and sang the song, 'Khud jiyo auron ko bhi jiney do' ('live and let live')." However, such visits by troupes from outside can but scratch the surface of the vast rural audience. It will be next to impossible, not to speak of the expense, to organise message-oriented performances at frequent intervals in each cluster of villages in the country.

Ideally, the extension personnel of the development departments should locate, establish rapport with and persuade resident practitioners of the traditional media in each group of villages to perform frequently at nominal remuneration. This will require a high level of motivation on the part of the extension workers, and ability to get the village composer-singer or other artist to internalise the meassage and give it creative expression. This is rather much to expect.

If radio and television had been expanded at the district level, primarily for area-specific communication on a decentralised basis, and if both had been made accessible to the rural poor through community listening and viewing, it would have been possible to utilise the traditional modes through these modern media. Traditional forms being highly specific to each cultural region even within linguistic States and within the Hindi zone, and development information itself having to be area-specific, mass media programmes using traditional forms will have to be made and delivered on a decentralised basis. This is ruled out by the urban-elistist pattern of growth of the electronic media.

However, as political parties have demonstrated during recent elections, there is immense scope for utilising modern communication technology in the non-broadcast mode, through audio cassettes and video films. These can be used to convey development messages through traditional modes of expression, racy to the soil, both by official agencies and by voluntary organisations.

PART 3

As Communication, So Development

In contrast to elitist communication which buttresses the status quo stands consciousness-raising communication. It serves to widen, deepen and democratise the development process. Consciousness-raising communication is practised by a section of the non-governmental mass media, by some exceptional individuals in the official agencies of extension and information, and by voluntary social activists. For the voluntary worker, communication is not a career but part of his or her engagement in social action as the result of conviction and commitment. Action-related communication helps the common people to improve their conditions of life through their own co-operative effort as well as by bringing pressure on the authorities to implement laws and programmes such as those relating to land reforms and minimum wages, adult education, and assistance for self-employment.

Chapter VII

NON-OFFICIAL MEDIA : DIVERSE VOICES

The Second Press Commission noted with appreciation what it described as a 'conspicuous feature' of the Indian Press-- "the great diversity of opinion expressed in newspapers, a diversity that should be expected on the part of a free Press in a democratic country ... There can be no single voice of the Press in a free society. It has to be a conversation involving many voices, reflecting the needs and interests of different sections of society. Variety of ownership and opinion is the test of a free Press."[1]

(i) The Press and Development

The eleven members of the Commission were deeply divided, seven against four, on issues pertaining to newspaper ownership and the propriety or otherwise of governmental intervention in newspaper economics. But they were at one in paying a handsome tribute to the role played by the Press in relation to development. "It is to the credit of the Indian Press", the Commission's report said, "that, despite its predominantly urban and middle class moorings, it has evinced interest in the problems of farmers, agricultural workers, artisans, tribal groups and other sections of the rural population. Though, judged by readership or by ownership, it is not necessary for most of our newspapers to highlight the issues of poverty, the Press has made a major contribution by reminding readers of those who live below the poverty line and giving the ruling middle and upper classes a feeling of guilt.

"Many newspapers have, from time to time, drawn attention to such matters concerning the weakest sections of society as non- enforcement of mimimum wages and the failure to revise them to keep pace with the fall in the purchasing power of the rupee; the persistence of bonded labour despite its abolition by law, or its emergence in a new guise as contract labour; the generation of black money and its use, frequently entailing the involvement of corrupt officials and politicians, etc. Such creditable instances deserve wide emulation."[2]

(a) Local Press : a Bhopal Study : An analysis was made during the present study of the contents of four newspapers that are published from Bhopal and circulate in Madhya Pradesh. The newspapers are: *Nav Bharat, Dainik Bhaskar* and *Nai Duniya* in Hindi, and *Madhya Pradesh Chronicle* in English. The issues dated 1 to 9 June,1988, were examined. The wealth of news and analysis of local problems which the newspapers carried was incomparably greater than what All India Radio could offer in its regional news bulletins and talks. The question of local coverage by Doordarshan did not arise. Till the time of the present study the TV transmitter at Bhopal was linked exclusively with Delhi. Bhopal is among the thirty places where studio facilities were to have been provided under the Seventh Plan. These facilities had not been established till the end of June 1989.

The State was reeling under drought, which therefore figured prominently in the news as well as editorial comment. It is noteworthy that the newspapers carried both the reports of the administration's efforts to relieve suffering by providing drinking water, and complaints voiced by the people. In the latter category was a news agency report of the non-energising of a tube-well in village Chilwani in the Vijayapur tehsil of Morena district, resulting in what might have been the avoidable death of nine children, ranging in age from one to nine, because of thirst. A denial of this report was also carried; the denial attributed the deaths to measles. Also highlighted was a report about the municipal authorities distributing stamped postcards to residents in colonies served by tankers carrying drinking water, inviting them to report whether the tankers were arriving with the full supply of water or only half or less, and also whether the tankers came at the scheduled time.

A defect noticed was that many news items did not mention the source. For example, while the report of the death of children from thirst was credited to the UNIVARTA news agency which in turn identified its source, the denial--which was apparently from the State administration--was not sourced.

Numerous other subjects of local interest besides the drought situation were covered. These included publicity puffs, like 'Remarkable progress by Improvement Trust' of Itarsi, and 'State to have more vet hospitals by 1990' (in *Madhya Pradesh Chronicle*) as well as reports critical of the administration, such as "Roaring business in 'pan masalas' under different brand names."

National and international news was carried by the newspapers in addition to the coverage of problems of local interest. An interesting item concerned Doordarshan. It reported the findings of a survey of public reactions to Doordarshan news bulletins, carried out by Ms. Sura Roade, Sub-Divisional Officer (Revenue), Dhar, for her examination in the journalism course conducted by the Devi Ahilya University, Indore.

The survey, which was carried out in the Dhar and Indore districts showed that 92% of television viewers think the Doordarshan news bulletins are biased, while 94% favoured an autonomous status for Doordarshan. Fifty-five out of the hundred people surveyed said the signature tune before and after every newscast was quite 'un-Indian' and wanted a more melodious tune. Thirty liked the present tune, while 15 expressed no opinion.

(b) Pressures on the Press: Devoting a whole chapter of its report to Pressures on the Press, the Second Press Commission in listing the sources of pressure referred first to: "Physical attacks on the editor or the offices of the newspaper or its employees by mobs feeling aggrieved by the publication of particular items of news or views in a newspaper, or by mobs incited against a newspaper by political groups." Since 1982 when the Commission gave its report, the tragic developments in Punjab and in Kashmir Valley have underlined the threat to feedom of the Press from gun- wielding fanatics, and the government's imperative duty to maintain law and order.

Government itself was acknowledged as one of the sources of pressure on the Press "through selective and politically motivated exercise of powers under the law, or through extra-legal actions such as discrimination in the selection of newspapers for advertisements and/or in the rates fixed for such advertisements." To aviod bias in the choice of newspapers, the Commission recommended that the handling of government advertisements should be taken away from DAVP and entrusted to an autonomous corporation in the public sector. This recommendation was not accepted by the Government. An 'action taken' report on the recommendations of the Second Press Commission, laid on the table in parliament on 14 May 1986, said: "The working of an autonomous corporation in the public sector cannot ensure greater impartiality, rationality and objectivity than the Government." This is of a piece with the unwillingness of the Indira Gandhi and Rajiv Gandhi governments to let radio and television be run by autonomous corporations.

Government's direct handling of the electronic media has been, over the years, a potential source of pressure on the Press. All India Radio happens to be the largest single media contributor to the revenue of Press Trust of India and United News of India, the country's two main news agencies. AIR's payment for its use of the services of the agencies in its news bullletins is several times the amount of subscription paid by the largest of newspaper groups in the country. It was the threat to discontinue AIR's subscription which brought the news agencies to their knees during the internal emergency of 1975-76. They had no option but to agree to merge themselves in the government-sponsored 'Samachar' news agency. Since newspapers rely to a very large extent on the news agencies for the staple of news, governmental pressure on the news agencies can be a threat to Press freedom.

In normal times it is not necessary for the Government to go so far as to threaten discontinuance of AIR's subscription to news agency services. By reducing the scale of payment, or offering to pay more, the government can influence the way in which the news agencies treat news items bearing on the image and interests of those for the time being in power. An autonomous AIR and Doordarshan cannot easily be used in that way to twist the arms of the news agencies. The Press as a whole and the news agencies thus have a vital stake in the insulation of the electronic media from manipulation by the Government.

The Press, for its part, needs to guard against becoming so partisan in its muck-raking and opinion-building campaigns as to miss the distinction between news and views. Some newspapers have tended to become participants in, rather than critical observers and analysts of, the power game in which rival princes of the State, at the Centre or in the States, ally themselves with competing captains of industry and landed interests. Of interest in this connection is the advice which Jawaharlal Nehru gave while addressing the All India Newspaper Editors' Conference at Allahabad on 16 February 1946: "A newspaper must, whatever its views might be, maintain a certain integrity about the news. It must give all the news worthy of being given, and without any distortion."

(c) Economism: The Enemy Within: The concluding paragraph of the chapter on Pressures, in the Second Press Commission's report, is significant. The Commission says that the Press "should be able to resist not only external pressure but also inducements which would undermine its independece from within. Journalists should be on guard against the temptation to enjoy favours, whether from Government authorities, employers, advertisers or others."[3]

As an example of the enjoyment of undue favour from the government, the Commission refers to the case of those journalists in Bhopal who stayed in government accommodation at concessional rent and were in heavy arrears, with the government not bothering to collect even the concessional rent. Apart from such individual instances, there is a disturbing ambivalence in the attitude of journalists' organisations towards the Government. On the one hand, they want no curbs on the freedom of expression. When the Defamation Bill was introduced in 1988, they joined hands with newspaper publishers and editors, and with leading public figures concerned at the threat to Press freedom, in a massive protest movement which made Prime Minister Rajiv Gandhi drop the Bill. On the other hand, the organisations of journalists want the Government to intervene in their favour by modifying the awards of tribunals constituted from time to time since parliament passed the Working Journalists (Conditions of Service) Act in 1955. Members of no other profession and workers of no other industry in the private sector enjoy the benefit of such periodic improvement of salaries, perquisites and working conditions. The latest demand is for governmental intervention to enforce a scheme of pension for journalists. They also want that the Government's decision modifying in their favour the final award of the latest tribunal headed by Justice Bachawat should be put into the Ninth Schedule of the Constitution to protect it from challenge in the courts. They want all this, and freedom too.

(ii) Feature Films

In terms of the number of feature films produced each year, the Indian film industry is the biggest in the world. It is foremost among the mass media in the country as a source of entertainment, directly in cinema halls and indirectly through the film songs broadcast extensively by All India Radio and the films and film-based programmes telecast regularly by Doordarshan.

(a) Mixed Bag of Values: Entertainment is not value free. There are certain values implicit even in a film--or other programme on the stage, radio or television--whose ostensible purpose is nothing beyond entertainment. It is a mixed bag of values that are promoted by Indian films.

The Working Group on Doordarshan Software observes in its report: "The output of the Indian feature film industry is as large as its quality is uneven. The output includes films with a patriotic or social reform message conveyed competently and with aesthetic appeal. There are others which offer clean and healthy entertainment. But there are a very large number which are made to a formula of sentimentality, melodrama, violence and sex. They are an assault on aesthetic sensibility, and have a vulgarising and brutalising effect on viewers. It is a surprise that such films should get past the censors, and a greater surprise that Doordarshan should choose to screen them."[4]

(b) Stars in Political Wars: Much before Ronald Reagan became President of the U.S.A., Tamil Nadu began to have Chief Ministers who entered politics after attaining popularity with film-goers as script-writers (C.N. Annadurai and M. Karunanidhi) or actors (M.G. Ramachandaran). Some of the latter's fans were so frenzied in their devotion that they committed suicide when M.G. Ramachandran fell seriously ill and was flown to the U.S.A. for treatment, and several more when he eventually died.

It is no wonder that political party managers have found it profitable to flatter popular film personalities, dead or alive. M.G. Ramachandran's death came on the eve of the elections to the Tamil Nadu State Assembly in January 1989, in which the Congress (I) hoped to stage a come-back. The country was stunned when the President of the Republic, acting on the constitutionally binding advice of Prime Minister Rajiv Gandhi who was also president of the Congress (I), conferred posthumously on M.G.R. the nation's highest honour, the award of Bharat Ratna.

Earlier, in 1984, Rajiv Gandhi drafted into politics his close friend Amitabh Bachhan, the matinee idol. This was in order to pit him against H.N. Bahuguna in the parliamentary constituency of Allahabad in Uttar Pradesh during the Lok Sabha elections of December that year. The film star, popular on account of his good looks and love scenes, fight scenes and buffoonery, trounced his rival, an experienced politician who had served as Chief Minister of Uttar Pradesh.

Other stars who have been drafted into political wars include R.K. Govil, who played Rama in the cinematic and immensely popular TV serialisation of the Indian epic Ramayana. Congress (I)'s Govil was countered by the opposition front during 1989 with another popular film actor, Raj Babbar.

NOTES

1. Report of Second Press Commission, Vol. I, p. 19.
2. ibid., p. 20.
3. ibid., p. 66.
4. Report of Working Group on Software for Doordarshan, p.159.

CHAPTER VIII

INTER-PERSONAL COMMUNICATION

(i) Official Sector : Extension Personnel

The agricultural and health extension services have made a signal contribution to the increase in agricultural production and improvement in average expectation of life over the period of planned development since independence.

a) Combining Service with Advice : Qualified and trained extension workers, unlike persons engaged in communication per se, not only offer advice but render a service or practical guidance and demonstration. The service dimension of their activity makes their counsel more acceptable than it would otherwise be.

Foreign Christian missionaries working in India knew this. While travelling on their proselytising mission through the tribal tracts of the north-eastern region, for example, they would invariably carry a medicine chest and treat simple ailments. It was after a long and painful experience of failure that the family planning authorities in post-independence India learnt the truth about communication linked with practical service that the Christian missionaries knew.

In May 1972 the Department of Family Planning constituted a Study Group, with the present writer as chairman, to advise on improved utilisation of the mass education and extension staff of family planning at the district and lower levels. We found that the Family Planning Health Assistant, who was the peripheral male family planning functionary expected to work in coordination with the Auxiliary Nurse-Midwife, had come to be regarded as the weakest link. In some States there were moves to terminate the services of a large number of FPHAs for failing to achieve even a small fraction of the targets of sterilisation assigned to them.

After examining the reasons, the Study Group came to the conclusion that the category of FPHA should be mended rather than ended. The reasons for his failure were various. In the first place, though he was designated as a Health Assistant, there was no health function whatever in his job description. Secondly, the qualification prescribed was only 'middle-pass' (8th standard) though he was expected, among other things, "to carry out family survey, prepare eligible couples' register...to coordinate the work of family planning with activities of Village Level Workers, Panchayat Secretaries, Auxiliary Nurse Midwives, Block Health Workers, etc., and mobilise the support of community organisations by participating in their meetings..." Thirdly, many of the 13,500

FPHAs in position were virtually untrained. Finally, the responsibility given to him of covering a population of 20,000 was too heavy, specially where the density of population is low and the terrain difficult.

In addition to upgradation of the minimum qualification from middle-pass to matriculation, corresponding increase in scale of pay, and training of all those in position followed by weeding out of those found unsuitable at the end of the training, the Study Group recommended in the report given by it in December 1972:

(i) Change of designation from FPHA to Family Welfare Worker (this was much before the name of the Department itself was changed from Family Planning to Family Welfare) in view of the new functions proposed by the Study Group: "This will more truly correspond to the revised functions which are not confined to family planning but include education for family welfare; inculcation of the value of educating children (specially girls) and deferring the age of marriage; nutrition; personal and environmental hygiene."

(ii) FPHA should be trained and equipped to render first-aid and treat common ailments, which would enable him to establish rapport with the families he visits: "The principal reasons for the poor performance of FPHA include the fact that he has nothing to offer to the people except the message of family planning."

(iii) "Since FPHA will have to hold public meetings, it will greatly facilitate his work if he is provided with a transistorised megaphone and a relatively inexpensive means of purposeful entertainment in the form of a cassette tape-recorder containing music (including songs on family planning) carefully selected from the point of view of local appeal from out of All India Radio recordings as well as special recordings that should be arranged by the Block Extension Educator and the District Extension Educator."

(b) Role in Agriculture and Health : Unlike the poor FPHA of old, extension workers in agriculture and in the health programmes, both preventive and curative, have generally combined the ability to render service with the giving of advice. The increase in the production of foodgrains from about 50 million tonnes at the time of independence to more than 140 million tonnes in 1986-87 owes a great deal to the agricultural extension personnel from the block to the village level. Similarly the health extension network has contributed substantially to the increase in the average expectation of life at birth from about 32 to more than 54. During 1985-86, as many as 27,700 doctors were working at Primary Health Centres and at allopathic dispensaries in rural areas. The para-medical manpower in rural areas during the same year included 95,600 Auxiliary Nurse Midwives and Health Workers (female). The contribution made by extension work to development, compared to that of the mass media, suggests that in the circumstances of a largely agrarian and poor country like India, people in the next village are better reached by foot and spoken with face to face, than by aduio and visual signals broadcast terrestrially or via satellite.

Extension work has its own problems, however. In some areas where qualified pesonnel are not locally available for recruitment, the language barrier affects person-to-person communication. On a visit to Rajasthan with the Study Team on family planning communication, the present writer found that a large percentage of the Auxiliary Nurse midwives were drawn from the far-away Kerala State. These young women knew Hindi but not its locally spoken variant. They said they could make themselves understood, but could not follow what the local women told them in Rajasthani.

In family planning, as in other spheres of development communication, it is necessary to relax educational standards to the extent necessary to enable the recruitment of local personnel for work at the village level. The lag in formal education or prior training can be made good through intensive functional training after recruitment and before they are put to work.

(ii) Voluntary Workers

The field work undertaken in Madhya Pradesh as part of the present study included interviews with many experts and change agents as well as intended beneficiaries in the field of health, in the districts of Vidisha and Hoshangabad. These discussions brought out some fundamental differences in the approach of the government system in Vidisha and of the health care project of Kishore Bharati, a voluntary organisation, that is in operation alongside the government system in Hoshangabad district.

In the government system, priorities are set by policy makers sitting far away in the national capital, and to a lesser extent by those at the State capital. Local problems and needs do not dictate the priorities, as they do in the case of the voluntary organisation whose project directors are themsleves the policy-makers. A doctor at a Primary Health Centre said, for instance, that the crying local needs in the area of health were village sanitation and the provision of safe drinking water. But these were not at the top of the agenda of policy makers at the national level. To them, family planning and the eradication or control of communicable diseases were what mattered most.

The attitudes and beliefs of the rural people, who are overwhelmingly illiterate, need to be changed before there can be a significant improvement in sanitation and health. Interviews with patients and with health workers conducted as part of the present study showed that most village people are yet to realise the danger of leaving roti or other food exposed, and the need to cover over with earth the children's excrement after they have defecated. They do not know that flies that have sat on the faeces can infect the exposed food.

Many villagers still believe that diseases are due to the wrath of God. They first try to get over the disease by appeasing a local deity. Only after several days do they go to the nearest available health centre or private doctor. Often the delay aggravates the disease. Again, many are so poor that they cannot afford the expense of taking the patient to a health centre or doctor.

These basic needs of social education, literacy and economic improvement are outside the ken of the health programme in the government system.

In the voluntary sector, a health team goes round the villages on periodic visits, and the local volunteer notifies the health centre in case of urgent need. The idea of a trained health worker at village level, drawn from the village community, was first conceived as part of the community health and rural development project at Jamkhed in the Ahmadnagar district of Maharashtra. Dr. R.S.Arole, pioneer of the Jamkhed project, said in an interview in the course of the present study that a local advisory committee was formed with representatives of all segments of the population: women, Harijans, political parties, and minority communities. This helped to strengthen local cooperation and participation. Kishore Bharati adopted from Jamkhed the idea of training a health worker, preferably a woman, drawn from within the village. The project director, Dr. Meera Sadgopal, said that as women, the landless poor, and Harijans were most in need of health care, it was best to secure volunteers from these groups.

Targets set from above dominate the life and work of health personnel in the government sector. This is because their performance is evaluated in terms of the degree of fulfilment of those targets. Voluntary workers, on the other hand, are free to work at their own pace. They do not try to push people into accepting a new practice. They do not preach or prescribe behaviour, but seek to bring about change in desirable directions through patient discussion and dialogue. This inter-personal communication provides constant feedback which the government system lacks, and which it does not in the first place seek. The friendly attitude of change agents in the voluntary sector makes a great difference to the response from the illiterate rural poor. The information material used by voluntary workers is locally prepared, relevant to local needs, and easily intelligible.

A striking contrast was thus found between the contrally directed government system and the area-oriented approach of the voluntary sector to development in the field of health. There was a corresponding difference in the approach to and practice of communication. In the government sector, communication was part of official duty along lines laid down from above. For Kishore Bharati workers, communication was part of their engagement in voluntarily undertaken social action. It was part of interaction with the rural community, and meant talking with the village people and not talking at them.

PART 4

An Agenda for Renewal

What can be done to correct the course of development and of related communication, so as to bring them in line with the Gandhi-Nehru vision that prevailed during the freedom movement and in the early years of independence?

CHAPTER IX

RECASTING PUBLIC POLICIES

The remedies are implicit in the survey, in the foregoing Chapters, of the public policies that have fomented separatism, and of the elitist, centralised and urban bias of planned development and of officially organised communication.

(i) Countering Separatism

During the colonial period, the British rulers of India deliberately fomented social divisions on the basis of religion, caste or ethnic origin in order to buttress their rule. After independence, ironically, the temptation for political parties to gain votes by pandering to feelings of separate and special identity has resulted in the continuance of socially divisive policies. Most of the political parties have, in their pursuit of power, not hesitated to appeal for votes in the name of religion, caste, language or ethnic origin. A notable exception to casteism is the Communist Party of India (Marxist). West Bengal, ruled for many years by a coalition headed by the CPI (M), is the only state in the country not to have made any special provisions in educational institutions and public employment on a caste basis for what are called the Other Backward Classes. It has preferred to adopt the economic approach to the removal of social inequalities.

Even as the CPI (M) is opposed to a caste-based approach to the problem of social backwardness, the Bharatiya Janta Party--which the CPI (M) denounces as 'Hindu-communal'--opposes a religion-based approach to social, economic or political problems and favours instead a generalised approach based on citizenship rights. The following extracts from a statement of the BJP's position by L.K. Advani[1] are informative, and raise issues which call for thoughtful consideration:

> "The BJP is an ideological party which has a distinct approach to several matters. On some issues, it is practically a loner, even though among the people these issues command wide support. Thus the BJP is today the only political party in the country which holds that Article 370 of the Constitution, which confers a special status on Jammu & Kashmir State, ought to be scrapped. We regard this provision as a big barrier in the psychological integration of the State with the rest of the country...
>
> "Whenever my senior colleague, Mr. Vajpayee, raised this issue of Article 370 in Parliament, Pandit Nehru would invariably reply that a gradual erosion of the Article[2] was taking place and in course of time the Article would go. Early in 1964 a discussion took place in the UN Security Council in which, on behalf of Pakistan, Mr. Bhutto urged that 'the Security Council should interdict India from carrying on further integration'. Soon after, Minister of Education M.C. Chagla made a speech in the Rajya Sabha (24 February 1964) in the course of which he made this observation: 'The Prime Minister (Pandit Nehru) the other day spoke of the gradual erosion of Article 370 of the Constitution. I only hope that the erosion is accelerated and I also hope that very soon that Article will disappear from the Constitution of India. After all, it is transitional and temporary. I think the transitional period has been long enough...'
>
> "The BJP's stand on the question of the Minorities Commission is yet another matter which our critics glibly dub as 'communal'. The Janata Party manifesto of 1977 had promised a Civil Rights Commission which was to deal with infringement of civil rights of any individual or group, irrespective of whether the victim or victims belong to the majority or to the minority. The Janata Government erred when it deviated from this commitment

and instead of a Civil Rights Commission, set up a Minorities Commission.

"The error would only be compounded if, as is being suggested by some parties today, this Commission is elevated to constitutional status. The BJP is strongly opposed to this and regards the proposal as an example of crass electoral opportunism. Instead, the BJP would like to see the Minorities Commission replaced by a Human Rights Commission.

"It may surprise many to know that a similar proposal was strongly made to the National Integration Council by none other than Justice M.H. Beg, then Chairman, Minorities Commission. Justice Beg observed: 'Naming Commissions as being meant for minority communities etc. is by itself misleading and encourages divisiveness.'

"Justice Beg went on to suggest, instead, the setting up of a 'National Integration-cum-Human Rights Commission for the Promotion of Secular Traditions and National Integration'. He argued: 'If separate electorates were politically disastrous and joint electorates preferable, is the suggestion of a common means of meeting all complaints of discrimination, similary, not a better method of emphasising the common interests of all in the removal of discrimination?'

"These days whenever the BJP speaks about the above two issues, or suggests that Article 44 be implemented and that there be a uniform civil code for all citizens, we are accused of playing the Hindu card. The fact is that the BJP stand on these issues is prompted by national interest, and, generally speaking, those who oppose it are actuated by sordid electoral expediency."

Prior to independence, Jawaharlal Nehru regarded economic restructuring as the basic remedy for social backwarness. Discussing the problem of Harijan emancipation in the course of his presidential address at the Lucknow Congress on 12 April 1936, he said: "For a socialist it presents no difficulty, for under socialism there can be no such differentiation or victimisation. Economically speaking, the Harijans have constituted the landless proletariat, and an economic solution removes the social barriers that custom and tradition have raised." By the same reasoning, a socialist transformation of the economy would remove the backwardness of other backward castes and ethnic groups. But Nehru went along, while the Constitution was being framed, with a two-pronged policy of reservations-- political, and socio-economic. The political aspect of the reservation policy, which has caused little controversy or social tension, consists of the reservation of seats in the State and national legislatures for the Scheduled Castes and Scheduled Tribes. The reservation is limited in terms of both size and duration. What has proved controversial and even explosive is the blanket sanction accorded by the Consitution for special provisions in the social and economic spheres in favour not only of the Scheduled Castes and Scheduled Tribes but Other Backward Classes. These special provisions have in practice taken the form of reservations in admission to educational institutions and in public employment. The special provisions are left to executive discretion, without the requirement of legislation. The are without a time limit, and in many cases without a means test such as would confine the special treatment to the poor and economically deserving.

(a) **On Minorityism : Amrit Kaur, M.C. Chagla:** Rajkumari Amrit Kaur, herself belonging to the religious minority of Christians, said in a memorandum to the sub-committee on minorities of the Constituent Assembly's advisory committee on fundamental rights: "The primary duty of the committee appointed to look into the problem of minorities is to suggest such ways and means as will help to eradicate the evil of separatism, rather than expedients or palliatives which might, in the long run, only contribute to its perpetuation...Privileges and safeguards really weaken those that demand them. They are a definite bar to unity, without which there can be no peace, as also to efficiency without which the standards of good governance are lowered...In order to ensure maximum efficiency, it should be a sine qua non that promotion shall be only and strictly according to merit.

"Axiomatically there is no reason why the interests of any individual or community should not be safe in the hands of a good person or persons, irrespective of their personal religion. Rather than say for how long any safeguards are necessary, I would plead with the minorities to say that the necessity for safeguards should only be considered after a period of, say, five or seven years, if their trust in the majority communities has, in this interval, been proved to be wholly unjustified." Rajkumari's advice was disregarded.

The reservation policy has not generated conflict in respect of general education up to the higher secondary or even graduate level. But it has stirred up social tensions in the context of admission to institutions of higher education and training, in medicine and engineering particularly, which are highly subsidised from public revenue and in which the availability of seats is severely limited in relation to the demand. In public employment, there is not much opposition to the reservation of quotas in favour of the S.C. or S.T. or O.B.C. at the stage of initial recruitment. However, the out-of-turn promotion of members of these groups is fiercely resented.

Deploring a socially divisive instead of economic approach to problems, Jawaharlal Nehru said in the course of one of his fortnightly letters to the Chief Ministers of States, in September 1962, following the general elections held early that year to the Lok Sabha and the State Assemblies: "It amazes me that some people in this age of swift transition should still cling to ideas which have no relevance today; should be attracted to communalism and provincialism; and should be powerfully influenced by caste. It is distressing that elections should turn on caste and communal aspects...Many of our opposition parties, and sometimes even the Congress, approached the electorate in a narrow way."

Like Rajkumari Amrit Kaur, another distinguished member of a minority community, Muhammad Currimbhoy Chagla who served as Chief Justice of the Bombay High Court and a member of the Union Cabinet, was against minorityism. He wrote in 1973: "I have often strongly disagreed with the government policy of constantly harping upon minorities, minority status and minority rights. It comes in the way of national unity, and emphasises the differences between the majority community and the minority. Of course, it may serve well as a vote-catching device to win Muslim votes, but I do not believe in sacrificing national interests in order to get temporary party benefits such as getting a few more seats.

"The Congress government has also often followed what I can only call the old British policy of communalsim. In my view, if it is communalism to pass over and ignore a man with merit simply because he happens to be a Muslim or a Christian or a Parsi, it is also communalism to appoint a person merely because he happens to be a Muslim or a member of some other minority community. It is injurious to the interests of the minorities themselves to have posts and offices filled by men who have no merit, merely because they want representation in high offices. The minorities come to expect that they will get certain posts whether the men deserve to get them or not. It is much better that they learnt to work hard and deserve the post

"When I am told that there is no minority representation in any particular post, I often ask the question: Is there any deserving person who has been passed over? If so, it is injustice, and we must fight against it. But if there is no deserving person, then to clamour for a post is really to be communal. And to yield to the clamour is also to betray a communal spirit. It amounts to a reproduction of the bad old days and of discredited British policies.

"Consider the attitude of the Government to the question of a uniform civil code. Although the Directive Principles of the State enjoin such a code, Government has refused to do anything about it on the plea that the minorities will resent any attempt at imposition; unless they are agreeble it would not be fair and proper to make the law applicable to them. I wholly and emphatically disagree with this view. The Constitution is binding on everyone, majority and minority, and if the Constitution contains a directive, that directive must be accepted and implemented.

"Jawaharlal showed great strength and courage in getting the Hindu Reform Bill passed, but he accepted the policy of laissez faire where the Muslims and other minorities were concerned. I am horrified to find that, in my country, while monogamy has been made the law for the Hindus, Muslims can still indulge in the luxury of polygamy. It is an insult to womanhood; and Muslim women, I know, resent this discrimination between Muslim women and Hindu women."[3]

Justice S. Ranganathan, sitting Judge of the Supreme Court, said in the course of the Dr. Alladi Krishnaswami Endowment Lecture at Madras on 23 December 1988 that it is necessary to make a "close and thorough examination of the whole issue of reservations" and to evolve "just and equitable criteria" for ensuring that social and economic justice is meted out and protection afforded to "truly backward citizens". Often, he said, "only the more dominant, powerful, fortunate or affluent sections among the classes enjoying reservations manage to secure the reserved seats. And this privileged access was at the expense of "the truly backward or economically barren members of even such communities."

Also noteworthy is the point made by more than one speaker at a Seminar on Nation Building, Development Process and Communication, held in Delhi in December 1988, that the real issue is the right of all citizens to work; reservations whether for religious or caste minorities or for women only deal with the symptom of the disease which is unemployment and under-employment.

In this context of the need to maximise employment opportunities, the policy with regard to the introduction of high technology requires reconsideration. If it is acknowledged that the provision of work for all should be one of the central aims of development, there can be no reckless pursuit of science and technology for their own sake. "What I object to", Gandhiji said, "is the craze for machinery as such. I want to save time and labour, nor for a fraction of mankind but for all. Mechanisation is good when hands are too few for the work intended to be accomplished. It is an evil where there are more hands than required for the work, as is the case in India."[4]

(b) Nehru and Secularism: In a summative evaluation of the great contribution made by Jawaharlal Nehru as the first prime minister to the growth of a democratic and secular ethos, as well as of some of his failures in this area, Dr. S.Gopal said at a seminar on Jawaharlal Nehru and India's Quest for a Secular Identity, held under the auspices of the Indian Institute of Advanced Study, Shimla:

> "It must be said that there are certain steps which, under pressure of circumstances, Nehru took or failed to take, which do not fit squarely with his promotion of secularism as the root of equality and the basis of democracy. Special treatment of minorities is in itself a weakening of the secular ideal. If caste, as Nehru said, is a violation of secularism, so is reservation of seats for particular castes. But this can be explained as temporary measures to remedy longstanding injustices, although Nehru would have preferred affirmative action of different kinds. Reservation by itself perpetuated division and confirmed lower status and standards.
>
> "Then there was the question of communal political parties. In 1948 Nehru committed the support of the Government to a resolution in the Constituent Assembly calling for the ban of such parties. This is an obvious aspect of secularism. As the State does not interfere with religions, so religious organisations should not interfere in politics; nor should religious grounds be postulated for political actions. But this resolution has not been implemented. In 1961 he directed the Law Ministry to examine the matter and was told that it was difficult to define communal parties and any such attempt might be questioned as an infringement of fundamental rights.
>
> "An even greater inadequacy in Nehru's implementation of secular principles was his restriction of the insistence on monogamy to Hindu men, and the grant of the rights of divorce and inheritance only to Hindu women. In his keenness to win the confidence of the Muslim community, he failed to provide equality before the law to all Indian women and to promulgate a common civil law. But there is no room in a secular society for inequalities which claim religious sanction. Religion has to be separated not only from politics but also from the law. To deny rights to Muslim women which are available to women of other

> faiths is a violation of the provision in the Constitution that the State shall not discriminate against citizens on grounds of religion. The Constituent Assembly had declined, by a resolution in 1948, to accept that Muslim personal law was an inseparable part of the Islamic religion, and rejected attempts to exempt it from the directive principle regarding a uniform civil code. Nehru, of course, knew all this but felt that the time had not yet come to impose in this matter on Muslims decisions taken by what would necessarily be a non-Muslim majority. A start should be made with the Hindu Code, thereby preparing the ground for the extension of its principles to all Indian women. But what Nehru postponed in the fifties has now become even more difficult."[5]

(ii) Area v. Sectoral Planning

If the correction of political and social approaches that perpetuate separatism is the major task in the area of public policy, the correction needed in economic planning may be summed up as the adoption of the area approach in place of sectoral planning.

Sectoral planning perpetuates distortion of priorities, since the annual and five-year Plans have come to mean an aggregation of incremental growth in each sector rather than radical reconsideration of inter-sectoral priorities. Under sectoral planning, every Minister and his or her officials seek the maximum increment they can get for their sector. Thus, domestic civil aviation has over the years enjoyed a priority it would not deserve if the eradication of poverty and illiteracy was the central aim of planning. It continues to grow from year to year and from Plan to Plan. Rural sanitation and drinking water, which never got the priority they should have been given in a scheme of people-oriented development, also get an increment in the Plan outlay--which continues to be egregiously small and an insult to the rural poor.

Area development, on the other hand, will compel attention towards local needs. If existing local resources are inadequate for meeting the needs, area planning will stimulate the examination of means of mobilising more resources from within the area. Some areas may need resource supplementation from outside. The principal need and justification for central planning and coordination is resource allocation for different areas, from a national point of view that acknowledges the right of people in every part of the country to the fulfilment of basic needs.

The 'area' for the purpose of planning will depend on the agro-economic and social conditions prevailing in various parts of the country.

It may, but not necessarily, be the district. The appropriate area may well include more than one district and also cut across district boundaries. In the controversy generated by the suspected political motivation of the Constitution (64th Amendment) Bill, 1989, because of its being initiated in an anticipated election year, the underlying assumption of the district as the unit for planning did not receive the notice and critical examination which it needs.

Whatever may be the area, it is in support of area-specific development programmes that communication can be meaningful and fruitful.

NOTES

1. *The Communal Card* by L.K. Advani, 'Indian Express', Pune, 14 August 1989.
2. Article 370 occurs in Part XXI of the Constitution, initially titled 'Temporary and Transitional Provisions' and amended in 1963 to 'Temporary, Transitional and Special Provisions'. The Article itself is sub-titled: 'Temporary provisions with respect to the State of Jammu & Kashmir'.
3. *Roses in December*, Bharatiya Vidya Bhavan, Bombay, 1973.
4. *Harijan*, 16 November 1934.
5. No. XLII in the series of Occasional Papers on History and Society, Nehru Memorial Museum & Library, New Delhi, May 1987.

Chapter X

COMMUNICATION AND SOCIAL ACTION

Those who are engaged in development-promoting communication may be categorised into three broad groups: offcials of the information and development departments; missionaries inspired by a religion or an ideology; and voluntary workers impelled by pure humanism, who may be described as missionaries without a church.

(i) The Official Communicator

Once upon a time, before the Central Information Service (now known as the Indian Information Service) was formed in 1960, the Ministry of Information & Broadcasting used to recruit for journalistic posts in its media units persons with experience of and proven aptitude for journalism. Some of them got bureaucratised and let their skills rust; others tried to function as professionals even within the governmental framework and were agreeably surprised to find that they could do so--till the regime of internal emergency proclaimed by Indira Gandhi in 1975 led politicians in power, and their bureaucratic underlings, to exercise brute power.

Recruitment to the Indian Information Service is now through the combined examination for the Indian Administrative Service and allied Services such as Police and Audit and Accounts. Ranking in the list of successful candidates, not aptitude, determines whether they go into policing or into information work. This writer has heard a C.I.S. trainee at the Indian Institute of Mass Communication remark with self-pity that he narrowly missed the I.P.S. One felt sorry for the young man, and also for the C.I.S. Another traince was a young lady who, during the training, switched her option from C.I.S. to I.P.S., and eventually got into the I.A.S.

Non-testing for aptitude is compounded by the fact that communicators in the official sector, whether Central or State, are generally not accountable for results in developmental terms. If they are judged at all by results, it is in terms of publicity for a Minister or official in the Press, radio and Doordarshan.

(a) Low Self-Image: An essential part of the training of official communicators in the context of development is to correct the low self-image of the information/publicity/public relations/journalist functionary as a megaphone of the government's achievements and intentions, and painter of a flattering image of those for the time being in power.

It is possible for information officials, as for other public servants, to deserve the name by serving the public. They are not, and do not have to behave like, servants of Chief Ministers or the Prime Minister. There is a certain elbow room for individual discretion, initiative and creativity which is available to official communicators, as to other civil servants, which they can exercise if they are willing and able. By doing so, they will gain legitimate self-esteem and also help to correct the image of the official publicist as a 'propagandist' in the pejorative sense of the term.

(b) Media Autonomy and its Exercise: Autonomy for the official media is a necessary but not sufficient condition for their contributing to an informed society and to the mobilisation of the people for the tasks of development. The human factor is decisive.

There was a Director General of Doordarshan who, at a meeting chaired by the Minister of Information & Broadcasting in Indira Gandhi's Cabinet after her return to power in 1980, said in all seriousness that Doordarshan did not ignore the opposition. The Minister, who had called the meeting in order to get briefed in preparation for a meeting of the Consultative Committee of M.P.s attached to his Ministry, wanted to know more. The D.G. then reeled off a long list of opposition party leaders who had been mentioned in Doordarshan's news bulletins. He explained that they had all issued statements condoling the dealth of Sanjay Gandhi in an air accident, and Doordarshan had taken due notice of them!

Even after autonomy has been granted to AIR and Doordarshan it will not be exercised by such crawlers--to employ an expression used by L.K. Advani, Information Minister in the brief-lived Janata government. He said at a meeting with journalists: "They (the authorities during the emergency) wanted you to bend; some of you chose to crawl."

Jawaharlal Nehru invited C.D. Deshmukh, not long after, and notwithstanding, the latter's resignation from the Cabinet over the question of Maharashtra and Bombay City during the process of States reorganisation, to take up chairmanship of the University Grants Commission. Deshmukh wanted to be a assured that the commission could function autonomously. Jawaharlal Nehru wrote in reply to the effect that it was for him (Deshmukh) to exercise autonomy, and for him (Nehru) to respect it. It takes autonomous individuals to exercise autonomy.

(c) Professional Skills: So cast iron is the security of government service, with promotion from one scale to the next virtually guaranteed, that the official communicator has little need to acquire communication skills and to keep them honed. The impulse for excellence in performance as a communicator has to come primarily from within. But training can help.

As part of pre-service training as well as in the course of a development department's activity of information and motivation, it will be useful to arrange for exchange of ideas and experience between official communicators and persons in the private sector of communication. Of the latter, men and women working in advertising agencies have in particular to be on their professional toes since their performance is amenable to evalution by results.

A rare instance of such interaction was when the Department of Family Planning secured the collaboration of the Advertising Agencies Association of India, in 1974, in devising campaigns to promote family planning in selected States. For the first time, a team of advertising persons made available by AAA undertook a study of the audience, and the characteristics of different segments of that audience, before formulating the content and form of the messages through appropriate media. Unfortunately, even as the consultants were making their presentations, the declaration of emergency made persuasive communication redundant.

Though the emergency did not last more than 18 months, it resulted in a coarsening of approach from which the official media have yet to recover. They are being utilised by politicians in authority almost as crudely as during the emergency. When better days return, as one must hope they will, give-and-take between communicators in the public and private sectors should be resumed. Greater professionalism in the official media will make them more cost-effective than they now are.

(d) Skills and Values: Professional skills are means that are useful for the promotion of certain ends. To the 'pure' professional it matters little what he is called upon to sell: it could be something commercial like soap and cigarettes, or something altruistic like blood donation; it is a thin line that divides the professional and the mercenary. The official communicator is in the same position as the advertising person. He may be called upon to put across the virtues of socialism today and of privatisation tomorrow; of confrontation or war with a neighbouring country when it suits those in power, and of conciliation and accord if it is desired at another time by those in authority; of the virtues of democracy or of authoritarian rule and censorship. At such critical points of moral choice it is for each person to do as his her conscience dictates. In normal situations, however, it is possible for the official communicator with a social conscience, in a democratic country, to apply his professional skills to good purpose. He can contribute his mite to human development by propagating the values professed by the government such as social justice and equality of the sexes, and making known to the unprivileged their rights under the law, or the assistance they are entitled to under the anti-poverty programmes.

(ii) Proselytising Communication

In contrast to the professional communicator whether in the private or official sector is the proselytiser. His purpose is fixed, unlike the variable purpose of the professional communicator. He engages in social action as part of communication, and practises communication as part of social action. A pre-eminent example is afforded by some of early Christian missionaries in India. The earliest bilingual dictionaries and grammars of Indian languages compiled by them, and accounts of the customs and manners of Indians based on close observation, as by Abbe Dubois, bear witness to their anxiety to know the target audience and their 'language' in its multiple senses.

A similar effort to know the Indian masses and speak to them in their language, for winning them over to Marxism, was made by Communists in the middle period of the 20th century. Indicative of this was the affirmation by Kishen Chander, the novelist, that when Kranti (revolution) comes to India, she will come wearing Kum Kum (the auspicious mark in red worn on the forehead by Indian women), and the employment of traditional folk forms of communication like the Jatra of eastern India and the Burrakatha of Andhra.

Constructive work and comunication with the masses at the grassroots level is undertaken by some other groups, like the Ramakrishna Mission in Arunachal Pradesh or by those inspired by the Rashtriya Swayamsevak Sangh, to preserve vulnerable sections like Harijans and the tribal people from conversion to Christianity or Islam or to Marxism in any of its variants including Naxalism. Their benignancy, like that of the proselytisers, is not motiveless. But constructive work and the stirring of consciousness, whether generated by proselytism or by reaction thereto, are preferable to social indifference and acquiescence in an unjust status quo.

(iii) Missionaries Without a Church

Of a higher order is the social action and communication undertaken by workers, like those encountered in the course of this study in the Hoshangabad district of Madhya Pradesh, who are actuated by the impulse only of human goodwill. They 'sell' nothing--no product or service, religion or ideology. Missionaries without a church, their rapport with the community among whom they settle and work is deep, precisely because they are relaxed and willing to observe and to learn, and in no hurry to reform or teach. The action-communication they engage in is empathic rather than manipulative.

There have been in the official sector of information and extension work some who have tried to relate to and serve the people instead of merely delivering homilies. These are career communicators with a social conscience--a faint reflection, in the official sector, of action communication in the voluntary sector. It was respect for the audience that impelled the experiments in localised communication in the field publicity organisation in the early 1970's. Social concern was the impulse behind the Pij experiment in localised terrestrial television during the Satellite Instructional Television Experiment of 1975-76. The ongoing experiment in development broadcasting from the Kota station of All India Radio is another example of communication informed by social conscience.

(iv) Media Technology at Community's Service

Available now, for supplementing and augmenting the effect of inter-personal communication by all the three orders of change agents, are media technologies which obviate reliance on the government-owned radio and television systems. Not too expensive, they enable audio and video presentations to be made in the non-broadcast mode, employing locally prevalent speech and with the participation of men and women of the community.

Audio cassettes, with a combination of music, locally popular forms of dramatic narration, and explanatory talks, lend themselves to more highly area-specific programming than even a district level local radio station can achieve. Ideal for group listening in a school or mahila mandal or panchayat ghar, the cassette taperecorder can serve as a mobile local radio without the cost of transmission and of installing a community listening facility at fixed points.

In the early 1970's, the technology of Super-8 mm. film seemed to hold the promise of light-weight equipment for relatively inexpensive production of localised films. Experimentation with the use of Super-8 projectors was part of the effort made by the field publicity organisation at that time. Since then, the vastly more potent technology of the video cassette has become available. The VCP is today a more versatile and less expensive mode of exhibiting area-specific video films, on a standard TV or large screen, than through telecasts, whether terrestrial or via satellite.

These possibilites of utilising modern media technology in the service of the community are of special interest to all those--whether professional communicators in the official sector, or the cadres of a religious organisation or political party, or voluntary social activists--who work among the unprivileged in the villages and in urban slums.

CHAPTER XI

JOINING OF HANDS BY THE HUMANE

The scarcest of resources for people-oriented development is not rupee finance or foreign exchange or scientific manpower but consciousness-raisers and organisers for working among the deprived masses. Had such men and women been available in large numbers, political parties and the governments formed by them in the States and at the Centre would have been compelled to act on their promises. Instead, each successive election sees the politicians promising again, and yet again, to remove poverty and illiteracy.

It has been evident from the time of the community development programme in the early 1950's that persons with zeal cannot be recruited by governments on the basis of prescribed qualifications and pay scales to work among, educate and organise the rural and urban poor. It is only a very few among the ever-increasing staff of the development and welfare departments who bring to their work the sincerity of purpose needed for contributing to human development. Their effort has to be supplemented on a massive scale by non-official volunteers.

These may be from non-party associations of men and women of goodwill, from organisations inspired by religion, or from the cadres of political parties. A vast difference will be made if all such, in every village, urban locality and city would join hands in tasks dictated by bare humanity and beyond ideological controversy. Among such would be: adult literacy and social education; organising and participating in Shramdan (donation of labour) for projects to improve sanitation and provide drinking water; exercise of vigilance to see that anti-poverty programmes are implemented without political bias, corrupt practices, or discrimination on grounds of religion or caste; promoting girls' education and acceptance of equality of the sexes and of the desirability of fewer children in the interest of the family's health and well-being; and making the legally prescribed mimimum wages widely known and helping to organise workers collectively to refuse to offer their labour for less.

Unfortunately, men and women of goodwill who would like to volunteer for such causes do not find suitable local organisations through which they could work. Moreover, they stand divided by walls or prejudice and suspicion.

(i) Harnessing Youthful Idealism

Despite the misconceived banishment, from the public education system, of instruction in values to live by (discussed in Chapter II (iv) (b), and despite the daily invitation to hedonistic self-indulgence by seductive advertisements in the mass media, such is the innate idealism among young persons that, every year, there are large numbers among those who leave high school or college who would like to apply their talents and energies to improving the condition of those less fortunate than themselves. Some of them are ideologically inclined towards this or that political party, but many are non-aligned in religious or ideological terms. They look for organisations through which they can render constructive social work without surrendering their judgement to a religious orthodoxy or an ideological system.

If youthful idealists do not find an organisation that can utilise their services and maintain them on a modest allowance, they turn like most others of their age group to a remunerative career. However distasteful they may find the rat race initially, they soon get sucked into careerism. Their social concern evaporates and they begin to look back on their early enthusiasm with mixed feelings of guilt and cynicism. This should not be allowed to happen.

The work of a voluntary organisation is much more cost-effective than that of bureaucratically structured departments. The lack of commitment among most of the personnel in the latter leads to seepage of funds on a vast scale. Moreover, voluntary workers raise the level of social consciousness among the people besides promoting productivity and welfare. This is known to potential donors who would like to help voluntary organisations with money even if they cannot give their own time to social causes. There is crying need today in every part of the country for local and contemporary versions of organisations like the Ramakrishna Mission, the Servants of India Society, the many volunteer corps which Gandhiji and Vinoba Bhave raised, and the social service leagues organised by Christian and other religious groups.

Besides the larger organisations that can maintain full-time volunteers and support their work, small neighbourhood associations can attract other voluntary workers: men and women who can apply some of their free time for social work, and those who have retired from full-time remunerative activity and would like to render honorary service.

(ii) Religion as Humanist Resource

There are men and women of humanity, tolerance and compassion among the adherents of each relgiion. They have more in common with their counterparts professing other religions than with those, in their own religion, who are filled with intolerance, cruelty and greed. Yet the humane rarely join hands across religions.

There was a mingling of the egalitarian Hindu Bhakti movement and Muslim Sufism at the time of Kabir and Nanak, in the 15th and 16th centuries. Gandhiji popularised in our own century the prayer line *Iswar, Allah, tere naam* ('Iswar and Allah are both Your names'). It is to India's great credit that there have been such inter-religious affirmations of humanism, not witnessed on comparable scale in any other part of the world. However, it is also India's misfortune that co-operative co-existence has not always prevailed. It was the social distance, if not cleavage, between the different religious communities which enabled the British to divide them politically; and the sedulous encouragement of Muslim separatism culminated in the partition of the sub-continent amidst carnage in 1947.

It is again to the credit of India that, despite the circumstances of the partition, its leaders framed a Constitution based on full democracy and freedom of religion. But the continued outbreak of Hindu-Muslim conflicts from time to time, in various parts of the country, underlines the need to recover the non-absolutist and syncretist approach to religions which Gandhiji stood for. "After long study and experience," he wrote in 1928, "I have come to these conclusions: (i) that all religions are true; (ii) all religions have some error in them; and (iii) all religions are almost as dear to me as my own Hinduism." Gandhiji wanted Hindus to be good Hindus, Muslims to be good Muslims and Christians to be good Christians, and thereby live in harmony and co-operation. This was in accordance with his philosophy of Swadeshi, which meant among other things the acceptance and improvement of one's inherited religion. Gandhiji defined the term thus in February 1916: "Swadeshi is that spirit in us which restricts us to the use and service of our immediate surroundings to the exclusion of the more remote. Thus, as for religion, in order to satisfy the requirements of the definition I must restrict myself to my ancestral religion, that is, the use of my immediate religious surroundings. If I find it defective, I should serve it by purging it of all its defects."

Since Gandhji saw in religion the source of individual and social ethics, there was no question of religion being separated from politics. "Indeed", he wrote, "religion should pervade every one of our actions. Here religion does not mean sectarianism. It means belief in ordered moral government of the universe. It is not less real because it is unseen. This religion transcends Hinduism, Islam, Christianity, etc. It does not supersede them. It harmonises them and gives them reality."[1] Again, "For me, politics bereft of religion are absolute dirt ever to be shunned."[2] These words sound prophetic as we consider the dirty state of public life after four decades and more during the greater part of which the country has been ruled by a political party professing its faith in 'secular' democracy. Those who talk glibly of keeping religion out of politics do so either in ignorance of Gandhiji's life-work and teaching or with tongue in cheek. Political parties which are loudest in their protestations of secularism have not hesitated, in their pursuit of power, to play the communal card.

(iii) Ending Political Untouchability

Among the ersatz religions which have sprouted in the modern age of science and industrialism, a major manifestation after European Marxism is Indian secularism. Like the traditional religions, the pseudo religions have their own hagiology and demonology. If, after Marxism was established in power, whoever was branded by the Kremlin as a Trotskyite or counter-revolutionary became an outcaste to be hunted and liquidated, in India the high priests of secularism anathematise their political rivals as 'communal'.

The new, political untouchability prevents the joining of hands by the humane among the different political parties. The development publicist needs to expose the hypocrisy of those who, like the Brahmins of old, claim spiritual virtue merely because they chant the Gayatri Mantra of 'democracy, secularism and socialism' and proceed to brand their competitors for political power with the guilt of communalism or of associating with communal pariahs.

Secularism is not a word that was current during the freedom movement. It came into use after independence. It denoted in the beginning that even though the sub-continent had been partitioned at the insistence of a majority of representatives of the Muslim community, India would not be a Hindu theocratic state. There would have been no confusion if the word had continued to retain its acknowledged dictionary meaning. But it came to be invested with special meanings.

Jawaharlal Nehru wrote in 1956: "We call our state a secular one. It means freedom of religion and conscience, including freedom for those who may have no religion. The word 'secular', however, conveys something much more to me, although that might not be its dictionary meaning. It conveys the idea of social and political equality. Thus, a caste-ridden society is not properly secular."

While this was an extension of the meaning of the word in a liberal direction, over the years since Jawaharlal Nehru's death secularism as practised by the Congress (Indira) has come dangerously close to meaning encouragement of a sense of separate identity among Muslims and appeasing the conservative leadership of the community as a means of wooing Muslim votes. During Indira Gandhi's second tenure as Prime Minister she drew up a special 15-point programme for the minorities, aimed specially at the Muslim community. In 1986, during Rajiv Gandhi's prime ministership, parliament enacted a special law to circumvent a unanimous decision of the Supreme Court and exempt the Muslim male from payment of maintenance to his divorced and needy wife. This caused as a backlash the assertion of Hindutva, or the country's ancient cultural heritage symbolised by Rama, hero of the Ramayana epic and the beau ideal of India in whose praise the poet Mohammad Iqbal wrote early in his career before becoming a Muslim zealot and separatist. The Vishwa Hindu Parishad is spearheading a campaign for reconstruction of a temple at Ram Janmabhoomi, believed to be the birthplace of Lord Rama, where now stands a mosque built in commemoration of the victory of Babur who invaded India in the 16th century and established the Mughal empire. The BJP's support to this campaign, in which heads of Hindu religious establishments are taking a prominent part, has made it vulnerable to the charge of fomenting Hindu communal feeling.

It is not only the Congress and the BJP which have been tempted to play communal cards. The Communists, who are vociferous in their profession of secularism, have entered into alliance at various times with the Muslim League and with the Sikh party, the Akali Dal. A Muslim-majority district was carved out in Kerala when the State was under a Communist-led coalition government. The Janata Dal, another loud exponent of secularism, has repeatedly and unabashedly sought Muslim votes through the Imam of Delhi's Jama Masjid.

(iv) Forging a Human Chain

Development publicists must expose the low-level motivation of contestants for political power who pander to reactionary communal elements, whether among religious minorities or the majority. The attention of men and women of goodwill, whatever may be their political inclination, must not get diverted from the central problems of our people.

Even as there are many persons of goodwill and human compassion among religionists, alongside others who are fanatical and narrow-minded, so there are the two kinds of persons among the members and sympathisers of every political party. This is as true of avowedly communal parties like the Muslim League and the Akali Dal, and parties based on caste or ethnicity for that matter, as of professedly secular parties and the BJP which is neither avowedly communal nor is on the bandwagon of post-independence secularism which it regards as dubious.

Indeed, the two Communist parties and the BJP between them have the largest potential stock of constructive workers. This is because they have committed cadres, in contrast to the hired crowds of supporters whom the other parties mobilise from time to time. Yet it is the Communist and BJP workers who are most bitterly opposed to each other, in hostility which is gleefully encouraged by the forces of the status quo.

The enlightened among the adherents of every political party must recognise the primacy of humaneness. Ideologies of the Left parties being but religion minus god, what Gandhiji said about Anekantavad, the Jain doctrine of non-absolutism, is of contemporary relevance: "I very much like the doctrine of the many-sidedness of reality. It is this doctrine that has taught me to judge a Muslim from his stand point and a Christain from his." The honest and the humane among secularists as well as religionists must likewise learn to understand each other.

The true difference is not between those who believe in different religions, nor between the so-called secularists and the adherents of 'communal' parties, nor again between the supporters of one political ideology and another. It is between the socially concerned and the unconcerned, the self-transcending and the self- centred, the humane and the not-so-humane. The humane must--if necessary in spite of their power-engrossed leaders--join hands to form a human chain against mindless violence and work together in every village and urban locality for overcoming poverty and illiteracy and promoting respect for the human personality irrespective of religion, caste and gender.